The Dad I Never Knew

A War Orphan's Search for Inner Healing

by

Bruce Brodowski

I have made every effort to contact the copyright holder *Ralph Zuljan of* www.onwar.com for chronological information from his website, but have received no reply. Since it appears that *Ralph Zuljan* has no desire to assert his rights over this material, I am using it in this book with proper attribution to the author

Revised Edition
ISBN: 978-0-9826581-0-9

Carolinas Ecumenical Healing Ministries
Matthews, NC 28105
www.angelfire.com/nc3/chm

DEDICATION

In honor of Edward Brodowski
and all soldiers
that gave their lives for freedom
against tyranny and evil

ACKNOWLEDGMENTS

To my children Tammy, Tricia, and grandchildren for whom this novel has been written so that they will know the father that I never knew.

To John Langdon, professor of History at Lemoyne College, published author, and life long friend for his invaluable input.

To Lloyd "Dick" Kemp and his faithful help over many years of which without I could not have completed this novel nor understood the final events. He is greatly missed. DOD February 2008.

To John H. my dads tank driver for his helpful information and itinerary of his and Ed Brodowski's destinations during the war.

To my loving wife Ellen who so graciously put up with me during the long hours of research and frustration for this novel.

To the many American World War II orphans for allowing me the honor to include stories about their dads which contributed to the personal aspect of the book.

To God and His healing grace

TABLE OF CONTENTS

Preface

I never knew my dad. It didn't really seem that important to me over the years. It just didn't seem unnatural not to have a dad around. I was told that dad was a tank commander that was killed in WWII and was buried in Margraten, Holland. So that was it. No more information was necessary. It was too painful to talk about and it is still too painful for my family to this day. I think it bothered the grown ups more than me. You know, "Oh that poor boy doesn't have a father." So therefore, I was raised by my mom, my grandmother and all my aunts. My uncles tried to help as substitute fathers, with little success.

In addition to dad dying in the war, my mother became very ill with cancer in 1950 and so her life was consumed with constant trips to the doctor's offices and many hospital visits for surgical procedures and radiation treatments. During this time, she tried to explain to me about dad, especially when she knew she would not be around much longer. The hospital scene in the movie "Terms of Endearment" where the dying mother of cancer holds her children for the last time to say goodbye also happened to me in 1955. Mom passed on to greener pastures in October of that year.

I always thought that all the men in my dad's tank were killed. Then in 1997, John H. stopped at a gas station off the New York State Thruway in Utica, New York. John H. was my dad's tank driver and his best friend. He was looking for me and made contact with my family. He wanted to tell me about dad. What he was like, his personality, places where he had been, stories of things they had done, and everything else that a son would want to know. However, I was living in North Carolina at the time. My family notified me about John's visit. It was then that I felt a nagging piece of my life was missing and was longing to be found. There was an empty hole that needed to be filled

There are 183,000 World War II American orphans according to Veterans Administration records. I am just one of them. Some of us have experienced the same orphan heart that encompasses a deep dark black empty hole of some missing piece in our lives. This was the consequence of the war. However, every fatherless orphan, whether male or female, experiences that same orphan spirit.

Ann Bennett Mix, of AWON, wrote in her book "Touchstones" that "when we were children and asked questions about our fathers, we made grown ups around us uncomfortable; and seeing this, we quit asking. If we mentioned to others outside of our family that our fathers were killed in World War II, the reactions we received were very strange. People would stop talking. They too became uncomfortable. They would change the topic. We learned not to bring the subject of our fathers up." This was the wall of silence.

It is human nature as adults to want to know everything about the father. That is the way we were created. However, many of us have experienced mothers and relatives who have accused us of digging things up, hurting their feelings, ripping them apart by having to relive the horrors of the war, or ask us just what we are trying to prove. They do not understand that sons and daughters need to know who they are. They need to reconnect to their past. For those who seek inner healing, the wall of silence must be broken.

Only by knowing the father can they fill the need to be loved by the father. We have developed an orphan's heart because of the void of a father. In order to heal the orphan's heart of a war orphan, he/she must FIRST learn everything there is to know about his/her dad. Only then, can the inner self-healing start to take place.

As a trained healing prayer minister, I was well aware that I needed to discover everything there was to know about my dad. It was only then that inner healing could start in my life. Through my story, others may find the path to inner healing.

The 8th Armored Division was activated at Fort Knox, Kentucky, on 1 Apr 1942. This story is an account of the 8th Armored Division and the life of one soldier from Camp Polk La. to Germany. It is a story that is told through his actual letters, which correspond to the historical dates of the Division. It is one of many stories of the 8th Armored Division, their training, their struggles, and their battles. It is also the story of a marriage separated by war and their growing love for each other through their emotional strain of WWII.

In the beginning, my intention was to learn all about my dad. In the end, I ended up learning all about myself. This journey has continued down a path for me of inner and self-healing. Now I am able to say that in certain ways, I am just like my dad. Some people, such as Dick Kemp, who were over there with him, call my dad a hero. Heroism is in the eye of the beholder. In dad's words, "As all I do is my job."

All information used in writing this story is factual and true to the best of my knowledge. However, when comparing details of dates, destinations, and battles with several soldiers from the 8th armored division, sometimes the stories did not coincide. The years have eroded the accuracy of their memories.

The events during World War I and II over the span of years would tell the story of inhumane horrors and unthinkable massacres of human beings all for the idealisms of a few. Never in the history of humanity has so much destruction been experienced nor should it ever be revisited again. Who could have ever imagined the extermination of Jews in concentration camps or the instant vaporization of Japanese at Hiroshima and Nagasaki? "It is a known fact that Hitler devoted his life to the occult and the study of the art of Black Magic. Hitler redefined the concept that death of the right people, like the Jew, could be beneficial; even more than beneficial, such death could result in the "healing" of the nation. His genocidal "Final Solution" became the obvious necessary step to achieving this "healing" of the German body. Hitler considered Christianity to be weak, beggarly and Pauline Jewish! Therefore, he stated his objective to be to "tearing up Christianity root and branch". As soon as he was finished totally annihilating the Jews, Hitler planned to turn on Christianity with the same Hellish fervor."[1]

Was it a coincidence that all hell broke loose in Buer Hassel, Germany on Good Friday March 30, 1945 after 3 P.M. in the afternoon, the time that it is thought that Christ died on the cross 1945 years before? In the whole big picture of things in the spirit realm, there is no such thing as coincidence in Gods spiritual world. This is a fact I know to be true. Was World War II only about defending against the tyranny of a few governments or was it also a spiritual war against the principalities of darkness? I will let you be the judge of that. Many soldiers died in The Wars to right the wrong and fight the fight of evil that invaded the human race. Ed Brodowski my dad was one of them.

Bruce Brodowski

Chapter One

MARCH-JUNE 1943

Getting ready for The War

Camp Upton was an induction and training facility built in 1917 for new soldiers who were to fight in World War I. The camp was named after Major General Emory Upton, a Union general in the Civil War. In 1940, on the eve of World War II, the camp again served as a military training ground for new inductees. It was there that Ed Brodowski was sent for evaluation.

March from Camp Upton, N.Y.

Dear Honey,

Dropping a line but excuse the writing and mistakes as for the positions and conditions for writing this letter are a little hard to explain. Although I can say this much, I am in the Army. It may not be that same old Army in 1936 as when I was in the 33rd Infantry in Panama, but it is still the

Army. I won't write much about that as I will keep it for days when I come back and we find that we have nothing to do. Then I will tell you about it.

Well honey, I am smarter than I thought. On the I.Q. exam I scored a 117 which is enough to try out for Officers Training School. We had three exams in all. In the second, I scored a 107, which was based on mechanics such as electricity, machinery, and explains all sorts of designs. That isn't bad even though I am bragging. The last test was for the Signal Corps and I scored a 95 on that one. If I had got a 107, I would have had a chance to take up radio. So taking all into consideration, that wasn't too bad.

Now about "Aviation Cadet," I seem to have the qualifications but they don't give exams for it here. So I must wait until I get to my permanent station. So the only thing here for me is the paratroops. But I am getting ahead of myself. They checked up and found out that I was a cook in the Army in Panama and also have experience cooking at home. So you see where I stand. Cooking would probably catch up with me so I told the interviewer that if I couldn't get in the Air Corps, that I would volunteer for the Paratroops as I wouldn't ever get into the kitchen again. So they talked it over and finally suggested that I better not volunteer until I was sent to my permanent place. So here I am hoping that I can get what I want.

Well honey, how is everything at home. Now I sent my things home and I hope that you get them. Don't worry too much about everything. I made out an allotment for you so they will inquire about you. So don't be surprised if they do.

Well honey, I won't say more for the present. Give my love to all at home especially to mother and tell her not to worry as everything will be all right.

Loving you always,

Ed

Dear Honey,

Looks like I am writing you again. I know you won't. You don't have to answer all of my letters but we have to stay in the barracks because one of the fellows has the measles. I hope not for long. Well I got K.P. last night but I can tell you this, I haven't done enough to get a good exercise. I am only trying to keep out of sight. By the way, one of the fellows is from Utica and he is also our barracks leader. So I got out of work this afternoon. Instead I played softball this afternoon and made out swell. I was asked to go out with the boys but I refused. Last night (Utica) "The barracks leader" asked me to go to the show but I refused him. Also, there is a fellow by the name of Whitey. This fellow has already been across but was wounded and now is waiting for a new assignment.

I am making out swell and I am just waiting to get out of here so I can find out what and where I am going. Oh yes, I met a man who came in the same day I did. We sleep next to each other's bunks. It seems we got the same details and all. Pretty nice chap although he is an older fellow but he is rather nice to talk to. By the way, we have an outfit of W.A.A.C. here and wow do the fellows stare at them...Some push them around a little. They have dances for Permanent Party men. They also have the W.A.A.C. over there. The fellows seem to have a good time. There is nothing wrong in that. Maybe you understand now about your joining them. Well honey, you know how we talked about it. So I wish you would take everything into consideration before you do anything. I hope everything is well at home. Don't forget to let me know if you have any trouble regardless of what it might be.

Well honey, you know that I miss you. Just before you know it, we will be together again. With lots of luck finding a job. I remain.

With Love,

Ed.

Edward Brodowski was born September 19, 1918 in Forestport N.Y. He graduated the eighth grade in June 1935 at the age of 16. In 1936, he enlisted into the Army's 33rd Infantry and was at Fort Lilium, N.Y. in May 1938. In September of 1938, he was stationed in Fort Clayton, the Panama Canal Zone. The 33rd Infantry's purpose was to guard the Panama Canal against any enemy takeover. He was discharged in 1940 and in that same year started a job at Savage Arms, in Utica, N.Y. Ed was called back into the Army in March of 1943.

The Savage story is a long and honored one. Formed in 1894 by Arthur Savage, the company marketed the first "hammerless" lever-action rifle with the action enclosed in a steel receiver. By 1915, Savage Arms was manufacturing high-powered rifles, rimfire rifles, pistols and ammunition.

During World War I, Savage merged with the Driggs-Seabury Ordnance Co., and made Lewis machineguns. Savage purchased J. Stevens Arms in 1920, and later acquired the assets of the Page Lewis Co., Davis-Warner Arms, Crescent Firearms, and A.H. Fox. At the time, according to company history, Savage was the largest firearm company in the free world.

During World War II, Savage made heavy munitions for the war[2] However, Savage Arms went out of its way to do its part in the community and help out in the war effort. The following memo was sent out to the employees:

Savage Athletic Association to Organize
a "Family Party" Local Radio Show to be Broadcast
over WIBX from Stanley Theatre, Sundays at 12:30 Noon

Among the Savage Arms employees there is a great deal of musical and other talent which would welcome an opportunity to express and develop itself in actual practice and performance.

In addition all of us are anxious to help along the war effort in any other way we can besides making guns.

A way has been found to accomplish both these worthy objects. We plan to organize a weekly Radio show, consisting of our own talent, which will provide a vehicle to assist locally on United States Government and other war efforts, such as salvage drives, bond sales, Red Cross and war chest campaigns, "Books for Soldiers", "Victory Gardens", etc.

By these programs we can give our men and women with special talents a chance to keep them alive and perhaps develop them further by public appearances in a theatre before their fellow employees and their families, and to the public at large via radio; and at the same time help the war effort.

By arrangements made with WIBX and the Stanley Theatre, it is planned to put on a half-hour Savage radio show, each Sunday from 12:30 to 1 P.M. at the Stanley. Free admission tickets will be given to Savage employees and their families.

For this purpose we hope and confidently expect to organize a good orchestra or band, a glee club or chorus, a dramatic group and a variety of specialty talent and acts suitable to radio.

The purpose of this letter is to locate suitable talent.

Are you a musician, singer or actor or with any other talent you think could be used on a radio show? Would you like to take part in this activity on a voluntary basis? If so, please fill in the attached questionnaire and drop it in the nearest suggestion box or send it to Harold Howell.

Philip Sheffield, who so successfully directs the Players' Club, will soon hold auditions, set up programs, select the talent and acts, supervise rehearsals and the broadcasts.

Please respond promptly. We plan to have the first broadcast as early as possible. If you think you can be useful in the programs, please don't hesitate to apply, or if you know of some Savage employee with talent send in his or her name. It's a chance to develop your and their talents, help the war effort and provide entertainment for your fellow Savage workers and their families -- and the community.

Sincerely yours,

Savage Athletic Association

February 27, 1943

"In 1942 high level military planners realized the need for a program to train men for armored combat. One essential part of such a program would be an armored unit to train cadre personnel for armored divisions yet to be activated. April 1, 1942 at Fort Knox, Kentucky, The Armored Forced, officially activated the 8th Armored Division."[3]

Division History[4]

History

The Division was initially called the 'Iron Snake', but subsequently adopted the 'Thundering Herd' moniker and another, its war code name of 'Tornado'. From June 1942 until January 1943 it served as a training division. It trained cadre and replacements for many other armored divisions. While stationed at Fort Knox, the Division was the official military guardian of the United States Gold Vault.

In January 1943 it moved from Fort Knox, KY to Camp Campbell KY, and in February 1943 it was relieved of its cadre-training mission and directed to attain combat-ready status. In March, the division was moved to North Camp Polk, LA, where it took over vehicles and equipment of the departing 7th Armored Division. While in North Camp Polk, it began training for combat service.

In October 1943, it moved from garrison to bivouac and conducted extensive field exercises.

1942-1943

1 Apr 1942 - the Division was activated at Fort Knox, Kentucky, with Brig. Gen. Thomas J. Camp as commanding officer.

13 Apr 1942 - Brig. Gen. William M. Grimes replaces Gen. Camp as commanding officer.

- Jun 1942 to Jan 1943 - the Division conducts training of 10,833 cadre personnel for the 9th to 14th Armored Divisions.
- While stationed at Fort Knox, the Division was the official military guardian of the United States Gold Vault.
- Jan 1943 - moved from Fort Knox, KY to Camp Campbell KY.
- Jan 1943 - sent over 4,000 replacements to the 1st Armored Division after the Battle of Kasserine Pass in Tunisia.
- Mar 1943 - moved to North Camp Polk, LA. Took over vehicles and equipment of the departing 7th Armored Division.
- Mar 1943 - Sep 1943 - took part in the Mobilization Program designed to mold the Division into an effective combat organization.
- Sep 1943 - completed reorganization from the old style triangular division to the new 'light' armored division.
- Dec 1943 - participated in the 'D' Series training exercises preparing for full scale mane

From February to April 1944 it participated in Louisiana maneuvers which lasted three months. The Division stayed in the field after maneuvers were completed. Shortly after this most privates and Pfc.'s were shipped out and new replacements were received.

The Division ended almost six months of duty in the field as they moved to barracks at South Camp Polk and continued training for combat. In September 1944 it was placed in top priority for overseas movement. It departed for Camp Kilmer, New Jersey in late October 1944. Departure from New York began on 7 November with arrival in England on 18 November 1944.

1944

- 7 Feb 1944 - began the Sixth Louisiana Maneuver period which consisted of seven phases.
- 2 Mar 1944 - received 1,200 replacements from cancelled Army Specialized Training Programs (ASTP)
- 3 Apr 1944 - completed the last phase of the Sixth Louisiana Maneuver period but the Division stayed in the field.
- 19 Apr 1944 - most trained privates and PFC's were shipped out to other units.
- 28 Apr 1944 - the Division ended almost six months of duty in the field as they moved to barracks at South Camp Polk
- May - Sep 1944 - participated in various training and classroom exercises and firing range activities.
- 30 May 1944 - the Division assembled to pay tribute to the 32 men who had died in training since 4 Mar 1943.
- 15 Jun 1944 - Infantry Day - the 3 infantry battalions made a 125-mile march to Shreveport to set up exhibits and participate in the parades and other activities.
- 4 Jul 1944 - all-day sporting activities were conducted. The 58th AIB won first place and also broke the all-army wall scaling record during that event.
- Sep 1944 - the Division was placed in top priority for overseas movement.
- Sep 1944 - The 58th AIB topped the Division in four of seven combat firing tests and was far ahead of other infantry battalions in anti-tank platoon, rifle platoon and infantry platoon tests.
- 5 Oct 1944 - Maj. Gen. Grimes was replaced by Brig. Gen John M. Devine who previously served as CG of CCB of the 7th Armored Division.

- 9 Oct 1944 - infantry battalions participated in series of tests for the Expert Infantry Badge. The badge was worth $5 extra pay per month.
- Oct 1944 - received the official alert for movement to the Port of Embarkation for overseas deployment.
- 27 Oct 1944 - began boarding troop trains for movement to Camp Kilmer, NJ located near New Brunswick.
- 7 Nov 1944 - sailed from New York on the HMT Samaria, USAT George W. Goethals, USAT Marine Devil and SS St. Cecelia.
- 19 Nov 1944 - disembarked from troopships in Portsmouth and Southampton for movement to Tidworth Barracks, near Salisbury.
- Nov - Dec - Received vehicles and began training exercises on the Salisbury Plain.
- Dec 16 1944 - 'Battle of the Bulge' begins. Received orders shortly thereafter to prepare for deployment to the continent.

After a six week stay at Tidworth, England the 8th Armored landed in France on 5 Jan 1945 and assembled in the vicinity of Pont-a-Mousson, France to organize a counterattack against an expected enemy strike in the Metz area.

On 22 Jan, after failure of the German attack to materialize, the Division joined the fighting in support of the drive by the 94th Infantry Division against the Saar-Moselle salient. Six days later, it was relieved and moved north to the Maastricht, Holland area to prepare for participation in 9th Army's attack toward the Rhine.

January, 1945

- 1 Jan - began moving across the English Channel, landing at Le Harve, France.

- 4-7 Jan - moved across France to Bacqueville just north of Rouen.
- 8-10 Jan - moved 175 miles from Bacqueville to vicinity of the cathedral city of Rheims.
- 11 Jan - attached to 3rd Army under Gen. George A. Patton.
- 12 Jan - moved 105 miles from Rheims to vicinity of Pont-a-Mousson, France in anticipation of German attack on Metz.
- 14 Jan - the 148th signal Company, the last unit across the English Channel, joins the division. They had been stranded on a ship in the channel until 11 Jan.
- 17 Jan - Cleared mines and removed dead, both American and German, from Pont-a-Mousson area.
- 19 Jan - CCA began battle indoctrination and are ordered to attack German towns of Nennig, Berg, and Sinz in a joint attack with 94th Inf. Div.
- 22 Jan - CCA units launch attack on Nennig in conjunction with units from the 302nd Inf. Reg. of the 94th Inf. Div.
- 24 Jan - Nennig is captured and cleared during a blinding snowstorm and bitter cold..
- 25 Jan - the attack on Berg is begun and the town is cleared by noon except for a strongpoint in Schloss-Berg which was captured that evening.
- 26 Jan - the attack on Sinz began in the morning. Engineers build a treadway bridge over an anti-tank ditch in the evening.
- 27 Jan - the battle for Sinz continues throughout the day. CCA is relieved after midnight and ordered to rejoin the Division
- 28 Jan - CCA returns from assisting 94th Div. and goes into reserve. Casualties were 23 killed and 268 wounded. Six tanks were destroyed and four were disabled.

The Division crossed the Roer 27 February and assisted the 35th and 84th Infantry Divisions in their push eastward, taking Tetelrath, Oberkruchten, Rheinberg, and Ossenberg against stubborn resistance. Crossing the Rhine at Wesel 26 March the Division attacked east to help form the northern arm of the Ruhr encirclement.

February, 1945

- 1 Feb - the Division was detached from 3rd Army and assigned to the XVI Corps of the 9th Army in Holland 250 miles to the north.
- 2-4 Feb - The 250 mile long march to Holland began. The winter of 1944-45 was the worst in the past 40 years and the roads were icy, resulting in many accidents as vehicles slid off the road.
- 8 Feb - received orders to relieve the 137th Inf. Regiment of the 35th Div. but orders were later postponed for two days and finally cancelled.
- 17 Feb - received orders to relieve the British 7th Armored Div. (the Desert Rats) on 19 Feb.
- 23 Feb - Operation Grenade started. This operation was planned to cross the Roer River and to clear the area between it and the Rhine River.
- 26 Feb - CCR leads attack to capture Roermond, Holland. One platoon of Co. C, 58th AIB is cut off for nearly 24 hours until contact is made by Co. C, 7th AIB. CCR suffered 64 casualties during the operation.
- 26 Feb - The 35th Inf. Div. secures a bridgehead across the Roer and the 8th Armored begins crossing.
- 27 Feb - CCA crosses the Roer River via the Hilfarth Bridge which had been captured by the 35th Inf. Div. and headed for the town of Wegberg.
- 27 Feb - CCB moves through Sittard, Gangelt, Geilenkirchen, Randerath, and Brachlen to arrive at the Hilfarth Bridge.
- 27 Feb - 15th Cavalry Group (Mechanized) began relieving CCR in the Hiede Woods near Roermond and they began moving to the vicinity of Huckelhoven.
- 28 Feb - CCA tanks and infantry destroy fifteen pillboxes, capture Tetelrath, and cross the Swalm River.

- 28 Feb - CCB attacks and captures the towns of Arsbeck and Ober Kruchten
- 28 Feb - CCR joins up with CCA and they begin crossing the Roer River and move to assist the attack on Wegberg.

Taking Dorsten and Marl on 29 March, it crossed north of the Lippe Canal on 1 April and raced east to reach Neuhaus on the 3rd. At that point, it veered south, then attacked west into the Ruhr Valley in an effort to help eliminate the Ruhr Pocket.

March, 1945

1 Mar - Co. A, 53 engineers clear 90 Regal and Teller mines from the road and opens the way to Amern-St. George.

- 1 Mar - CCR is restricted to use of one road in trying to assist CCA near Lobberich. Request to pass through the 84th Inf. Div. area was denied by them.
- 2 Mar - CCA captures Lobberich. Moves through the 35th Inf. Div. and secures the town of Wachtendonk on the north bank of the Niers Canal.
- 2 Mar - CCB attempts to move to the left flank of CCA to aid in the attack but could not find suitable roads.
- 2 Mar - CCR captures Grefrath. Co. C of the 53rd Engineers worked through the night to bridge the Niers Canal which was holding up the advance on Moers.
- 3 Mar - CCB moves through CCA area and captures Alderkerk.
- 3 Mar - CCR captures Saint Hubert, Vinnbruck and Saelhuysen in the advance toward Moers.
- 3 Mar - The Division receives orders to cease forward movement. It was 'pinched out' by the 35th Inf. on the right and the 84th Inf. on the left.
- 4 Mar - CCB was detached and assigned to the 35th Inf. Div. so an attack could be mounted in the direction of

Rheinberg and Wessel to prevent Germans from crossing the Rhine River.

- 4 Mar - CCA relieves CCB in the vicinity of Alderkerk so CCB can join up with the 35th Inf.
- 5 Mar - CCB attacks Lintfort and Rheinberg. Heavy fighting in and around Rheinberg resulted in 199 casualties and the loss of 41 tanks while the Germans suffer 350 men killed and 512 take prisoner.
- 6 Mar - CCB continues to attack northwest from Rheinberg to Ossenberg. The area (nicknamed '88 Lane') was under direct anti-tank and heavy artillery fire and each house had to be cleared by dismounted infantry.
- 7 Mar - The attack continues against heavy resistance throughout the day and a foothold is secured in the vicinity of Grunthal that evening.
- 7 Mar - The 9th Armored Division captures a bridge over the Rhine at Remagen. The 130th Panzer Division was pulled out of the Wesel area and moved south to counterattack.
- 8 Mar - The Solvay factory on the outskirts of Ossenberg is captured. Fighting continues throughout the day.
- 9 Mar - The town of Ossenberg is secured and the towns of Borth and Wallach were cleared. CCB is relieved at 2400 and ordered to the Venlo, Holland, rest area, the relief being completed on 10th and 11th of March.
- 11 Mar - The Division was assigned to cleanup operations in the rear areas of the Rhineland which had been bypassed during the movement to the Rhine River.
- 11-20 Mar - The Division became the first unit to uncover the existence of a secret 'Werewolf' organization when several cleverly camouflaged bunkers were discovered, each containing 12 to 15 fully equipped German soldiers.
- 11-20 Mar - The German 180th and 190th Volks Grenadier Divisions and the 116th Panzer Division succeeded in withdrawing across the Rhine from the Wesel area.

- 11-20 Mar - Cleanup patrols and river crossing training operations continued. Patrols had trouble sometimes moving through convoys of Navy LCVP's and LCM's moving up to the west bank of the Rhine in preparation for crossing.
- 22 Mar - Division Artillery units moved into firing positions in preparation for the assault on the east bank of the Rhine River.
- 23 Mar - All artillery units fire over 130,000 rounds preceding the initial crossing of the Rhine River to be made by the 30th Infantry Division.
- 24 Mar - The 18th Tank Bn was ferried across in support of the 30th prior to the Division's crossing. An 18th tank was the first across the Rhine in the 9th Army area and assisted in the capture of Spellem, the first town to fall east of the Rhine.
- 26 Mar - The Division is the first armored division to cross the Rhine in the 9th Army area, crossing at bridge sites 'G' and 'H'.
- 27 Mar - Orders are received to secure the road running from Hamm to Soest.
- 28 Mar - CCA attacks on the left flank and captures Im Loh and moves on to bypass Dorsten. Heavy house-to-house fighting slows the attack.
- 28 Mar - New orders are received late in the day to capture Dorsten so that the Lippe River could be bridged to allow armor to move northward.
- 28 Mar - CCR, located near Bruckhausen launches an attack on Zweckel and Kirchellen to the south. The 116th Panzer Division is defending both and the approaches have been heavily mined.
- 28 Mar - CCR captures Zweckel in the afternoon and launches an attack on Kirchellen which was secured by nightfall. An advance unit of the 80th Tank battalion that was surrounded in Kirchellen since early morning is relieved.

- 29 Mar - CCA captures Dorsten early in the morning. CCB moves in to cleanup so CCA can join CCR in the advance to the east toward the town of Marl which was cleared by nightfall.
- 29 Mar - CCA swings southeast from Dorsten heading for Polsum. CCR attacks and captures the towns of Scholven and Feldhausen.
- 29 Mar - The German 180th Volks Grenadier Division and the 116th Panzer Division withdraw and set up new defensive lines running through the fortress town of Recklinghausen.
- 30 Mar - CCR crosses the Rapphotz-Muhlen Canal and captures Buer-Hassel. Co. C, 53 Armored Engineers builds a bridge across the canal in 44 minutes.
- 31 Mar - CCR captures Kol Berlich. Heading east, it passes through Westerholt and Langenbochum, approximately 2,500 yards from Recklinghausen.
- 31 Mar - The Division is relieved by units of the 75th Inf. Div., crosses the Lippe River, and assembles at Selm south of Dorsten.

In mid-April, when the XIX Corps drive to the Elbe was threatened from the south, the Division was pulled out and rushed east to provide right flank protection against fanatical remnants of the German 11th Panzer Army grouping in the Harz Mountains. Assembling in the vicinity of Halberstadt, it attacked south against the German force, taking Blankenberg on the 20th of April, and seizing Ottenstedt on the 21st in the division's last coordinated action of the war.

April, 1945

1 Apr - Orders are received from XIX Corps to set up two spearheads for an attack to the east, the 2nd Armored and 30th Infantry in one and the 8th Armored and 83rd Infantry in the other.

- 1 Apr - CCA is assigned to attack Delbruck.
- 1 Apr - CCB moves to attack Paderborn but runs into heavy resistance as they approach Neuhaus.
- 2 Apr - CCB is stalled by fierce German resistance at Neuhaus.
- 3 Apr - 9th Air Corps provides close support in the Teutoburger Forest and Neuhaus areas.
- 3 Apr - CCR moves up to attack Elsen to help CCB repel strong German counterattack launched from Sennelager.
- 3 Apr - CCA attacks in an attempt to reduce the enemy strongpoint at Sennelager.
- 3 Apr - The Division is relieved by the 83rd Inf. Div. and receives orders to attack towards the west to help reduce the Ruhr pocket.
- 3 Apr - the Division turns 180 degrees and CCR attacks west toward Recklinghausen.
- 4 Apr - CCR continues west capturing the towns of Stripe and Norddorf, and continue through Vollinghausen, Oberhagen, and Ebbinghausen stopping for the night in front of Horne.
- 4 Apr - CCA attacks Erwitte, a center of Nazi political and ideological indoctrination.
- 4 Apr - 9th Air Corps provides close support as the Division assults the Ruhr Pocket in the Lippstadt area.
- 4 Apr - Col. Wallace, CCR commander is captured during the night.
- 5 Apr - Col. Vesely assumes command of CCR and continues westward capturing the towns of Horne, Klieve, Schmerlacke, and Serlinghausen.
- 5 Apr - CCB relieves CCR and they move to the vicinity of Lippstadt. CCB continues the attack westward toward Soest capturing the towns of Schallen and Lohne.
- 5 Apr - 9th Air Corps provides close support for the assult on Soest.

- 5 Apr - CCA continues attacking south capturing the towns of Anrochte, Mensel, Drewer, and Altenruthen.
- 6 Apr - CCB makes a 25-mile 'end run' around Soest to the outskirts of Ost Onnen and cuts off the Germans breakout path from the Ruhr pocket.
- 6 Apr - CCA clears the area north of the Mohne River so glider troops can be landed in case of an attempt to break out by the Germans. They capture the towns of Wamel, Brullinggsen, Ellingsen, and Westendorf.
- 6 Apr - CCR outposts all roads northeast of Soest to facilitate an attack on the town by the 94th Inf. Div.
- 6 Apr - troops of the 194th Glider Infantry Regiment arrive to help clear the mountainous wooded terrain in the area. They capture Nazi diplomat Franz von Papen.
- 7 Apr - the 2nd Armored moving east and the 8th Armored moving west create a gap of 180 miles between the two fronts. A breakout of the Ruhr pocket which would cut off the 2nd Armored.
- 7 Apr - Troop A, 88th Reconnaissance Squadron captures the Mohne Talsparre Dam and prevent the Germans from flooding the Mohne Valley.
- 7 Apr - CCB begins attack on Werl in the afternoon and captures Gerlingen. The burgomeister of Ost Onnen surrenders the town.
- 8 Apr - CCR moves to secure the road between Werl and Wickede and capture the towns of Parsit, Bremen,Vierhausen, Schluckingen and Wiehagen capturing 238 PW's, one Tiger tank, and three 88's.
- 8 Apr - CCB captures Werl by late afternoon after heavy resistence during the day. They move on and capture Ost Buderich.
- 9 Apr - CCB moves on Unna capturing Holtun and Hemmerude. The threat of a German breakout has passed due to the buildup of troops in the area.
- 10 Apr - CCB continues the attack on Unna and captures Lernen. A ten minute air strike is laid on Unna to soften it

up. The Germans move reinforcements, including Hitler Jugen to Unna from the Mulhausen garrison.

- 10 Apr - CCR advances 7,000 yards and secures Stentrop, Bausenhagen, Scheda, Beutrap Wemen, and Fromern.
- 11 Apr - CCA joins in the attack on Unna and CCB goes into reserve. CCB has had 198 casualties this period.
- 11 Apr - CCR captures Hohenheide and Frondenberg after an air strike drives 4 German tanks out of the town. The town of Billmerich is also captured.
- 11 Apr - After receiving air support, Unna finally fell in the afternoon. The Germans lost 160 PW's, two tanks and a battery of 88's. The surrender finally finished the 116th Panzer Division.
- 12 Apr - CCA continues cleaning up operations in Unna.
- 12 Apr - CCR captures the towns of Hengsen, Ostenforf, Ottendorf, and Dellwig.
- On 12 Apr, 1945, elements of the division liberated the Langenstein-Zweiberglager concentration camp near Langenstein, Germany and continued on eastward. After the war, all information about the camp was sealed and stamped classified, presumably because the camp contained a tunnel leading to a site where an improved version of the buzz bomb was being developed13 Apr - CCA is relieved and ordered to move east of Unna across the Weser River to the vicinity of Wolfenbuttel. CCA had lost two tanks, one halftrack and one jeep.
- 13 Apr - CCB is assigned to protect right flank of the 2nd Armored and the 83rd Inf. Div. as they move east. They move 170 miles to Wolfenbuttel.
- 13 Apr - CCR is relieved and ordered to move to the vicinity of Denstorf. On the drive west, CCR had 203 casualties and lost eleven tanks, three jeeps, nine halftracks. The enemy lost six Mark V tanks, four 20mm guns, one large railroad gun, and three tons of small arms.
- 13 Apr - As the Division moves east, it participates in the liberation of the Halberstadt-Zwieberge concentration

camp near Langenstein, Germany, a sattlelite of the Buchenwald camp.

- 14 Apr - Most of CCB moves on to Halberstadt with some units remaining in Wolfenbuttel until the rest of the Division arrives.
- 14 Apr - the remaining units of the Division begin moving to an assembly area in the vicinity of Braunschweig with CCA going to Wolfenbuttel and CCR going to Denstrof.
- 15-18 Apr - CCB begins clearing the area near the Hartz Mountains of remnants of the 11th Panzer Army then grouping in the area.
- 16 Apr - guards were placed on the Herman Goering Plant and the Ruhrchemie Plant at Gebhardshagen.
- 16 Apr - CCA began moving to Seehausen to support the attack on Magdeburg by the XIX Corps.
- 17 Apr - CCR moves from Denstrof to Braunschweig and continues screening the rear areas.
- 18 Apr - CCB completes clearing resistance from the edge of Forest Heimburg south of Derenburg.
- 19 Apr - units of the 2nd Armored relieve CCR and it moves into the vicinity of Strabeck in preparation for reducing resistance in Blankenberg.
- 19 Apr - CCA is relieved and returns to Wernigerode from Seehausen where it relieves the 330th Inf. Reg. of the 83rd Inf. Div.
- 19 Apr - CCB moves to Westhausen and CCR moves to Aspenstedt to clear the remaining woods around Blankenburg.
- 20 Apr - the Division begins to attack Blankenburg. At 1000 a 13 plane squadron attacks Blankenburg and afterward the burgomeister is contacted about surrendering after a show of force.
- 20 Apr - by nightfall, most of Blankenburg had surrendered except for a few strongpoints that were either fanatics or who had not received word to surrender.

- 21 Apr - CCR clears the woods south of Blankenburg and contacts elements of the 1st Inf. Div. of the First Army.
- 22 Apr - the last organized resistance ended with the capture of Gen. Heinz Kokott, CO of the 26th Volks Grenadier Div. He was a brother-in-law of Gestapo Chief Heinrich Himmler.
- 23 Apr - 8 May - The Division, assigned an area of 90 kilometers long by 30 kilometers wide, goes on occupation duty. Some additional cleanup is required as small pockets of resistance and stragglers are found.

It continued mop-up operations and performed occupation duty in the Harz Mountain area up to and immediately following VE day. Then, in late May, it was ordered south to Czechoslovakia to assist in processing prisoners of war, operating displaced persons camps and guarding vital installations including the Skoda Munitions Works.

The Division closed in the Pilsen area 6 June, 1945 and remained there until departure 19 September for return to the United States and inactivation at Camp Patrick Henry, Virginia, on 13 November, 1945

May-November, 1945

- 1 May - the 58th Inf. loses two men to snipers which are then killed since they would not surrender.
- 2 May - the 58th Inf. loses an officer and three more men when a powder plant blows up in Munchshaf. Sabotage was suspected. It is believed that these were the last official wartime casualties of the Division.
- 8 May - 30 May - The Division remains on occupation duty and continues to cleanup stragglers and small pockets of resistance.

- 30 May - The Division is assigned to Third Army. It is relieved by units of the British Army and begins to move to the Pilsen, Czechoslovakia area.
- 1 Jun - 19 Sep - As the point system went into effect for returning home, many men were shipped out during this period. Those remaining were sent to various I & E (Information and Education) training schools. Very little other training was done.
- 19 Sep - The Division began the 600 mile trip to Camp Oklahoma City near Rheims,France for deployment home.
- 26 Oct - The last 180 mile trip from Camp Oklahoma City to Camp Phillip Morris at LeHarve, France was started and the Division was officially dismounted, but no one cared.
- 13 Nov - The Division was deactivated on 13 November 1945 at Camp Patrick Henry, VA by Gen. Charles F. Colson.

"A change of station came in January 1943 when the division made a tactical march of 200 miles to Camp Campbell, Kentucky. While there, news arrived of the losses suffered by allied tankers in the Battle of Kasserine Pass. In the next three weeks the 8th, the only armored division having available trained replacements, shipped more than 4,000 men directly to Tunisia to help launch the drive which ultimately pushed the "Desert Fox," Field Erwin Rommel out of North Africa."[5]

Battle of El Guettar

"The Axis army commanders had become aware of the U.S. movements and decided that the 10th Panzer Division should settle them. Rommel had flown to Germany before the battle, leaving von Arnim in control of the newly-named Panzer Army Africa. Von Arnim held Rommel's opinion on the low quality of the U.S. forces and felt that a show of force would be enough to clear them from the Eastern Dorsals again.

Patton attacks

On 19 March, the British 8th Army launched their attack on the Mareth Line, at first with little success.

At 06:00 on 23 March, fifty tanks of Broich's 10th Panzer emerged from the pass into the El Guettar valley, followed by Marder tank destroyers and panzergrenadiers. The Germans quickly overran front line infantry and artillery positions. Major General Terry de la Mesa Allen, Sr., commanding U.S. 1st Infantry Division, was threatened when two tanks came near his headquarters, but he shrugged off suggestions of moving, "I will like hell pull out, and I'll shoot the first bastard who does."

German efforts took a turn for the worse when they ran into a minefield. When they slowed to clear the field, U.S. artillery and anti-tank guns opened up on them, including 31 potent M10 Wolverine tank destroyers which had recently arrived. Over the next hour, 30 of the 10th Panzer's tanks were knocked out, and by 09:00 they retreated from the valley.

A second attempt was made starting at 16:45, after waiting for the infantry to form up. Once again the U.S. artillery was able to seriously disorganize the attack, eventually breaking the charge and inflicting heavy losses. Realizing that further attacks were hopeless, the rest of the 10th dug in on hills to the east or retreated back to German HQ at Gabès.

However, on 26 March, a force sent via an outflanking inland route arrived to the north of the line, and the Mareth defenses became untenable. A full retreat started to a new line set up at Wadi Akarit, north of Gabès. This made the U.S. position even more valuable, since the road through El Guettar led directly into Gabès.

Over the next week the U.S. forces slowly moved forward to take the rest of the interior plains and set up lines across the entire Eastern Dorsals. German defenses were heavy, and the progress was both slow and costly. However by 30 March they were in position for an offensive south from El Guettar. In order to start a breakout, the two original Italian strongpoints on Hill 369 and Hill 772 had to be taken, one after the other.

The U.S. plan involved the U.S. 1st and 9th Infantry Divisions, and one "Combat Command" (1/3rd) of the U.S. 1st Armored Division, collectively known as "Benson Force". This force attacked Hill 369 on the afternoon of 30 March but ran into mines and anti-tank fire, losing 5 tanks. The 1st and 9th attacked again the next day taking several hundred prisoners. However an Italian counterattack drove them back with the loss of 9 tanks and 2 tank destroyers. A further attempt the next day on 1 April also failed, after barely getting started."

APRIL

Thursday, April 1, 1943

In the North Atlantic... The Italian blockade-runner *Pietro Orseolo* is attacked off the coast of Spain by British Beaufort and Beaufighter torpedo bombers. Escorting German destroyers shoot down 5 of the aircraft. After dark, the US submarine *Shad* hits the ship with a torpedo, causing substantial damage [6]

Dear Honey,

Well here is another card but good news. I am leaving tonight. So if you don't hear from me for a while, don't worry, as I may be unable to write. Hoping it will be where it is warm. Lots of love.

Love,

Ed.

Back in Africa, Patton received orders to start the attempt on Hill 772, even though Hill 369 was still under Italian control. The 9th was moved to Hill 772, leaving the 1st on Hill 369. By 3 April, the 1st had finally cleared Hill 369, but the battle on Hill 772 continued. The Italian commander, General Messe, then called in support from the German 21st Panzer Division, further slowing progress. The tempo of the operations then slowed, and the lines remained largely static.

On 6 April, the British 8th Army once again overran the German lines, and a full retreat started. On the morning of 7 April, Benson Force moved through the positions held by the 1st and 9th, and raced down the abandoned El Guettar-Gabès road, where it met the lead elements of the 8th Army at 17:00.[7]

The War Department training Memorandum summed up the 8th Armored's next task: to develop itself rapidly into an integrated, highly trained, aggressive combat team. For this new mission the 8th was transferred from Camp Campbell to Camp Polk, Louisiana. The Thundering Herd spent March taking over the vehicles and equipment of the departing 7th Armored. From March 21 to April 5, 1943, the Division received fillers, a total of 11,497 soldiers. On April 5 the first phase of the Mobilization Training Program got under way."[8]

April 5, 1943

In Tunisia... The Axis defenses on the Wadi Akarit Line have been improved over the course of the past few days. The line is occupied, mostly, by Italian troops. The German 15th Panzer and 90th Light Divisions are held in reserve behind the line. Most of the Axis armor is further north, engaging the US 2nd Corps around El Guettar. In the evening the British 4th Indian Division begins a night advance against the Djebel Fatnassa position. Good progress is achieved.[9]

Tuesday, April 6, 1943 Camp Polk, LA.

Dearest Honey,

First chance in which to write. enclosed is a picture of a tank which will describe what I am in. Haven't anything to say. As you may know, you have no choice in your situation but take what you get. I am just letting you know that I am safe and sound.

Well honey, I was on the road from Thursday night (April 1) to Sunday Morning (April 4). Remember when we saw the picture of soldiers traveling on the train. Well that is the way we traveled to here. Dear, I wish I could find a place for you here as I do miss you but I am afraid that it would be impossible. As we are suppose to train for at least six months and then after that only God knows. One thing is for sure, this outfit is the toughest that I have ever seen. And I believe that I am much dumber than I thought I was. As you know that I consider myself to be pretty smart but now I think that differently. If things turn out as I see them, then maybe, now honey, just maybe, understand this, I may be rated. As the Lieut. that I spoke of, he seems to think that I am pretty good. As he was an enlisted soldier but a few short months ago. But you know the Army. You just never know what happens from day to day. Well honey, I am stopping again as I must fall out. It seems we don't get time to ourselves. So if anyone asks why I don't write, please apologize for me. As I don't get any time to myself.

I just received your letter and am I glad to hear from you. Well hon, I don't have to tell you how I feel. Just stop and think about how you feel and I am sure that you will realize how I must feel, but perhaps twice as bad. As I wrote, I am now in a tank division and I have nothing to say about it as the army had changed quite a lot since I have been in. But honey, do not worry about me. I will keep smiling and I know that we will carry on someday where we left off. Right at present, they are having quite a time about me. As you see, my Lieutenants are in charge of platoons. I have been moved from one platoon to another and the Lieutenant is burned up about it. Honey, I am stopping this letter tonight as it is about 10:30 P.M. and I have been moving for quite some time.

Honey, this is the next morning and I am trying to drop a few lines to you at any time I get a chance. This place isn't bad. Only one thing, it is a brand new outfit and they don't know what they want to do from one day to the next. I hope I can make something out of myself here as I am afraid that all I hoped to dream for is now gone with the wind. No officers training School, No Aviation Cadet School. But honey, I believe that what ever becomes of me will be for the best. And we will soon be together. Now honey, you do what ever you think is best but I am telling you to stay at home and I mean don't go and join the W.A.A.C. Take care of everything at home and we will do the things that we wanted to do very soon, I hope. Now honey, I am sending those papers for Dependency of Insurance, so keep them as proof that I have taken.

Honey, I still miss you perhaps more as I write to you. So that is why I hate to write as it makes me feel so very blue. Now honey, if things should turn out where I am somewhere near to you, I'll have you come. So don't worry about that as that will be the first thing that I will do. But for the present time, do as you think fit. As I don't know what to tell you. Or what the circumstances are. But honey, write as often as you can as I want to hear from you. Tell all the others to write to me, however, it may be days before I will be able to answer. But I'll answer as soon as I can. I may not answer individually but you can do that for me. And I know that it will have to do, because it seems that we don't have time to turn around and that is no joke, I assure you. Well honey, I am starting again as I just came back from getting a shot. As we have to get seven all together but as of yet I have three to go.

Now honey, buy for me a leather kit but not too expensive. But something which is small in size and deep. Don't get the articles for the kit as I have all of them I want here. Send my soap case and tooth brush case. Now honey, send to me about six wire hangers. Not more than that as it will make too big of a package. A couple small towels, a few handkerchiefs, and bed room slippers. Oh yes, send that sewing kit that I had there and my shoe brush. Now honey, take out the hunting knife and the soap and keep them home. As I will not find use for them. Now honey, please don't send anything else as I have no place to keep them.

Darling, I love you more now than I can imagine. I guess I didn't realize how lucky I was until too late. But if we pray hard enough we will be home again and together. Give my love to mother and your folks, as I don't find time to write separately. So then, ask them to write. Well honey, with all my love and kisses. I remain.

Your Loving Husband

Ed

In Tunisia... Axis forces are rapidly retreating from the Wadi Akarit Line. Patrols of the British 8th Army and the US 2nd Corps meet on the road toward Gafsa.

In Germany... Hitler and Mussolini meet at Salzburg over the course of the next five days (April 7-11). Among other topics discussed, they decide they must continue to hold on in North Africa[10]

Saturday, April 10, 1943

Lonesome again so I am writing, if you get time and feel like it, make a cake or some cookies, as I would like to have some of your baking again. Something else you didn't know, but your cooking was tops even if I didn't praise it much. Well honey, I have made a little success. It seems that the Colonel told the Major and the Major told the Company Commander, well anyway, I was recommended for Lance Corporal. You probably remember I told you about a Lieutenant Fry. Well he came running over and told me. He seems to like me. It is just acting Corporal and I don't get paid for it. So honey, maybe I'll get along better than I thought. Just seen a couple of W.A.A.C. and all the boys ran for the windows.

Oh yes, I better tell you about what I did today. Well I'll start from the first part. We wake up at 5:00 or 5:30 A.M. It all depends on the first Sergeant. Breakfast is about six and then by 6:30 or 7:00 A.M. we are out for exercise and drill. From that we get explanations on guns and how to use them. We only have about one hour for dinner. Then sometimes we haven't time to finish. Today, we had barracks clean up for inspection. Also today, I had a detail to take to the Company area and while marching the men down there, I run into our Company Commander. He stopped and watched me. Boy was I scared because it was the first time I even did that here.

Oh yes, my hair is cut and I mean cut. It is only about one inch or better than 1/2 inch. My face is sunburned and is it red. Boy do I look like heck but then no one will see me here. I hope that I can look like some one before I get home. It seems that we will get a furlough before we ever go across. So I was planning already that if I should stay here long enough to be entitled for a furlough, I'll have you come down as they have a guest house where you could stay. But that is only for three days. Then I could have my furlough start on your last day here and then we could go back home together. That way I would get full benefit of the time off. As it takes quite some time to travel from here. But I guess I am way ahead of myself. But it helps thinking that maybe we will be able to get together.

Now honey, if I should ask for anything and it is to much trouble for you, then forget about them. But here is one thing, whenever you get time and want to send me anything like candy or cake, but don't put yourself out as I don't need it that bad. But it is good to be able to have someone who cares enough to want to go through the trouble of sending things. Until you write, I remain.

Your Loving Husband,

Ed

In Tunisia... Axis forces are now established in what will be their final defensive positions. They occupy the ring of hills around Bizerta and Tunis from about Cape Serrat to Enfidaville. British 8th Army units are moving up from the south to pressure Djebel Garci and Takrouna. The US 7th Division is preparing for deployment in North Africa. [11]

Thursday, April 15, 1943

Dear Honey,

Haven't to much time to write so I am hurrying a little letter to you. It has been sometime since I have heard from you. The boys have been getting mail but as of yet I have only received three letters. Is there something wrong or haven't you time to write to your husband? I have received the packages of candy. It was rather a mess as the box was just about gone but the cookies were swell and now I am waiting for more.

Well, it has been made official that I am acting Corporal but for how long, I don't know. Hope I can get more promotions before to long. We took our hike today and it was only for two hours so we didn't go very far. They probably will be much harder on us later on.

Oh yes, I sent a letter to Savage Arms for that pay. As soon as I get it I will mail it to you. Now don't forget, if you have any trouble at all, you let me know as I want to keep in close touch with the going ons at home. So please write as often as possible as you are the only one who writes to me. I guess all the rest of the relatives and friends just don't give a damn.

I hope that this darn training was over. Than I may be able to come home at least once. As that is the only thing which keeps me going. I have very little interest in the events that take place. I am unconcerned at what the outcome may have for me. I don't exactly dislike it but I sure don't care for it. As you have asked me to tell the truth, well, there it is.

Well it is nearly time to fall out. Will wait till tonight to finish this letter. Maybe I will get one letter tonight from you. I better or I'll be mad.

Well, no letter from you but at least one letter from mother. Tell her I was very glad to hear from her. I understand that you are now working. It doesn't make me happy. In fact, I feel pretty bad thinking that I am unable to take care of you. A hell of a husband I make but I know that you will feel better if you do something. But don't forget, if it is to hard, quit the job or I'll get sore. And don't work too hard, as I don't want you killing yourself. Now honey, tell me all about the job. What, when, and where. Now don't forget, as I will be worried until I hear from you. With all my love.

Loving you always,
Ed

Sunday, April 18, 1943

Dearest Honey,

I am in Charge of Quarters. That means that I stay in the orderly room, take calls, and send out details that Headquarters may ask for. The only thing I don't like is answering the phone. As it consist of long and short rings and I can't make out which are long and which are short. But hoping I make out O.K. Oh yes, I went to church this morning. So the Army hasn't change me as yet. I will go to confession next week. But I haven't had any time to do any sinning or at least I don't think so.

Yesterday I had one platoon out and I drilled them for about an hour. At first I thought I would never make a go at it but towards the end, I was making out pretty good. Sometimes I think I will make out good and then again I don't know. But the only thing I can do is hope and pray for the best. Honey, please send to me the things I have asked for I know you must be getting tired of having me ask for things but if you were here you would understand. As it makes it hard with nothing to do with. As they don't give you as much clothing as when I was in the Army before

Honey, I hope your work isn't to hard as I wouldn't want you to work to hard because it is really unnecessary. As I make enough to keep you going or I hope I do. It is hell not to get any mail from you. As of yet, I have only received three letters from you and two from mother. But I suppose you are pretty busy at first looking for work and then getting the job. Please tell me all about the job, where is it and all the details.

I guess I wrote a lot to you and I don't remember as to just how many. Now I am expecting that many back and then some. Well honey, I'll close but don't forget that I love you.

With love,

Ed

Initially, Major Hobby and the WAAC captured the fancy of press and public alike. William Hobby was quoted again and again when he joked, "My wife has so many ideas, some of them have got to be good!" Hobby handled her first press conference with typical aplomb. Although the press concentrated on such frivolous questions as whether WAACs would be allowed to wear makeup and date officers, Hobby diffused most such questions with calm sensibility. Only one statement by the Director caused unfavorable comment. "Any member of the Corps who becomes pregnant will receive an immediate discharge," said Hobby. The *Times Herald* claimed that the birth rate would be adversely affected if corps members were discouraged from having babies. "This will hurt us twenty years from now," said the newspaper, "when we get ready to fight the next war." Several newspapers picked up this theme, which briefly caused much debate among columnists across the nation.

Oveta Culp Hobby believed very strongly in the idea behind the Women's Army Auxiliary Corps. Every auxiliary who enlisted in the corps would be trained in a noncombatant military job and thus "free a man for combat." In this way American women could make an individual and significant contribution to the war effort. Hobby's sincerity aided her in presenting this concept to the public. In frequent public speeches, she explained, "The gaps our women will fill are in those noncombatant jobs where women's hands and women's hearts fit naturally. WAACs will do the same type of work which women do in civilian life. They will bear the same relation to men of the Army that they bear to the men of the civilian organizations in which they work." In Hobby's view, WAACs were to help the Army win the war, just as women had always helped men achieve success.

WAAC officers and auxiliaries alike accepted and enlisted under this philosophy. A WAAC recruit undergoing training at Fort Oglethorpe, Georgia, whose husband was serving in the Pacific, wrote her friend, "The WAAC mission is the same old women's mission, to hold the home front steadfast, and send men to battle warmed and fed and comforted; to stand by and do dull routine work while the men are gone." [12]

Over Germany... The US 8th Air Force carries out a daylight bombing raid on aircraft factories in Bremen. Of 115 B-17 bombers employed, 16 are lost on the mission *In Tunisia...* A massive convoy of 100 transport aircraft leaves Sicily with supplies for the Axis forces. At least half the planes are shot down by Allied fighters. Another effort to supply the Axis forces by air suffers heavy losses. [13].

Monday, April 19, 1943

I just received your card and letter and boy was I glad to hear from you. As I was very worried. As I haven't heard from you in quite some time. How about telling me more about your job as all you say is your working and in Ilion, N.Y. I am afraid I won't be able to send you a card for Easter as it is hard to get anything here. As all the other boys also want them and when they do get a few in, they are all gone before word can get around. Now honey, tell me when you send the last of the things that I asked for as I do not keep track of what I write for. The only thing that you can send to me without me asking is things like a cake, cookies, or such. The fellows I sleep with, I mean in the same room. Oh yes, I sleep with another fellow in a private room. Boy do I rate. Well anyway, he got a big box of staff cakes, cookies, meat, and candy. He has a radio and we get music at night. I got another needle today so my arm is a little sore from the shot but I will be O.K. by morning. I suppose I am a big pest And for Pete's sake don't go joining the W.A.A.C. as we have a Sgt. here who is married to a W.A.A.C. and he never sees her and won't see her till after the war. So stay home because it won't be long, I hope.

Things here are about the same as it is drill and more drill. Now we are learning how to get into the tanks and that sort of drill. Yesterday I wrote a letter. Well it wasn't long after I wrote it that my Lt. came over and ask me why I hadn't tried for Air Corps. I told him about it and he said that he tried also but that he was too old. Then he told me I should try for the Officers Candidate School. I told him that I didn't think I could make it. He said not to be foolish as he thought I could make it. Also, if I would make up my mind to try for it, he would do all he possibly could for me. So it makes it that 2 Lts. are pulling for me. Maybe I will make out all right after all.

Well honey, I will close with love and kisses. Loving you always.

With loads of love,

Ed

In Tunisia... The British 8th Army (Montgomery) launches a series of unsuccessful attacks on Axis positions near Enfidaville. The Allied forces suffer heavy casualties. A series of Allied attacks are launched against the Axis positions in the hills. The US 2nd Corps (now commanded by General Bradley) attacks Hill 609 in "Mousetrap Valley," with the objective of advancing to Mateur. The British 5th Corps attacks "Longstop" and "Peter's Corner" and the British 9th Corps attacks between Boubellat and Bou Arada. Montgomery has been ordered to cease his attacks along the coast. Meanwhile, another Axis air supply effort results in 30 transports being shot down.[14]

Thursday, April 22, 1943

I am having a day of rest today so I am again writing. I was on guard duty last night for the first time so now I have a little time off today. The company has left for driving training, which will be all day. They are going to teach the boys how to drive the tanks. It makes me mad that they make me do things like guard duty all day, K.P. and Charge of Quarters. The only men who do this are the regular ones who have had this training so when I have to stay in all day, I miss valuable instructions and training. But I guess they think that I can learn the same as other fellows and do special work on the side. I don't know if I told you but the regular ones are only Sgt. and S. Sgt.s. The ones who are tracking us. There are only about 20 or 30 of them. The rest of us are all new men as we have about 160 all total. The weather at present is rather cool but it really gets warm during the day. Also, it is very bad when it is raining as it is clay soil.

Now honey, you were asking me about bonds. The only thing I can say about that is that you do as you see fit. As I don't know what goes on home. I mean can you afford to get one a week or not? Now don't forget that I want to see that new Easter outfit as I'll be mad if you don't get one.

Have you looked at my car? How is it doing? Have you noticed if the blocks are still the same or are they slipping anywhere? How about the oil? Do you have plenty? Please take good care of my car. If there is anything home that you don't know about, then write to me and maybe I can help. **You know honey, men are such fools when they have something and they don't know enough to appreciate it. But when this is over, I am sure you will find that I am a different man. I never realized what it could be like without you but it is better late than never. It seems strange not to have you around but only have around a bunch of fellows.** As yet, I haven't been to any movies. Only the Army pictures and I don't miss them. But there are a lot of things I miss. Mostly having you around to love up and talk to. I am quite sure that before I leave for anywhere, I'll have you come down for a few days regardless of the cost. I will close for the present as I will make a fool of myself if I continue. Loving you always.

With loads of Love,

Ed

Saturday, April 24, 1943

I received four of your letters today of which one you wrote on the 13th. So I will answer all now. Honey, I love your letters but don't get to lonesome as I know how you must feel. But I know that you will be all right. Don't think about me being away. Just think I am working nights and any day I'll be back home. Sorry honey, I didn't get you a card for Easter but I had mother get you something. I hope you like them. I am sending you a pillowcase. I hope it makes up for the card.

Honey, tell mother that the car engine block isn't cracked but that the water plug always leaked a little water. That she may have to add water every so often but I am sure it isn't the block. Tell her to take care of my car and not to let everyone fool around with it. As it is a good car but if everyone fools around with it, it won't be worth a darn.

I listened to the radio and they had Abbie's Irish Rose radio show on. It made me think of how you used to have it on every Saturday. Oh yes, now I won't be able to go to church as I am on Charge of Quarters again this Sunday and am I mad. They don't give me a chance to do anything. Yesterday afternoon I helped bring foot lockers from the station. I had a chance to drive a truck. One of those big ones. It isn't to bad. A little harder than a car but I managed to drive it there. The only thing is that I haven't got an Army permit yet. But we will all have to know how to drive a tank, truck, jeep, half tract, and fire a 75, 50, and 30, 45 sub machine. These are all guns. Oh yes a pistol. I have already had the 30, 45, and pistol training in the Army before so I am a little ahead of the other fellows.

You ought to see my face. It is sunburned all but a line where my helmet strap goes around my chin. You know what kind of helmet I mean. Those you see the boys have on in the pictures who are over across. Last night we never got to bed until after 11:00 o'clock. Boy do they work us. I'll be tougher than rocks when I get thru here.

Honey, you'll laugh at this. The other day I went on K.P. in the afternoon as the company was out learning how to drive tanks. Well, only one cook was on duty. It seems he couldn't get everything done in time so I gave him a hand. I made the biscuits and if I do say so myself, they were pretty good. So I will have to watch myself or I may be in the kitchen before I know it. I hope not.

It seems when I get started on these letters I can't stop. Well honey, have a good Easter and think of me as I will be thinking of you. Although, I think of you all the time. Love is a funny thing. They say absence makes the heart grow fonder. I hope that's true. As when we get back, we'll never be able to separate. Loads of love and kisses. Until we get together this will have to do. Seems funny not to see you or have you near to be able to take hold of and kiss you. Loving you always.

As ever,

Ed

Easter Sunday, April 25, 1943

Dearest Honey,

I just received your letter. Hon, I am just as lonely as you. Maybe more so as at least you have someplace to go. Here I don't have to much to do for amusement. The P.X. is overcrowded and so also are the theaters. As for town, I don't believe I'd care to go there. I have only been to a show once and I had seen the picture before. The only thing we can do is to bear it and maybe it wouldn't be to long before we may be together again. Today I spent the day thinking of you and how you must look in your Easter outfit. Gee hon, it's hard just thinking about it. Sometimes I get to feeling so blue that I could just pack up and leave here but I know better than that. You know, sometimes I almost wish I had kept **the old car**, as I liked it better than my new Dodge. Also, as you say, it brings back memories and what wonderful memories. You know honey, I believe we can truthfully say that we had a swell time in that car. Perhaps a little naughty at times but there was no damage done. I know that you would be willing to do it again if the opportunity occurred. I know that I would. The only thing that I am afraid of is that I may be a changed man when I get back. You know that war isn't pleasant and a lot of things can happen now that I am in this outfit. Almost anything can happen. Here is a small picture of what the tanks are like. The numbers on the picture mean the places of where the men are located. I am supposed to be where the number 5 is. In the position of number 4 and 5, **the** man has to stick his head out of the top of the tank. So you can imagine what this outfit is like. The only thing I hope is that I can go to Officers Candidate School. I am going to try very hard as I want to be promoted with stripes or bars.

The only thing, hon I want you to promise me that you won't join the W.A.A.C. as the fellows here talk a lot about them. Also, I have seen plenty and I don't want to think of you as one of them. In fact, I demand that you forget about it. As a husband I believe that I have the right to do that. So honey, stay home for me and put up with this situation the best you can. As you must realize I have to put up with a lot.

Well honey, I better close for now but remember I love you dearly and I hope to be with you soon. Love and loads of kisses.

Loving you,

Ed.

Easter Sunday, April 25, 1943

Dearest Ed,

Our Easter is a very rainy one and altho I have a day off, it isn't a happy day because of the rain. Received a letter with your announcement about Lance Corporal and I believe the right thing to say is "Congratulations." The talk about Officers Candidate

School is the best idea and I also think you're crazy to pass up a chance like that. I'm sure that if you did fail it wouldn't make any difference. If it was up to me, I'd still take the chance and let the rest come what may. I went to church today for the 10 o'clock (last) mass and thought of you all the time. Also, I lit a candle in your behalf. Here I'll say good luck to you. Thanks for the corsage you had your mother buy for me but I wasn't proud to wear it because I couldn't prove to the people that it was from you as they were knowing that you were not there in person.

Again I must tell you that in the past letters which have not as yet reached you 1 have described my work as well as I could. Otherwise, I am not allowed to say any more than only my job is called a "fuse job" and the little things that we are doing are used as caps to screw on to the end of torpedoes. My job is called threading and it is done on the outside of this gadget by a die, which makes these threads. We make $0.15 per hundred and they are about one inch.

I love you with all my love,

Maryanne

In Tunisia... "Longstop" hill is captured by the British 5th Corps. The Churchill tanks used in the attack have proven useful in the hilly terrain.

From Washington... New plans are approved for the Solomon Islands operations (code named "Cartwheel"). Admiral Halsey's South Pacific Area forces are to advance through New Georgia and Bougainville. MacArthur's Southwest Pacific Area is to continue its advance northwest along the coast of New Guinea until he and Halsey can link up to isolate the Japanese bases at Rabaul and Kavieng.[15]

Thursday, April 29, 1943

Dear Honey,

I am writing to you again, as I may not be able to write to you for a couple of days. As we are going out for the day and also the night. They say that it is going to be wicked at most. 87 boys that don't know anything about putting up tents and so forth. Gee I hate the thought of going out for those couple of days. Today we fired the machine gun. I made 106 out of 125, which isn't very much. Then I coached four men. Told them how to shoot and where to shoot. One made 111 and one made 114. The other two men made 89 and 90. Boy did I get heck for the two men who got the low scores, but it isn't my fault. After all, I can't shoot the damn gun for them. Boy I never have seen such a bunch of fellows. They seem to be helpless. But once they get overseas they'll learn what it is all about. I know you must be tired after working all day but you still don't tell me what you work at. You know honey, it seems funny that I worked on the gun parts at Savage Arms and now I use them. I had my blood typed today and it is type "O" which is universal or that is any one can use it. So I am good for something. Well honey, I will close for now. Happy dreams. Hope I am in them. Love and kisses for now.

I love you,

Ed

P.S. Wish I could be able to hug you now as I have that feeling to do so. But no dice. So I will dream of you.

In Tunisia... The Germans retake Djebel Bou Aoukaz. Farther north, the American gain a foothold on Hill 609. Alexander decides to switch veteran units from the British 8th Army to join a renewed attack between Bou Aoukaz and Ksar Tyr.[16]

Friday, April 30, 1943

Dear Honey,

Well today we went out in the field with the tanks and boy is it dirty out there. The dust is so heavy that you can't see the tank ahead of you. Well, to start the day, we got up at 3:30 A.M. and were out with the tanks by 6:00 o'clock. After we got there, the first thing to happen was for Brodowski to take four men and dig a latrine. As you may know, I don't do the work. As soon as I finished that job, I came back. It seems that they had the boys divided into groups and getting instructions in different things. So what do you think happened next? No, it was Brodowski again. Take this detail out. Give them Close Order Drill. All this until 11:00 o'clock. Then the Company Commander says, "Brodowski, come with me." So I followed him. We get to the peep and he drives with me sitting along side of him. He drives back to headquarters, which is about 5 miles. Then he says, "You drive the peep back to the Company and wait for me." Then I waited for about a ½ an hour. Then back we went to the tank training area. Then again the afternoon was wasted and the hardest part of it was that all the other fellows got to drive the tanks, all but me. Everybody was all set to go back to the barracks. All of a sudden, I hear "Brodowski" so I jump up and run over to the Lt. He says to me, "Take some men and cover the latrine." So off I go. After that is finished, we got to the tank garage, which is better known as the "Motor Park". Boy can those tanks cut down trees. The Sgt. driving the tank took them all down.

Well anyway, we get to the Motor Park and boy do I work hard. No kidding, I may not get the instruction some of the other fellows get, but I know what is suppose to be done so am I busy. I worked for about a half an hour when they go and get a couple of fellows to help. We don't get to the Co. until about 6:30 and are we dirty. No kidding honey, you wouldn't know me if you had seen me. Now we are trying to clean up the barracks or rather the boys are. You know it burns me up. I go out and get as dirty as any of the fellows, still I don't get a chance for instructions. It seems that whatever they do, I have to give some kind of instruction and as far as I am concerned, they know more than I do. I can't figure out what they are trying do. As I get all the marching detail and I don't like it. I would rather get instructions. If they keep fooling around, I am going to go to work in the kitchen. I mean it. I'll be dang if I'll get shoved around like that. Well honey, I guess I better stop finding fault. I will close this letter for now. Sending my love and a lot of kisses. Good night honey.

I love you,

Ed

MAY

In Tunisia... US forces complete the occupation of Hill 609 in "Mousetrap Valley." The Axis defenses hold American attempts to advance further.[17]

In May, 1943, Churchill was in Washington for the TRIDENT Conference, during which the Americans and British agreed to launch the cross-Channel attack in a year's time. He also made a second speech to Congress. Churchill reminded them that "the main burden of the war on land" was still being borne by the Soviet Army on the Eastern Front. He added that the final triumph, in spite of the recent victory in Tunisia, would come only after battles as difficult and costly as those that had followed the pivotal Battle of Gettysburg in the American Civil War.

"The five months from April to September 1943 at Camp Polk included various types of activity. During May and June all personnel of the Division participated in the Army Ground Forces physical training tests which measured the ability of the American soldier to exist 24 hours with no sleep, one canteen of water, and a very light meal of combat rations. All members of the Division ran through the infiltration course during the daylight and again in darkness. Small units held field exercises in the Peason Ridge, Rose Pine, or Slagle Training Areas."[18]

Saturday, May 1, 1943

Dearest Ed,

I am writing this letter to you in the cafeteria while eating at noon. Say what do you know but it's May 1st. It's snowing here and very cold. Did you get my letter with the pictures? How is the mail coming to you now? Did you get all the back mail yet? Please take Officers Candidate School. I know you'll like it and pass it.

So you think a man is a fool when he tells his wife how much he loves her. It makes me feel bad because I have been doing just that to you in every letter. I sent so many packages to you that I lost track so please dear tell me what you receive and when you receive them.

Before I go on, I must tell you of a plan I have. You know June 28 is our wedding anniversary. I would like to be with you. So if things go right, I will try hard to get there and I hope you are also looking forward to it. Please say yes for then I can tell you a lot of things I am holding back now and don't ask me what they are. One thing though, what would you say if your mother happened to trade **your Dodge** for another car. She claims there is a lot of expense on repairs for it.

Darling, please don't say anything to her about this for she will know who told you. Can't write much more as I am sitting with some girls and it would be very rude for me to ignore them. I love to get letters from you every so often so please don't forget me. I love you. till later. I remain,

Ever Yours,
Maryanne

Monday, May 3, 1943

My Dearest Honey,

Things here are about the same as always. Work and more work and nothing for it. I don't know really what is going to happen to me and I hear all kinds of rumors. The only thing is I hope they are all for the best. As I would like to come home being someone. Not a common private. Even being a Lance Corporal don't mean nothing.

Honey, I had the daylights scared out of me as some guy came over and asked me if my name was Brodowski, or so I thought he said. I said yes and he says your wife is here waiting for you. I looked at him and man was I shocked. I guess I must of showed it. Anyway, he hands me an envelope with the name on it and it was someone else. But for a second I thought you had come. Gee, I shook all over for a moment. Honest, I thought you had come. Don't ever do that unless I know ahead of time when you are coming. As if you come unexpected, I may be out or on duty.

Yesterday I went out and bought a dinner. It cost me $.90 and it felt good to be out to eat. The only thing bad was some of the fellows had their wives and I wished I had you here. Also, it makes me feel bad every time I see the fellows have their wives or girl friends with them. Then I think back what we did and the fun we had. Gee honey, I really miss you more than you may realize. I get a lump every time I think of you. Honest honey, I could do almost anything to get back home with you. So you must know by now how much I love you. Honey, I don't think anyone loves one another as we do. Well honey, I better close this letter as I may get foolish and put things in here that I may regret. The only thing I can say is I love you dearly. Honest honey. So good night and lots of love.

With love,
Ed

Wednesday, April 28, 1943

Dear Honey,

Well, I suppose the weather is getting nice at home. The grass is green and the rest is hay. Couldn't I have fun if I were home. What do you do in your time off? How about telling me? Not that I want to be noisy but I am wondering what you do in you time off? As for myself, I don't get to much time off. So I can not do much. I mostly write or should I say try to write. This coming week we are allowed off the post. They have a truck convoy going to Lake Charles, which is about 80 mi. from here. They can only put up 250 men with beds so the rest will have to carry their own on full field equipment if they want to go. As for me, I just as soon stay at the barracks and maybe get a couple of letters off. I hope you don't mind that it is mostly nonsense. I'll be glad when they get all this recruit training over with then maybe I'll get a break but for the present time it is pretty tough.

I guess you have a job trying to read my letters but you'll have to get used to it as I always was bad at writing. Wish I had the gift of writing so I could express my feelings in the nice way but all I can say is that you are the only one and that I love you with all my heart. You know honey, that I wish I could put in words how I feel. What I mean is how I feel towards you. But for the lack of speech and also the lack of words, well that is me. But honey, there will never be any one but you no matter where we are or how far apart we are. You will always be the only one for me. You know that I have been in different places in the army before I met you. Also hon, as of yet I haven't found anyone who could compare to you. I don't know what it is but there is something about you that gets to me. Perhaps that laugh or the way you smile. I don't know but there is something that does.

I don't even know if you remember but before we got married, we went to the show. It was the Utica Theater and we had to wait, as it was full. Up to that time I used to think about you, one time thinking yes she is the one and one time thinking no. But this time I watched you from the side. From then on I knew what I wanted and was determined to get you. It was the way you looked or something but from then on I was sure that I was in love with you. I'll bet you think I am screwy or something but honest honey, I am telling the truth. Hon I love you dearly and the only thing that matters is that you love me. . Don't know what I would do if something should come between us. I hope that nothing will ever come between us. That nothing will ever change either of our minds. Especially while I am away. Because honey, as for me I am sure of my love for you. So honey, don't forget that you have someone who loves you. So I hope that you never think of finding someone else as it must be hard for you being home alone. I don't want you to think that I don't want you to enjoy yourself for I do. I think that you should go out as much as possible as it may be a long time before we'll be able to go out together. But I know one thing and that is that I am going to see you again even if I have to have you come down here. Time will tell. It all depends on the situation over across. I can say this much, I think the whole world is crazy having people fighting each other and many never coming home.

Your Loving Husband,
Ed

Monday, May 3, 1943

My Dearest Darling,

I have 3 of your letters, which came as on Sat., and two today. These letters make me so happy that I don't understand how I can sit here instead of running for the first train to take me to you. It's funny how we write to each other because we can't answer each others letters on account of they are meeting each other on their way. Funny but now I feel that all you have told me is truly from the bottom of your heart and you can just take all that vice versa for I feel the same way about you, dearest. I dread writing letters for then I become a silly crying woman. But I do all I can to hold it back. I lose plenty of sleep just imagining that you are with me and in my mind I talk to you, something like this. Oh darling, please say over and over that you love me for it is so hard for you to not repeat those words. And yes my sweet, I love you and always will. Then I make believe that we are planning for the future and say that we figure out what money we spend to build the home which will be "our home" etc. You see darling, it sounds swell but it is so far away. This letter must sound as if I'm a stuttering person for I repeat things over and over. If the letters sound unreasonable forgive me for my thoughts are so full of you that I forget to reread them, as is my habit. Did you receive my pictures yet? I wish those darn letters and packages would reach you in accordance to the way I sent them. Honest darling, I write ever so often. Sometime I write 2 letters for each one of yours. So you see, I'm quite anxious that you should receive them for otherwise you do not know what I write to you.

Golly, it makes me mad the way things are. Why must it be? Why must we be apart? I long to be able to hold you in my arms and smoother you with kisses. I cry myself to sleep at night. I miss you so much.

And about the 1 year and 10 months of our marriage that has gone by, I thought about it and of you all day also and how sacred those months were to us. And dear, when you tell me how you feel, don't call it nonsense or any such thing because when you do, you spoil all of it that you write. Maybe I'm shameless in saying this but I know you love to hear these fancy words from me and before God, I say I do also. After all we truly are in love but now is one awful time for us to find out how much and what we have missed.

Golly darling, I wish you had talked to me like this when we were together. Altho, I do understand that it is easier to write down on the paper than to tell a person to his face of love. Now do you understand when I begged you in the past to tell me these things for our marriage would have been so much easier with just a few words of love? Remember the first time you asked me if I loved you and to say it. I do remember it very plainly. I also remember it didn't go over very big with you because there wasn't enough feeling in it. Then too, I wasn't to sure about us but now darling I am and how much I am. I wouldn't even think of making any dates with any man. I'll wait darling, even if it takes a lifetime. As things go, the situation in Africa is perfect so maybe God will stay on our side and grant us our wish. But the biggest wish is that you wouldn't go across. That if you do go overseas scares me the most. Darling, I'll pray so hard because I'm afraid to let you go.

There is something else you to wrote me a while back. You said you would show me how good you will be to me when you get back by showing it through your actions. But as I remember, it was the lack of words, not actions, that we needed and sweetheart, we will have to learn to talk (to each other) for we proved our love already by actions. You could never be any better to me for you were the best to me and the only thing that kept between us was a wall which was that lack of words of love. Remember when I felt blue and cried telling you that I didn't understand what the wall was between us? That kept us somehow apart altho we were close otherwise? I knew what it was but I was afraid to talk about it.. But now you know so that is the only change that will have to be done when we see each other. I am hoping that it will be very soon.

I have received the first dependency check from you. You know thru the War Dept. Tomorrow and Wednesday are my days off. (Tues) Tomorrow I will go to cash the checks, which are my pay, and the War Dept. check, which is for $50.00. This Friday when my pay comes I will get around $52 to $55. Isn't it grand? And I'm so anxious but not as anxious as me wanting to come to you on our anniversary. So please just give me a yes as a gift. For seeing you and being with you will be like going to heaven on wings. Oh darling, you haven't written me the answer but I have taken it for granted it is yes. I am saving all the money and I am already visioning how we will meet. It will be such a grand meeting and I just can't wait.

Now I must close and go to bed for it is late. So goodnight darling. I love you so much and here are all those kisses you used to get when we said goodnight together in bed. xxxxxxxxxxxxxxxxxxx etc.

Ever Yours,
Maryanne

Sunday, May 9, 1943

In Tunisia... The last organized Axis resistance is eliminated. Large scale surrenders, of Axis troops, begin.

From Berlin... Hitler approves Operation Citadel, the attack on the Kursk salient, despite expressing misgivings and news of Soviet defensive preparations. [19]

Dearest Honey,

This morning I was admitted into the hospital and had my eye dressed. Also, they gave me some pills to kill the pain so I came back and laid down for a while and feel better now. If they don't do something beside put drops into it, I am going to raise hell as I don't want to become blind. Not yet anyway. It started the same way as at home, remember? But this time it closed up and the whole eye is red and sore. So I don't know what the outcome is going to be. But don't worry about it as otherwise I am fine.

Oh yes, I have driven a tank. Nothing to it. Almost as easy as driving a car. I have to laugh as they say, "to bad you're not a regular man as we could make you this or make you that." So I don't know just what will become of me. As I am able to do almost anything there is to be done. Yesterday, we had full field inspection on bunks which means all your equipment displayed on bunks. Well, I not only did mine but almost all the other fellows to. The Company Commander came through and all he said was O.K. Brodowski. It makes it tough to be an old soldier as they are all waiting for you to do something wrong. But I will fool them and do everything right (I hope).

Honey, today is Mother's Day so tell yours and mine that I am thinking of them. Also, send them my love. I hope they received those cards I sent. Let me know if they did. Like you said, there is a lot of things you will tell me when you come down. So, also, I have a lot of things which I can say and not write. So they will wait until you arrive. But honey, as I said yesterday, get all details before you try to come, as it is very hard to make arrangements here. The only thing, I hope I can arrange to get a couple days off. I will try hard to. So I am counting the days until I see you.

Honest honey, I miss you more and more. The Army before wasn't to bad for me for I didn't have you waiting for me. But now, I have you and it seems a lifetime that I have been away. So if this damn war don't end pretty soon, I'll be an old man at an early age. You won't even recognize me. But you don't mind do you? I mean being old at an early age. Until we meet hon,

I love you,

Ed

Tuesday May 11, 1943

The US troops attack Japanese at Attu in the Aleutian Islands

Wednesday, May 12, 1943

In Tunisia... General von Arnim surrenders to the Allies. Italian General Messe is promoted to Field Marshal by Mussolini in hopes of encouraging him to continue fighting. [20]

In Washington... The Trident Conference. Roosevelt and Churchill meet to discuss strategy. The Americans seek a commitment to an invasion of western Europe. The British seek a commitment to an invasion of Italy and possibly the Balkans.[21]

My Dearest Darling,

I am afraid that when you read this letter you will be worried but don't as everything will come out O.K. You know I wrote about my eye. Well yesterday I was sent to the hospital with it where I am now. It makes me so damn mad to stay in a hospital but it doesn't pay to argue, as they know best. As for the eye, I will know in a few day just what really is wrong. At present, they are calling it, "Iritis." which is the inflammation of the iris treatable with eye drops. I now will lose a lot of chances for advancement by being here but I guess that what is to be will be.

Now I don't have anything to do but think and the only thing I can think of is you and home. But I wish I'll be out by the time you decide to come down. It would be hell if you come to see me and I'm in a hospital. Will try to give you information day by day. But this is a lazy mans life. Nothing to do but lay around. If they had sent me when I first came in, I may have had a better chance. But now they kept putting drops in for 4 days and then decided that I should see an Eye Specialist.

But honey, now don't get alarmed as I'll be O.K. If you should carry on, I won't write another thing that happens to me. So hold fast and I'll be writing where everything is fine. Love you more every day. Lady, I am writing to your picture. I have it laying on the cot along side my writing material. Hon, how are chances on having a picture made of yourself. A post card size, colored and in a paper frame just like the one you had made before but post card size. I know you'll have one made. Or I'll be mad. Well honey, closing my one eye for now. Love and kisses.

I love you,

Ed

Ed spent the next month in the hospital because of an eye condition while the rest of the soldiers received training that Ed was going to miss. Missing this training eventually cost him the promotion he so dearly wanted. The war continued on and the soldiers at Camp Polk continued to prepare for the inevitable day in the future of being deployed overseas.

Thursday, May 13, 1943

In Tunisia... Italian Field Marshal Messe orders the remaining German and Italian troops to surrender. About 250,000 Axis troops have been taken prisoner in the past few days[22]

Sunday, May 16, 1943

Over Germany... During the night (May 16-17), a specially trained and equipped RAF bomber squadron (No. 617) carries out successful precision bombing raids on the dams on the Mohne and Eder Rivers. A third target, the Sorpe dam, is not attacked. The targets are believed to supply the majority of electricity used in the Ruhr industrial area and a significant quantity of the water. However, 8 of the 19 aircraft are lost and the damage is far less than had been hoped.

In Occupied Poland... The Warsaw Ghetto Uprising. The synagogue is blown up. S troop, the SS commander responsible for putting down the uprising, claims that since the uprising began, on April 19, 14,000 Jews have been killed in the ghetto and another 40,000 have been sent to Treblinka to be killed.[23]

Monday, May 17, 1943

In Occupied Yugoslavia... Operation *Schwarz*. The Germans launch their fifth major offensive against Tito's partisans. German forces are commanded by General Luters. They include the SS Division Prinz Eugen, 1st Mountain Division and the 4th Brandenburg Regiment. The latter two units have been deployed in the area for this operation. Other Axis units hold an encircling ring. In total, there are about 120,000 Axis troops engaged against, at most, 20,000 partisans led by Tito[24]

Wednesday, May 19, 1943

My Darling,

I received your letters yesterday. Also the package of cookies were swell. Will be waiting for more of them. Now about my eye. I have been here 8 days today and it seems a little better. I hope by next week to be out. You know, by being in the hospital kinda knocks a hole in my plans. As I am missing training and I don't know how the Company Commander will take it. As I was quite sure of a rating after seven weeks so now I don't know.

I was going to write yesterday but I got a shot for the eye and it put me in bed for the day. Altho, they wanted a better reaction, the shots don't seem to work on me. In fact, they increase the dose yesterday and it still didn't take the proper effect. The doctor said I was a tough one.

You asked about Officers Candidate School. Well it seems you have to complete your basic training first before you can apply for it. I suppose I'll never get the chance to go as my luck was never that good. And the Air Corps, that is entirely out. Once you get in the Armored Force you stay there. So you see you'll have to be satisfied with a private for a husband. The Army is funny as whatever you want, you can never get. But fellows who don't give a darn get the best of the choices. Oh well, will have to make the best of it. Just hoping the war ends soon so that we can be together again. That is the only thing that counts.

Honey, do you miss all the fun we had last year. The lake and all. I guess you do as I know I'm missing it all. You know, after our 13 weeks of Basic Training we are supposed to start maneuvers for the same amount of time and I dread the thought of them. As you'll live like animals and not humans. The only thing I am living for is the idea of seeing you again. Otherwise, life just wouldn't be worth a dime. I mean it. If it wasn't for having you to go back to, I wouldn't give a darn for anything. But the thought of you keeps me pushing ahead. So don't let me down. I can't wait till next month. I hope nothing happens that I may not be able to stay with you. So you better pray on the side that I get off for a few days.

Now honey, I am going to try to explain how you will have to get here. The fellows I talk with seem to say that by going from Utica to Chicago, then down to St. Louis, Mo. From there down to Alexandria. Then I believe you will have to take a bus to Leesville. Then from there either send word into camp and I'll try to get out or take a North Camp Polk bus right into Camp and I'll have arrangements at the guest house. But as I said, try and get here for Friday night so that we can have the weekend together. Now honey, listen carefully. Go to any gas station and get a Southwestern United States map. This map will have Texas, New Mexico, Louisiana, and Arkansas on it. On this map you can just about find where I am at. But you will have to get off the train at Alexandria and take the bus to Leesville. Also a bus to camp.

Your Loving husband

Ed

Thursday, May 20, 1943

Dearest Sweetheart:

Have just had a lovely supper in the dining room as I am ashamed to eat in front of the men putting up the chimney. They are working upstairs already and soon will reach the attic. Our weather here has warmed up a bit but again it looks like rain. We have had so much rain that we are still waiting to see a few sunny days in succession. I have a little over $130.00 so far and I should have another $100.00 by the time I start out. But now I have 2 worries on my mind. One is that I do have to ask the M.P for a written pass before I get to walk on the Camp grounds to reach the Orderly Room and Co. Comm. don't I? And the other is, isn't your basic training about due then or how long after the 13 weeks do you go for the other 13 weeks of maneuvers? Something else, is if there is no chance of you getting your days off or any possibility of my seeing you, even if to the last day, wire me or call Pop Putney and leave a short message for me not to come. Don't worry about the money for these things mean more to me than the old do re mi.

Talking about going to Hinckley Lake and all that stuff, you needn't think to much about it for pleasure driving has been banned again as of this afternoon. So you see you'd stay home anyhow. Gosh it's kind of hard to write as my arm and wrist feel lame. Work has been monotonous and I'm beginning to feel dragged out at all times like on the laundry days. I'm not working hard at all and don't seem to able to make my $50. But oh how I'm looking forward to that trip and I hope dear God up in heaven hears my prayers and brings things out just the way we want them. If I start out on the 22nd at night or the 23rd, I should get there as you want me to. I hope that it turns out that you could meet me and that will clear matters immensely. Altho, I am going to try my best to do all I can to get there otherwise as you have described. Gosh, I hope all turns out for the best. Last night I got a cramp in my leg below the knee in the muscle and that makes it miserable all day for me and I'm quite tired. You may not like what I will say but if, now I'm not saying he won't, but if the boss refuses me my 2 weeks, I'll take it no matter what the cost of the job means. For I can get another one when I come back somewhere else. And anyway, this place has got me down. I just despise the way men will says things about a woman. But don't care much on what I write for I'll explain all when I see you and will make things more clearer.

Right now I can't think straight and will have to get ready for bed. I love you and only you forever my darling and in closing, I must say help me pray and days will go by faster and speed my time to get to you. So till the next letter, my darling, goodnight. God bless you, pleasant dreams and may our wishes come true. As ever.

Your loving wife

Maryanne

Thursday, May 20, 1943

My Darling,

Here I am writing again but this is the only way I can come close to you. So will try and make it an interesting letter. The doctor gives us an exam every morning. This morning he said I had improved a lot. I asked to be let out and go back to my company but no dice. So do not know just how much longer I must stay here. I do know I am very tired of laying around. They just had mail call and I didn't get any. It must be at the Company as it goes there first and then here to the hospital.

Honey, how is everything at home. Gee I'd give anything to be home if just for a weekend as that would be better than being here. Wouldn't it be a break if the outfit moved to Pine Camp. Boy that would be swell as then I could come down often. You know they had me examined from head to foot trying to find the cause for my eye. And all of them came back clean, nothing wrong. So I don't know just what will be the out come.

I could keep on writing how much I love you but I can't find the nice words to express it. But honey, you know that you are the only one and no other will do. Also, I am not worried about others making passes at you as I know you care to much for me to look at another. Also, you can feel the same about me. As you are the only one who I care for. So closing with love and kisses.

Your Loving husband

Ed

Friday, May 21, 1943

My Darling,

I'll say this much about my eye, there has been improvement quite rapidly. In fact I hope to get out very soon. I tried to talk the doctor into letting me out yesterday but no dice.

But hope that I will soon. Boy are they feeding me light. Really. No meat or heavy foods, mostly liquids. Even so, I get enough.

We are having some swell weather and it makes me want to come home all the more. Sometimes I think what a fool I have been. Always, I wanted to come into the Army. Now I would take any sort of discharge just to get back. I mean it. It makes it hard not knowing if you are well or if any things come up that you may need my help

One of the fellows from the Company came over to see me and he said that a lot of fellows have been promoted. So I guess I lose out by being in the hospital. Oh well, maybe I'll get lucky when I get back and might be able to get a rating.

Last night I was thinking of the evenings we spent in the parlor reading, eating, and even fighting. Those were the times we both enjoyed. At least I did. Now what do I have. A single bunk, a bunch of fellows, and heck, then no company. Lights out regardless if you are ready for bed or not. Everything is done to schedule. If you don't get ready, you get bawled out. And at home we did anything we wanted.

I am beginning to miss all things more and more. Heck, it is even hard to get ice cream here. Remember all the custard we had. Those are the things I enjoyed. I'll bet you miss them too. But don't worry, our day will come and then we can make up for all the time we lost. How is the heating oil coming along. Have you got plenty yet. Now don't be afraid to get yourself some clothes, as I know you need some. So get them. As there is no reason why you shouldn't. Is your father still working? Hey don't forget about that picture I asked for. You better have it or when you come here, you'll be in trouble.

How is the Savage Arms running? Any layoffs lately? You know honey, I wish I could find a place and have you stay here. But that is out of the question as in the early part of July we expect to go out on maneuvers and I am only hoping it is not before you get here. So that means I may be with you for a short time. As if they do, I think I'll go nuts as I am really planning on it. But if something should happen, we at least tried. That will be something. Why do people have to fight and make innocent people break up homes just to satisfy one or two. It seems unreasonable. We were just getting to understand one another. (after one year and 10 months of marriage) Now we will have to start all over again. But it will be so much easier now don't you think?

We can say this much we were lucky to have so much time together as we had. As others only have a few days or weeks together and then they leave. Honey, in closing this letter, I want to say that I love you more and more and no matter what should happen, I'll always love you. So let's hope that we may be together soon, very soon.

I hope you are able to read this letter as my eyes aren't quite well yet. Lots of love and kisses.

Loving you always,

Ed

Saturday, May 22, 1943

From Berlin... Admiral Dontiz orders all U-boat patrols in the north Atlantic to break off operations against the convoys. The submarine losses have grown too high. This decision effectively ends the battle of the Atlantic with an Allied victory. Some boats are moved south to the Caribbean and to waters off the Azores.

In the United States... Mississippi river flooding continues. In total, 150,000 people become homeless.[25]

Sunday, May 23, 1943

Over Germany... The Battle of the Ruhr. More than 2000 tons of bombs are dropped on Dortmund in the heaviest RAF Bomber Command raid to date[26].

Monday, May 24, 1943

Dear Sweetheart,

Received 3 of your letters today and was overjoyed to get that many in one day. First thing I want to say is I hope you are perfectly well by now and it is the same with me altho I have a slight cold. That kit and bed room slippers were sent out without being insured but how about you asking the post office to look around and maybe it was left in the 88th Armored Reg. Like your letters did for it went out about the same time. Otherwise, as you say, it has been lost. I will go to the place where I sent it from and will try to find out but I don't think it will do any good. Gosh, it makes me miserable to know that it didn't reach you and I hope God answers my prayers and that you do receive them soon. But please check up on your end also. Darling, right now I have a cake in the oven but I know you wouldn't care much for it. As of late I've been making the cake all chocolate. I will not send any more to you till I get back from my visit. Again I will say yes, I have received the Savage Arms check and put it in the bank.

Why don't you quit worrying about promotions and stripes. I didn't marry you as a soldier and I don't even care if you do come out a private for I'll still love you as much as ever. I'll try to get those socks you asked for. How was I to know what kind if you didn't tell me what kind you wear. I'll also take care of that car of yours and give her proper treatment of mothballs. I wish that after basic training they bring you closer to home. Darling, about those packages that are supposedly lost, I'm sorry and I've learn my lesson for I'll insure all that goes your way. When you get out of the hospital and you check up please let me know what I should do; if you'd like me to buy you another pair or what.

And again I'm sorry if this letter is short for I can't seem to think very clear. So tomorrow I'll try to write a longer letter. It is now time to take the cake out so I'll close with best of health, best of luck, and God Bless you, dearest. I'll love till eternity. And now goodnight and sleep well as I'll be thinking of you all the time. It is close to my bedtime and I'll be dreaming of you. Sweet dreams my darling.

Your wife,
Maryanne

P.S. XXXXXXXXXXXXXXXXXX etc.

Monday, May 24, 1943

My Darling,

Here it is Monday morning and .at present, I have been here 13 days and I get to hate this place. There is no reason why I shouldn't be able to go back to my Company, as what little they do for the eye, I could do myself. The doc came around this morning but all he says is that the eye has improved but still is slightly red. So I have to stay a little longer. But as far as seeing, I can read the chart 20-20 with either eye.

I read the paper this morning and it looked pretty good over across. I hope that it don't last to long. It would be great to get back home and do the things we use to. Stop and think what all we have done together and then realize that it may be some time before we will be able to do those things again. Honey, don't think that I am a quitter but I am just writing as I feel. And I believe that all the fellows in the service feel the same way regardless of how good or bad the branch of service is that they are in. I believe they would give anything to be able to be home.

Today we had three of the fellows have operations. Two had their eyes straightened and one had a nose operation. You wouldn't believe it but it seems simple for them to take an eye out, clean it, and put it back in the same socket. With cross-eyes or crooked eyes they cut some muscles and put bandages on it and a few days later the fellow has a straight eye. One fellow coughed during an operation, which spoiled that operation. He had to be operated on again. These doctors are what you call common butchers. They love to cut anything, just to cut.

But tell me how are you making out about coming down here? Have you already made all your plans as yet? And as the days go by, are you as thrilled with the thought of coming down here as you were at first? As I am just waiting for the day you will arrive here. Wishing it was now instead of next month. But by waiting a little will make it that much nicer.

Honey, just to hear some of these fellows talk about their wives, I don't know why they married them if they don't trust them. That is something, which doesn't worry me, as I know that I don't have to worry about you.

One of these fellows has his wife visit him and this one day she was here when they had mail call. He had one of the fellows get his mail so his wife wouldn't know he had any. Boy that is something when you can't get mail because you are afraid it may be from someone that you wouldn't want your wife to know about. By the way, they were married on our anniversary the 28th of June only last year.

Boy what I wouldn't give to have you here. Hon, I love you more than anything else in the world. Wish you could see me sometimes. You'd get a surprise of your life the way I just keep looking at your picture. Well honey, it won't be long and we will be together for awhile. Until then, I love you. Sealing this letter with love and kisses.

Your Loving Husband,

Ed

Tuesday, May 25, 1943

In Washington... The Trident Conference ends. Roosevelt and Churchill, and their staffs, reach compromises on all of the significant differences. Among the decisions taken is the target date for the invasion of western Europe (D-Day) -- May 1, 1944.

British General Morgan is appointed to prepare plans for the invasion. His is designated Chief of Staff to the Supreme Allied Commander (COSSAC). [27]

Thursday, May 27, 1943

In Occupied Yugoslavia... British officers are parachuted into occupied Yugoslavia in order to rendezvous with Tito's partisan forces in Montenegro, near Mount Durmitor. Tito's forces have been under attack by superior German, Italian and Bulgarian forces for ten days now and they are concentrating for a breakout. The desire to meet with the British representatives is one reason for the delay in attempting to disengage.

From Washington... Churchill and American General Marshall leave for North Africa for talks with General Eisenhower on the Italian campaign. Churchill wants to exploit opportunities in the Mediterranean and to get Italy to surrender. Marshall wants to avoid commitments that will interfere with the invasion of western Europe that is now being prepared.[28]

My Darling,

I don't believe I told you but I had an x-ray of my teeth taken and all he could find was those two teeth that I had the nerve taken out. So he claims that they may cause my eye to go bad. So he recommends to have them taken out and I was suppose to have them out today. But as yet they haven't called me. Hope they forget about them.

I don't believe I said this before but since I have been here they have had me x-rayed and all kinds of physical exams trying to blame my eye on something in my system. But the teeth are the only thing they could find and then they are not sure. And the only way they can tell is by pulling them out.

Read the paper this morning and all the news seems favorable for us. Hope it remains so as want to get back home as soon as possible. Hope you don't have to much trouble getting here. Don't forget just where I am located, the Company and all. The rest I have told you.

It seems a shame about all the strikes going on and us here in the Army. Why in the heck can't they get together and finish this war and then worry about striking. How is your job coming along? I hope it isn't to hard. If it is, quit. Don't work to hard as it doesn't pay and I don't want you to get sick or anything just because you don't know when to quit. How about that picture I am asking for? Have you forgotten it or aren't you going to send it? Honey, do you love me today. I'll bet you don't.

Here I am a physical wreck in a hospital. Heck you don't want a guy like that do you? But all joking aside, I miss you Hon.. So closing this with loads of love and kisses.

Your Loving husband,
Ed

P.S. Honey, don't ever stop loving me as I couldn't take it if you did.

Saturday, May 29, 1943

My Darling,

Well here it is another day, I feel about the same. The only thing is that I am minus those two teeth. They finally had me go to the Dental Clinic and have them pulled. My jaw feels a little sore otherwise am well. I hope that it is what caused the eye to go bad. It be hell if it couldn't be cured but it will be, as it is almost well now.

The examination board for the Cadets is around but now I am in the hospital. Hope it is still here when I get out. Also, they are sending fellows to different schools to get special training. Well I missed that as I am in the hospital. It seems my luck has gone wrong on me. As everything I want to do, I can't, as I am in the hospital. Just stopped for a moment in order to eat an ice cream cone. It tasted pretty good. Can you get ice cream at home or is it tough.

Oh yes, I guess everything will turn out for the best in due time It seems a shame to have two people who love each other as much as we do to be separated. It doesn't make sense. Here in the ward I am in, I have seen a lot of things such as eye operations. I have also seen fellows put on an act to get an Army discharge claiming they are not physically fit for Army Duty. Honest, I never would have believed it but now I do because I have seen it.

Honey, when you stop and think back, I guess we didn't realize how happy we were or should I say that I never realized it. As I guess I was a pain with the way I acted but I assure you that I'll be very much changed when we get together again. I do want you to know that I miss you and wish this damn war would end. So all of us could go back and live like human beings. So until next month Honey, closing with love and kisses. I think of you every night. Loads of love and piles of kisses. I will close.

Your loving husband
Ed

P.S. Aso your lonesome and sad husband, down in the dumps

JUNE

June 10, 1943

From London and Washington... The Joint Chiefs of Staff issue the Pointblank Directive to British and American heavy bomber forces in Europe. The document sets out formal instructions for the priorities and aims of the bomber offensive up to D-Day. The instructions reflect American thought more so than British but the guidelines are vague enough that both the US Air Force and British Bomber Command can continue their independent operations.[29]

Thursday 5:30 P.M.

My Dearest Darling,

Here I am writing again as have a few minutes and want to tell my troubles to someone so am picking on you. As you know, this is my first day on duty and I really got a working over. Boy am I sore but it'll wear off in a couple of days. This outfit doesn't give a damn for anyone. You are out one day and the next day they put you on K.P. They could at least give me a couple of days to get hardened but they won't give you any breaks. Also, remember how I was Lance Corporal. Well I guess that is also taken away as the K.P. can only mean that I am a recruit again and that is rather hard to take after all the time I have in the service.

This is the worst outfit I have ever seen. No consideration for a man and I don't care anymore. As I gave up everything I hoped for Officer Candidate School and Air Corps. I just lost interest in everything, as before I took sick, my attitude was much different. Now it seems I am just a piece of mud under their feet. Just some one to push around. So now I am going to do like the rest and that is as little as I can just to get it done. As before I put out showing them that even that I was out of the service for sometime, I could get it back into it in no time which I did. But now, since they are doing this to me, the heck with them.

But enough of my belly aching, how are you coming along. Also, what is your final decision on coming down here? Is it just as we planned or are you going to chance it ahead. I really don't know how to advise you as I want you as soon as possible and still I am afraid that you won't be able to get a place and then it will be hell. As you will have to go back. So honey, try and think for both of us as I am going nuts today and I mean nuts. I don't seem to know what I am doing. Also, they want me to be in the kitchen as cook. I don't want to do that again so you see I guess your Army man isn't so good a soldier after all. But never stop believing that I love you as I will always love you and I hope that no matter what I should do won't change it. As I may do almost anything.

Love

Ed

P.S. But don't worry as I won't do anything to get in trouble.

Wednesday, June 16, 1943

In the United States... Operation Husky. The first convoys bound for the invasion of Sicily leave port.[30]

Friday, June 18, 1943

My Dearest Darling,

Just got back from our over night outing. We also had another accident although it wasn't in our company. It was a tank. It went over a bridge and turned upside down. It was very lucky the fellows on the inside were able to get out through the bottom escape hatch which is located on the bottom of the tank. These accidents make me want to get out of this outfit more and more. I don't know what will become of me but in due time I believe I'll find out. I guess I worked as hard today as I ever have. At present, I am sweating so bad it is running down all over this letter.

Honey, I don't know just what will become of us next week but I hope and pray that everything turns out for the best. As I wrote before, I have a 3 day reservation for Friday, Saturday, and Sunday. After that I don't know but I will see what I can do. I will try and go out this weekend and look around .Also, don't forget your ration book. Make arrangements at home so in case you are able to stay awhile. So you won't have any worries.

Thanks for the cookies. I am eating as I write. Boy they re good. Also, I am very hungry for your cooking, as the chow we get is good but it never stands up to yours.

Look honey, I better close for now but I am expecting I will try to meet you. But if I can't, you will know what to do.

Love and good luck.

Ed

P.S. Telegram as soon as you start. Also telegram if anything should come up that you were unable to come

Wednesday, June 23 1943

A telegram was sent to PVT Edward Brodowski, CO. D 80 Armored Regt 258 NCP

Starting seven fifteen tonight. Reaching Friday eight evening. Maryanne.

Maryanne spent the rest of June, all of July and the beginning of August in Leesville, La to be close to her husband. They spent their wedding anniversary together on June 28, 1943. However, on August 4, 1943 a telegram was sent to Maryanne's mother: Maryanne expect to leave next week. Send Money at once.

Ed

Chapter Two

JULY-DECEMBER 1943

Friday, July 9, 1943
"In Sicily... Operation Husky. The invasion of Sicily begins. The landing force is concentrated around Malta. There are 1200 transports and 2000 landing craft which will land elements of 8 divisions. In the evening, there are airborne landings by the US 82nd Airborne Division and British units which cause disruption in the Axis defenses, although they do not manage to seize their objectives. The Italian 6th Army (General Guzzoni) is responsible for the defense of Sicily. There are a total of about 240,000 troops (a quarter of which are Germans)."[31]

"The landings took place in extremely strong wind, which made the landings difficult but also ensured the element of surprise. Landings were made on the southern and eastern coasts of the island, with British forces in the east and Americans towards the west. The British walked virtually unopposed into the port of Syracuse, but Canadian troops met increasing resistance by determined Italian troops from the 206th Coastal Division in the hills. Canadian war correspondent Ross Munro recorded his experiences of the first few days of the attack on the Italian 122 Infantry Regiment north of Pachino in a newspaper article printed on July 12:

Stubborn resistance has been put up by the Italians north and west of Pachino, and along other [Canadian] sectors of the front there were heated engagements. Big battles will probably come before long, but meanwhile large numbers of prisoners are being captured. (The Toronto Globe & Mail, 12 July, 1943)

Attacks by airborne forces were carried out just after midnight on the night of the July 9-July 10, as part of the invasion — two British and two American. The American paratroopers consisted largely of the 505th Parachute Infantry Regiment of the 82nd Airborne, making their first combat drop and the British glider-borne troops were from British 1st Airborne Division.[3] Strong winds of up to 45 miles per hour (72 km/h)[4] scattered aircraft widely off course, and half the U.S. paratroopers failed to reach their rallying points. The British glider-landed troops fared little better, with only one out of 12 gliders landing on target and many crashing at sea. Nevertheless, the scattered airborne troops maximized their opportunities, attacking patrols and creating confusion wherever possible. A company of British parachute soldiers had a desperate battle to hold on to Ponto Grande Bridge against what was incorrectly reported as German counter-attacks on July 10[5].With approximately 90 men, the British force held out till about 1500 hours until forced to surrender to Colonel Francesco Ronco's 75th Infantry Regiment, 54th "Napoli" Division.

A U.S. crew checks their Sherman tank after landing at Red Beach 2, Sicily on July 10

Despite the weather, the beach landings (three hours after the airborne drops) met only moderate opposition from Italian units stationed on the shoreline, because the defenders had been weakened by naval bombardments. However, the Italian Navy and Italian Air Force made several attacks against the invasion fleet with airplanes, warships, and submarines, sinking and damaging several warships, transport vessels and landing craft, at the cost of few of their own vessels and aircraft.[7] Italian SM.79 torpedo-bomber squadrons coordinated their attacks with the German Ju-87 and Ju-88 bomber units, and Rome reported as follows on July 12:[8]

Italian planes torpedoed three cruisers, one smaller unit, and three steamers. Two of them of 8,000 tons each sank. Enemy craft concentrations were attacked by Italian and German formations. Five steamers and several landing craft are reported sunk. Hit and set on fire were more than forty merchantmen and transports of various types. Axis fighters shot down more than thirty enemy planes. Eight more crashed after they were hit by anti-aircraft fire. From operations of the last two days thirteen of our planes and ten of the Germans failed to return.

As a result of the adverse weather, many troops landed in the wrong place, in the wrong order and as much as six hours behind schedule.[9] The British walked lightly opposed into the port of Syracuse, but by July 13 British armour and infantry met increasing resistance from R 35 tanks and then infantry from General Giulio Porcinari's "Napoli" Infantry Division.[10] Porcinari and his staff were captured, however, by elements of 4th Armoured Brigade on the 13th.[11]

In the American centre there was a substantial Italian division-sized counterattack at exactly the point where the airborne were supposed to have been. The German Tiger tanks of the Hermann Göring Panzer Division which had been due to advance with the

"Livorno" Division had failed to turn up.[12] Nevertheless on Highways 115 and 117 during July 10 Italian tanks of the "Niscemi" Armoured Combat Group and "Livorno" infantry pressed home their attack on the city of Gela, but guns from the destroyer USS *Shubrick* and the cruiser USS *Boise* destroyed several tanks and dispersed the attacking infantry battalion. The 3rd Battalion, 34th Regiment, "Livorno" Infantry Division, composed mainly of conscripts, is recorded by its commanding officer as having made a valiant but ultimately equally unsuccessful daylight attack in the Gela Beachhead two days later alongside infantry and armour of the Hermann Göring Panzer Division."[32]

July 10, 1943

Operation Husky. The Allied landings begin. Patton's 7th Army lands in the Gulf of Gela between Licata and Scoglitti. The US 7th Army captures Gela, Licata and Vittoria during the day, against slight opposition. The British land between Syracuse and the southwest tip of the island. They capture Syracuse by the end of the day. The Italian defenders have been caught off guard.[33]

July 11, 1943

The British advance almost unopposed. Palazzolo is taken. On the coast, there is a halt late in the day at Priolo. The American forces encounter resistance in their advance. The German Panzer Division "Hermann Goring" strikes toward American held Gela from its positions around Caltagirone. Allied naval bombardment forces the German forces to retire.[34]

July 12, 1943

The Panzer Division "Hermann Goring" resumes attacks on American positions in the morning but withdraws to face the more threatening British advance in the afternoon. The German 15th Panzergrenadier Division proceeds to pressure the Americans after arriving from the west of the island. The British continue to advance toward Augusta, in spite of Italian and German resistance, and capture Lentini.[35]

July 13, 1943

The British 5th Division captures Augusta. Other British units are engaged by the German Panzer Division "Hermann Goring" around Vizzini. During the night Dempsey's 8th Corps launches a drive toward Catania, attacking around Lentini.. General Patton forms a provisional corps to advance on the west of the island while US 2nd Corps (Bradley) drives northward. In Catania the Axis forces retreat behind the Simeto River.[36]

July 14, 1943

The US 3rd Division attacks Agrigento and Porto Empedocle. The Canadian 1st Division captures Caltagirone advances toward Piazza Armerina. The British 50th Division crosses the Simeto River. Its bridgehead is later reinforced by armor. American forces enter Palermo and isolate 50,000 Italian troops in the west of the island. The Axis mobile forces, including most of the German forces, escape to the northeast corner of the island. American forces in north encounter heavy resistance to further advances. British and Canadian forces launch converging attacks on Agira, in the central region. Allied reinforcements, including the US 9th Division and British 78th Divisions arrive from North Africa. US forces are engaged on the outskirts of Santo Stefano and Troina. British forces capture Catenanouva. Off the west coast, the Egadi Islands surrender to the Allies.[37]

AUGUST

August 17, 1943

Over Germany... The USAAF bombs the ball-bearing manufacturing centers at Schweinfurt and Regensburg in a daylight raid. A total of 51 bombers are lost. During the night (August 17-18), the German rocket research center at Peenemunde is bombed by nearly 600 British bombers. A total of 41 bombers are lost in the raid. This bombing creates a significant delay in the German rocket program. Also noteworthy about the raid is the British use of "window," dropped by Mosquito bombers, which causes about 200 German fighters to concentrate over Berlin.

In Sicily... General Patton's troops arrive in Messina a few hours before British troops. The campaign in Sicily is concluded. About 40,000 German troops with 50 tanks and 100 guns plus a large quantity of supplies and 62,000 Italian troops have been evacuated from the island to Italy, across the Messina Strait. About 10,000 Germans have been killed or captured. More than 100,000 Italians have been taken prisoner. Allied forces has suffer 7000 killed and 15,000 wounded.[38]

SEPTEMBER

Friday, September 3, 1943

In Italy... At dawn units of the British 8th Corps, part of Montgomery's 8th Army, land on the Italian mainland. The landings, north of Reggio, meet almost no resistance. Reggio, Catona and San Giovanni are all captured by the end of the day. In addition, Allied commandos occupy Melito and Bagnara.[39]

In Sicily... Italian General Castellano signs a formal surrender agreement with the Allies in Cassibili. No announcement is made in order to prevent any German occupation of Italy.

Tuesday, September 7, 1943

My Dearest Darling,

I am sending that check so please tell me as soon as you receive it. I hope that it helps you in case you need any money. How is every one at home? Tell me all as I am interested especially in your physical condition. Is every thing all right or has some thing developed since I came back to Camp Polk?

Honey I am glad that you decided to take the Savage Arms job as I am sure you will find it much better in the long run. Altho, I hope the night work doesn't get you down. I remember Coffee the cripple fellow. Does he remember me

I am always imagining that I am kissing you which makes it harder as I want to kiss you and not think about it. Sometimes I get so darn mad, all I can do is write and say how I feel about you, which sometimes I think you don't really get my meaning. But no matter how I write it, never forget that I love you and I could almost leave here so that I could be with you. As for these kisses, I'll wear you out kissing you so much.

Honey, I am going to close, as I want to get to the Post Office before it closes.

Your faithful husband,

Ed

Thursday, September 9, 1943

In Italy... Allied forces land at Salerno. The US 5th Army (General Clark) lands at on beaches to the south of Salerno. His forces include the British 10th Corps (General McCreery) -- the Northern Assault force, and US 6th Corps (General Dawley) -- the Southern Assault Force. Naval support for the operation is under British Admiral Cunningham and a covering force (4 battleships and 2 carriers) under Admiral Willis, a support group (5 small carriers) under Admiral Vian and Admiral Hewitt commands the landing ships. There is some resistance to the landings. To the north of the main landing, US Rangers and British Commandos land at Maiori and Vietri to secure mountain passes. In addition, the British 1st Airborne Division comes ashore at Taranto and seizes the port. To the south, the British 8th Army continues a slow advance. German forces near Rome engage the Italian garrison. The Italian government is forced to flee, leaving Rome under German occupation.[40]

Friday, September 10, 1943

In Italy... On the Salerno beachhead, the forces of the American 6th Corps advance inland. The forces of the British 10th Corps occupy Montecorvino airfield and Battipaglia. German counterattacks by local divisional forces recapture the British gains before nightfall. German forces south of the beachhead, including those engaging the British 8th Army, withdraw northward to reinforce the forces containing the Allied beachhead at Salerno. Rearguard forces continue resisting Montgomery's forces.[41]

Sunday, September 12, 1943

In Italy... On the Salerno beachhead, German forces mount their first major counterattack. Forces of the British 5th Corps are pushed out of Battipaglia, again. To the north of the beachhead, Allied forces holding the Molina Pass are under pressure from the German "Hermann Goring" Panzer Division. To the south, the British 8th Army captures Crotone and continues to make progress. Meanwhile, in a daring raid by a German parachute detachment led by Otto Skorzeny, Mussolini is freed from Gran Sasso in the Abruzzi Mountains and flown to Germany.

Monday, September 13, 1943

In Italy... On the Salerno beachhead, the German counterattack against the British 10th Corps sector is expanded to include that of the American 6th Corps. Elements of the German 16th Panzer and 29th Panzergrenadier Divisions capture American-held Persano and penetrate the American line in several places. The possibility of isolating the British and American Corps arises as the Germans reach to within one mile of the beaches. Allied naval gunfire prevents further German penetrations. The US 6th Corps headquarters makes plans for evacuation. Elements of the US 82nd Airborne Division (General Ridgeway) are parachuted on to the beaches to stiffen the defenses. To the south, the British 8th Army captures Cosenza in its continued advance.[42]

Tuesday, September 14, 1943

My Dearest Darling,

Got your card. The card got me kind of worried as I don't know what to make of it. Now for getting mad about what that fellow was saying to you, well I didn't really know just how you were taking it. As your letter was misread by me about his intentions. No harm done I hope. Let's forget all about it, shall we?

I am going to try and see if I can get out of here. No harm in trying. As I am hating this outfit more and more. Wish I was near you where I could talk over things. Then I would know just what to do. But I believe if given a chance, I may be able to get into something better.

Well honey, I am sending my love and kisses until the next letter. I am

Yours,
Ed

Wednesday 1:45 P.M., September 15, 1943

My Dearest Darling,

Well honey, we are going on another road march tomorrow morning. The same as the one yesterday, mostly running. Right now I'm on guard. Wasn't supposed to be on but one of the sergeants thought that by being on guard, he could get out of the march. So he put himself on(by the way he is company clerk). But finding out that regardless of being on guard you still have to walk tomorrow, he made a fast change and my name got on. Altho, I don't mind to much as it made me Corporal of the Guard which means no walking guard as the part I have to do. But still I have to take the hike tomorrow.

You know it is funny that when it comes to a rating, I am up for t-5, but the other few get line Corporal which has more authority as he rates higher. Altho he doesn't get any more money he still is considered a ranking man. But when it comes to taking over or being in charge, they always put me on it. Which makes these line Corporals mad and they get mad at me so I am an outcast when it comes to having friends. A few fellows who are older and realize the situation are O.K. but the younger ones, well you can't seem to be able to drive it into their heads. I do chum around with one fellow right now. He is on furlough and will be back sometime next week so until then, I will have to put up with these guys.

Well honey, I will close for now as it is nearly time to pass my relief and I can't miss that as it would mean trouble. So good night and pleasant dreams. Don't forget I love you and no matter how it's written, try and interpret it your own way. The way you would like me to say it. And then imagine that I am saying I love you that way.

Forever yours,

Ed

Thursday September 16, 1943

In Italy... On the Salerno beachhead, German General von Vietinghoff orders a renewed attack on the positions of the British 10th Corps between Salerno and Battipaglia. The attack fails. By midday, Field Marshal Kesselring, commanding the German forces in Italy, authorizes a withdrawal to the Volturno line. During the day, patrols of the US 5th Army and the British 8th Army make contact. In the afternoon the British battleship *Warspite* is seriously damaged by two German glider bombs.[43]

Sunday 8:45 P.M., September 26, 1943

My Dearest Darling Wife

Just came back from town but didn't enjoy myself at all. Went to that carnival that they have here but it brought memories of the times we use to have together. It isn't much of a place. Very small in comparison to the ones at home.

The reason behind this letter is very simple. I have been writing on how much I miss you and how much I want you here. I still miss you as much if not more but after going to town and seeing things, also knowing what you would lose by coming here, my better judgment tells me to forget it. So honey don't even think about coming here again. As it would be to hard on you and again my staying here is so uncertain. I almost wish that I could forget all about our future after the war and spend our money having you with me. As I miss you that much but honey, will have to be satisfied with your letters telling me of your love.

And no matter when I go, I'll always love you. And never will be happy until I am back with you. So darling, good night and always remember we have a future to look forward to.

Loving you forever,

Ed

"During the month of September, 1943, the 8th Armored Division successfully accomplished complete reorganization from the old style triangular division, armored, to the new "light" armored division. Following instructions contained in War Department Letter AG-322, dated 15 September, General Grimes issued General Orders Number 3 Headquarters, 8th Armored Division, Dated 20 September 1943, which effected the following major changes:

(4). The 80th Armored Regiment, less 3rd Battalion, Band, Maintenance Company, Service Company, and Reconnaissance Company, was redesignated the 80th Tank Battalion, under command of Lieutenant Colonel Forsyth Bacon.

Preparing the Division for combat required participation in field exercises and full-scale maneuvers. October and November were months of alternating exercises and maintenance in preparation for the most important "D" Series scheduled for December. Most November days and nights were spent in the field, but Thanksgiving was a holiday and the mess crews pulled all stops to give the men turkey with all the trimmings.

The famed "D" Series field exercises, described by veterans as the "most rugged hardships the State of Texas and the weatherman could devise," took place between 11 and 28 December."[44]

OCTOBER

Friday, October 1, 1943

In Italy... The forces of US 5th Army capture Naples. The British 8th Army begins its advance with the 13th Corps (78th and Canadian 1st Divisions).[45]

My Dearest Darling,

Well what do you know. At last my tank went out in the field. Boy what a job I had as I had no radio and had to keep climbing all over to give instructions to my driver. We are not sure just what we are going to do tomorrow or Sunday. I hope we don't have to work. As for myself, I won't go anywhere unless we get paid. As I am dead broke.

Honey, I had a funny feeling the last couple of days as I had no mail from you. I had a feeling that you were on your way down here and were going to surprise me.

You know I spend everything I get here. Can't seem to be able to save anything at all and the funny part is I don't know where it goes to. Will try to do better from now on. Honey, the boys are singing that song, "Somebody else is taking my place." Well at least that is something that doesn't worry me as I know I am the only one you love. I am sure our difficulties have been straightened out and that we wouldn't have any trouble understanding each other. I miss you honey and can't wait for the day we will be together. So for now, I'll close but remember I love you and will be back one of these days.

Always,

Ed

Saturday, October 2, 1943

My Dearest Darling,

Honey, just got back from town and it's pretty late. Borrowed a dollar so that I could get into town and back. The fellow I go around with did the same. Got a lot of trouble on my mind. First thing is that we have to work again tomorrow. It seems we don't get any Sunday off anymore. We also have to get up at 2:15 Monday morning for more of that foolish field work. We don't know just when but I have funny feelings. So I am going to write to you a suggestion. Please tell me what you think of it and let me know.

You know you will get my allotment this month and next month. You also realize you have a birthday coming up. Well, I don't know what to get you but was thinking very seriously and here is the answer. Why don't you take that hundred, add some more, and come down here and visit me? As money isn't everything in life. I also may tell you my main reason. Nothing certain but still you can never tell. Our maneuvers are going to start the last of next month and as soon as they are over, well they say the ride over water is pretty tough. Altho, all this is uncertain but still I believe it would be a worth while cause for you to come down here. If it is so, would kick myself for not having you here so that I can see you again before I have to leave. And if I don't leave, well then I still get to see you. No harm done. I am sure that if you spoke to Shane and asked him for time off, say two weeks. I know you wouldn't lose your job. Ask and tell me what they tell you. If you can't have your job back when you come back, well forget the whole thing. But honey, it may be a long time before we will have the opportunity to see each other again. If you should leave say on Saturday morning, you could get here Monday. Even better, do the same you did before.

But before you say yes or no, think it over and see what you think and then let me know. As we have a whole month to talk it over. Even if you do come, I may be unable to see you every day. But I am sure I could see you part of the time. Honest honey, this place is really driving me crazy as I don't know what takes place from one day to the next. Honey, miss you and please think it over and let me know what you think of my idea.

Love you and want you more each day. But don't think I am writing this way just because I may want you physically as I am only thinking of the space of time we will be unable to see each other. It makes me very lonely and sad. But first I'll have to be like the rest and bear it.

Also keep this in mind. It may be a rumor and nothing may become of it. So use your own judgment.

Loving you always,

Ed

P.S. All this would take place next month as we would make it your birthday present.

Sunday October 3, 1943

In Italy... During the early morning hours, the German 16th Panzer Division moves to counterattack the commandos occupying Termoli. However, the commandos succeed in linking up with the 78th Division as the battle continues.[46]

Monday, October 4, 1943

My Dearest Darling,

Well honey, we sure are getting the heck worked out of us. You remember me telling you in last nights letter that we were leaving at 5:00 this morning. Well we did and rode for 2 hours into the field. Boy was it cold and dusty. I nearly froze as where I ride there is no protection at all. And boy was it dusty. Man you couldn't tell us apart after we got there. We had our tactical problem to work on and it stunk. No system what so ever. Suppose to go out tomorrow. But right now I am on guard again. So I came in from the field early which was a break as right now it is 6:30 and the Company is still out in the field. So guard isn't too bad at a time like this. Well honey, here it is Monday night and we still didn't get paid. Will get it Saturday we hope. So if you have some time get me some cookies or something will you hon?

Well honey the more I think about you coming down the more I am in your favor of it as we are expected to work every day until we go out into maneuvers which will take place next month, the last of it. From there on it will be no telling. Just thinking of times we use to lay in the parlor before bedtime and the fun we had. Well honey, keep those times in mind as it may be soon (we hope) and we can take on where we left off.

Darling will close as am lost for words. Love you and can't wait until the day we will be together again.

Always,

Ed

A USO letterhead paper postmarked October 5, 1943

My Dearest, this letter is to explain why I sent for that money. Here is the story. Monday they told us that some could get passes this weekend so right away I put in for Friday, Saturday, and Sunday. Coming to town, I tried to get a hotel room but there was none here so I phoned DeRidder and there was nothing there. So I then thought I would phone Shreveport and see if I could get something there. But the phone line was busy. I then went to travelers aid in the USO and then sent a wire. They also tried to get me a room. Coming into night I find that they are having some sort of convention and that there are no rooms. I have tried every where but to no avail. So I am going to see if I can cancel that pass as without you, it is no good. Then if I must take it, I am broke as I loaned all I had to fellows going on furlough. So that is why I am sending for money. If I had been able to get that room, I would have you come down. I was sure if I wired tonight that you would have been here Friday. Then we could have stayed there and tried to come to Leesville during the day and see about a room. But that is all off.

We are going back into the field for at least another month. So you can see where you and I will have to do with out one another for some time yet. I'll send for you. There doesn't seem to be a place anywhere here so the best thing is for you to wait until we do get into camp.

I realize it must be a big disappointment but I don't believe that you are half as disappointed as I am as I already pictured you with me.

Honey, it is getting time for the truck so will have to close. I hope everything is fine at home. Hold on as you are until I know for sure what is going to happen to me. Until tomorrows letter.

Love you, Disappointed husband

Ed

XXXOO

Wednesday, October 6, 1943

Envelope addressed to Corporal Edward Brodowski

Dearest Ed,

Don't know of much to write. All's well at home and about the same. Will let you know if dad will go to the hospital this week. My sister-in-law, Stella's father was run over by a car last

Saturday night. After an x-ray, it shows that a bone was broken on his left foot. Ed Lewis at the shop was telling me how much he liked you when you worked at Savage Arms and said he'd rather have you around than me. He told me particularly to let you know this but I'm glad the fellows think so much of you. It makes me puff up with pride to hear it. They are laughing at my hands because they look like a woman's of fifty years old. Lewis said if you had to see them now you'd leave me and I told him you didn't mind what my hands are like.

Baked a couple of pies over the weekend. One was apple and one chocolate meringue. I know you wouldn't care for them but I made a hog of myself and now they are about all gone.

I miss you a lot dear and I wish for all that you wish for. To be together would be heavenly but honey you mustn't be hurt if I refuse to come where you are because you yourself know what the situation is here. I am just beginning to better myself at work and you know I'm not happy if I can't be doing something. And we haven't that much cash that we can spend as expensively as we did in June when you were home.

But don't get me wrong, I love you very much and always will. I don't know how to tell you but I'm afraid you'll get a wrong slant on our love and then think that something is wrong. Let me assure you that <u>I can be trusted.</u> I'm still waiting for the day in the future when you will come home for good or even another short visit.

Darling I will close now and you must let me know if you received the money I sent you. Do not try to pay me back but think that I'm with you and we are having a good time. ($5) should be enough till pay day shouldn't it? You didn't say how much to send.

Yours forever,

Maryanne

Monday, October 11, 1943

My Dearest Darling:

Having found a ½ hour space of time, I am writing to you. Today is Monday and I will be going to work soon. Don't expect things to go right as have had a bad day. Went downtown with mother and didn't get much. We do have a good supply of bananas around and now I am getting back to baking things again. If you receive the cookies I sent you this morning then I will start sending something every week. It is about a month ago I told you my brother Pete went across and then said that he was in California. Now it really has happened as Mom and Dad received a telegram and again a change of address. Dad has changed his day to go to the hospital because they couldn't make arrangements so he is waiting till next Monday. You should see him darling. He's so unhappy now and so changed.

You know darling, I baked an apple pie and took two pieces to the shop to Bill my machine setter and another old man and they just couldn't stop raving about it. They asked me to bake it so I gave in. Now there is a young fellow who doesn't know I did that is begging me to bring him a piece of banana cream pie. How come all this? I believe I told you about them razzing me to take Coffee to my house for dinner. They mentioned baking a pie and I said I could do it. Since then I'm caught in a trap.

I miss you and am looking forward to good news from you. Really my sweet, I am praying very hard and faithfully. There's a full moon out tonight. Remember how we used to take a walk down the road after putting the car into the garage. Someday soon I hope to do it again.

Your mother and I have had some serious talks and I finally got it thru her head that she is not wanted in my life. She got an awful shock as I told her I can't stand it living here with her any longer and maybe I will move before long. I could go to my mothers any time as she's lonesome without the big girls and yet think I'd first go to Utica for sure. I love you darling. Goodnight and try hard to be happy. God bless you.

Your loving wife,
Maryanne

Monday, October 11, 1943

My Dearest,

I am sure that we understand each other about me wanting you to come here. As I said, it all depends on your job. If you can keep your job and come here well and done. But I don't want you losing you job just because I want to see you. It will be great showing you around again. Will try and get a three day pass then we can go to Shreveport or Lake Charles. Only hoping that I can find time to spend with you. As for arrangements, will do all I can but you know how good I am in making arrangements.

Honey, I realize the trip will be hard. Look honey, how about thinking it over very seriously and if you believe it is more than you can do, don't come. Just tell me that it will be impossible and I will then know what the score is. I do know about the trip but I believe that you want to see me as much as I want to see you.

Will try and get the guest house when we are sure you are coming. Now honey, I do realize all about money but I don't believe we look at it in the same way. I do believe in saving for the future, but I also believe I would like to enjoy ourselves now. As when and if I go overseas the chances are slim to enjoy ourselves either way. We may as well face it now that it is any time now. And I don't believe money should be considered, do you.

As for rumors, well now we don't go out till February so you see that hasn't as much to do with wanting you here. Just that I miss you and I don't know what to do. It seems if I only could see you once a month, it would do the trick. It seems when I was home, I didn't appreciate what I had but now that I am so far away, I would want to be with you all the time.

I will always love you and think you are the most beautiful girl I have yet met. I mean it, honest. I know I'm not much but will always try to make you happy. I wish I was strong so that I wouldn't make you come down here to see me. But I guess I am weak and seeing you will fix me up.

It will be fun showing you around again. Hope that carnival in Leesville is still here. Want to take you there. On Saturday if you are here, you won't stay there alone. As they really get rough, the fellows I mean.

Well darling, I am going to close this letter but before I do, I want you to stop here and think it over very carefully. Take everything into consideration and do you think it is right coming here and are you able to take the trip. Just don't lose you job on my account as it wouldn't be worth it. So please honey, think of yourself and then of me. And do what you think will be best. As in my state of mind I am not in any shape to give advice. As I only think one way. Love you always no matter what you decide.

Forever and always

Ed

Tuesday, October 12, 1943

In Italy... During the night (October 12-13) the US 5th Army begins its assault on the German Volturno Line. Elements of the British 10th Corps (McCreery) make some progress on the coast but German counterattacks generally hold its attacks. The

3 divisions of US 6th Corps (Lucas), however, push forward. A combination of determined German defenders and poor weather restrict advances to the main roadways.

Friday, October 15, 1943
In Italy... The Canadian 1st Division (part of British 13th Corps, 8th Army) captures Vinchiaturo. In the US 5th Army offensive, the attack has moved beyond the river but the Germans have skillfully maintained their defensive front while being pushed back.[47]
Sunday 10:05 A.M., October 17, 1943
My Dearest,

Didn't write last night, as I was quite busy. I have this morning off but have to work this afternoon. May have to go out this afternoon in the field and stay until tomorrow night. Hope I don't have to go. As it really is cold out now. Almost froze last night. We are going to start wearing winter clothes soon as it really is cold enough for them. How is the weather at home? I'll bet it must be pretty cold. Have you gotten any new clothes as yet?

Honey, I won't be happy until I can see you once more. The only trouble is that then I won't want to let you leave me again. But I am sure we will have a grand time while you are here. Honey, will close for this morning but will write this afternoon if I don't go out. Love you forever.

Always,
Ed

Monday, October 18, 1943

Dearest Darling,

Well here it is Monday night. The fellows all came back from the field. Having quite a time as they are all busy getting clean. Boy am I glad that I didn't have to go also. As long as I can get away with it, I am going to do so.

We are suppose to get tomorrow afternoon off. If so, I will go to DeRidder to see about the Air Corps. Wish me luck as I certainly will need it. Went out and seen a show last night. I am getting extravagant lately. Came back about nine thirty and then went right to bed.

Honey, tell me just what your plans are as I want to know for sure. I would like to have you see Leesville. Boy what a surprise you'll get if you do come and go there. But I will take you where ever you want to go. Boy, this is hell being so far away from you. I don't know what we can do to be closer together but it just doesn't seem fair being so far away. But it won't be long and we will be together soon. I hope it will be the above. But that is up to you.

Well honey, I am running short of words so will close for now. Will write tomorrow and may have some good news. Pleasant dreams and good night.

Always,

Ed

Tuesday, October 19, 1943

In Italy... German forces defending Dragoni withdraw before a scheduled attack by elements of the US 5th Army begins.[48]

Friday, October 22, 1943

In Italy... The British 8th Army launches an offensive on the east coast. Elements seize a small bridgehead over the Trigno during the night. Meanwhile, the US 5th Army continues its offensive operations with limited success.[49]

Wednesday, October 27, 1943

In Italy... British 8th Army forces capture Montefalcone. A night attack expands the 78th Division bridgehead over the Trigno River. The main German defenses continue to hold.[50]

Guest House, North Camp Polk, Louisiana

Date Oct. 27, 1943

Received from: Mrs. Maryanne Brodowski $1.50

One dollar deposit and fifty cents

No. of days: 3 From: Oct. 27 to: Oct. 30

Room No. 14-1 Received by: Jerrie Binen

Maryanne arrived to be with her husband. She will stay as long as she can in hopes that they can see each other if for only a little while.

October 28, 1943

In the United States... As a consequence of a number of unresolved disputes, a coal miners strike gains momentum. About 500,000 miners are on strike at this point.[51]

NOVEMBER

Nov. 3, 1943 at 2:30 P.M.

To Mrs. Edward Brodowski

Room 14, C/O Bessie Lee Hotel,

DeRidder, LA

Wednesday, November 3, 1943

My dearest,

Well the sad news came. I found out I had to go out. I had a heck of a time getting ready. Now all I can find out is we are suppose to be back sometime Saturday. So use your own judgment. Sorry I can't see you between now and then. I hope you enjoyed yourself so until I see you.

Love,

Ed

P.S. Lets keep the plans as we planned. May be able to see you Sunday. Not sure.

Well honey, heard now we don't come in until late Saturday and go out again Monday November 8. So I don't think I'll get any time off. I guess it's better if you go home as I don't think I'll see you. Honey, it's against my wish but I guess there isn't anything we can do about it.

I had a wonderful time being with you even if it was short. Perhaps I can see you again soon. So hope you have a nice trip home. And I am sorry I made you come all the way here and won't be able to spend more time with you. But you know the Army comes first right now. So good luck on your trip and pray I may see you soon.

Loving you forever,

Ed

P.S. Send me word from DeRidder the day you leave so when I get back from the field, I will know that you have gone.

November 4, 1943

In Italy... Forces of the US 5th Army continues. The British 10th Corps holds Monte Massico and Monte Croce and moves against Monte Camino with 78th Division. The US 6th Corps captures Venafro and Rocavirondola as it advances to the German defenses of the Reinhard Line. The British 8th Army has the Germans withdrawing to the Sangro River. The Allied armies now have full lateral communications through Isernia.[52]

Thursday evening 7:15 P.M,. November 4, 1943

My Dearest Ever:

If you receive this letter instead of seeing me personally, you will well know I am on my way home. Oh God, if only you knew how dreadfully lonesome these days have been. It is so much harder to leave you now. But I am still hanging onto a thin thread of hope of seeing you before my departure. This is why I am not leaving till Saturday morning. I am writing this from the bottom of my heart so darling, please believe me. I have prayed all day to have you come back here but only I will get my prayers answered if God sees fit to do so. If only he would give us just one more chance to be together. I really don't want to go home as I know now it will be twice as hard to bear. I love you so much my head is splitting from crying and I don't care what happens unless I'm with you. I had a notion to stay here till you came back and didn't care about my job or any other thing. But I know you want me to go back as we aren't rich.

I've never written such a crazy letter but if you feel the way I do, I know it won't be hard to understand. I went to the movies this afternoon thinking I could forget. It helped but very little and now I'm back in my room. I feel just as bad. Every footstep I hear makes me say, "God let that be him," and then you know what a let down.

Even though this place is such a hole, it isn't too bad with you around. Darling, help me hang onto my bearings as I believe I am losing hold of myself. If this damned war lasts another year, I don't believe I could hold out as I feel that I'll crack up any minute and I'm not talking through my hat either. Oh God, why, why, why does it have to be like this?

If you get this letter before Saturday, 10 A.M. call me right away and I'll stay, honey.

I love you and will always love only you. Honest, I am very positive about how much I love you.

Your Loving wife,

Maryanne

Letter mailed from DeRidder on Nov. 5, 1943 at 10:00 A.M.

November 5, 1943

In Italy... The US 5th Army launches an assault on the German-held Reinhard Line. The German 14th Panzer Corps (Hube) defending here prevents significant gains. The defense is made easier by the difficult terrain and poor weather. Nonetheless, the offensive continues. Meanwhile, elements of the British 8th Army capture Vasto, Palmoli and Torrebruna.[53]

November 6, 1943

In Italy... The US 5th Army continues assaulting the German-held Reinhard Line. No gains are achieved.[54]

Wednesday, November 10, 1943

My Dearest Darling,

It is only noon but I am going to write as won't have enough time tonight. Haven't much to say as the same thing goes on every day. Having classes today and expect to go out this week end. Suppose to fire the 75 mm so won't have much time to ourselves.

Well by now you must have the feel of being back home. I hope that every thing is at the best at home. Tell me all that is going on as I am very lonesome for all the news especially where you are concerned. I want to know all that happened on your way home.

Tell me if you want to come back down and all information on that subject. The reason I say this is you may have changed your mind after you got home. I hope not as I miss you something terrible. Can't get use to having you gone.

Honey, they seem to talk a lot about giving out furloughs. I hope that I am on one of the groups. Regardless of which one just so that I can get home. I really miss you and home. As you are home. Wherever you are at, is home. Honey, I'll close for now as we are going to fall out pretty soon. So don't forget I love you and miss you.

Forever yours,

Ed

Thursday November 11, 1943

My Dearest Darling,

Well you should have a guilty conscience. I am surprised that you put off writing to me but I have done the same, as at times I can't seem to find anything to say. I'll bet you get tired of my poor way of saying how much I care for you. I know that I don't put it in words like it could be done. But I know that you know how much I love you. I'll never stop loving you. Someday you'll run into the house and find me there. Won't that be something?

Well honey, we had tests and I guess we passed as I haven't heard anything otherwise. Oh yes, I fired the 75 gun today.

I am telling you that they have me all over. One time as tank commander and then another as Gunner. So today I fired the big gun. Boy what fun. Yesterday we went out on the road march. It rained all day and did we get wet. Stayed that way until tonight and that is because we are in the barracks.

Will write again tomorrow, as I am very tired tonight. I can hardly keep my eyes open. So goodnight and may your prayers be answered. I remain.

Yours forever

Ed

Friday, November 12, 1943

In Italy... The US 5th Army assault on the Reinhard Line fails to achieve any further progress. The British 56th Division (part of 10th Corps, US 5th Army) is forced to withdraw from some positions on Monte Camino.[55]

My Dearest Darling,

I haven't had any mail from you but expect some tomorrow at the latest. We are having a party tonight but I am on guard so I won't be able to come. But it doesn't bother me as I don't drink.

Don't know what will become of us as they change things around here from day to day. I am suppose to be in the field but ended up in the Company as it was called off. But will go out next week. Also expect to go out in December. So don't know about the furlough. I hope I am one of the lucky ones to go home.

Honey, are there any good pictures on at home. I went and seen a couple in the last week but didn't enjoy them. As I didn't have you around. Gee honey, I miss you more and more. I wish I could find some way to be near you all the time. Any suggestions?

Honey, get something for mother from the both of us for the birthday gift.

Honey, I better close for now so good night and until I see you. Always will be yours.

Forever,

Ed

November 15, 1943

In Italy... British General Alexander calls off the US 5th Army assault on the German-held Reinhard Line. Casualties have been heavy. A determined German defense combined with rugged terrain and poor weather contribute to the decision to end the attack. To the east, elements of the British 8th Army achieve tenuous crossings over the Sangro River.[56]

Tuesday, November 16, 1943

My Dearest,

Just got your second letter and was more than glad to hear from you. And when I do get them I feel a lot better. As when I am waiting for mail I start to think that maybe I wrote the wrong thing in my last letter and a hundred other thoughts go through my mind. So I feel like a new man as soon as I hear from you.

You're kidding about gaining weight as you didn't look any heavier to me. Talking about thinking back, that seems all I do is think back when you were here. Wishing you were still here.

As for the money, heck it isn't any good unless you use it. And seeing one another is as good a reason to use it as any.

Boy, if I only could be stationed some where near home. I'd have you near me all the time. I don't believe I could do without you. Ever since I came from the Army and met you, remember how I was always hanging around. It seems that if I am not around you, I don't know what to do.

Well honey, I am going out in the field this afternoon. I just thought I'd drop you a line. Please don't think anything of it if you don't get any mail from me every day. As we are going to be out in the field quite a bit. Hope that I'll be able to see you soon.

Well love, I must close for now. Love you and that part you mentioned about trusting you, well you know better. I always trust you and always will. So don't worry about that. Must close.

Love,
Ed

Tuesday evening, November 16, 1943

Dearest Ed:

Haven't much to say so this may be a short letter. All is quite well at home except I am having a little trouble at the shop. They have made safety rules for all of us to keep all our rings off of our fingers. So I may be fired because I'm putting up a fight. But no darned fool is going to make me take my wedding band off, job or no job. So you see darling, I'm still wearing it. But will have to go thru with the argument again today. Shane said if he was me, he'd keep it on to. I'll let you know how I come out with it.

Gosh, I'm just stuck for news and such because I've said about all in the other letters. I've bought some candy and will buy you a fruit cake as they are ¾ less the price here than in Leesville. When I get around to sending it, I hope you'll like it as I had a pound fruit cake last week and it was delicious.

I miss you and am looking forward to that Christmas furlough. I do want to go back with you very much and believe that we could find a way out. Altho, it seems a bad idea right now. Will write again tomorrow as I have to go to work a little earlier to stop at surgery and have my finger taken care of. I hurt it on a bolt but it is not to bad.

Nothing more to say. I love you and only you. That trip did just the thing as I don't care to get interested in having fun with these guys like I did before. Only keep to myself as much as possible. Some have noticed and remarked that I have changed, but I don't care. Good night darling and God bless you.

Yours,
Maryanne

Wednesday 6:30 P.M., November 17 1943

Dearest Sweetheart:

No letters this morning but will wait another day. Things here are the same and all is well as could be expected. I awoke at 2:30 this afternoon and being ambitious, I cleaned up my house a bit. I plan to go to the movies by myself tomorrow to see Deanna Durbin in "Hers to Hold. I told you about hurting my finger. Well it is coming along swell.

Also, when I was down to see you, remember I said I put out 1180 pieces at work. Well, my highest quota now is 1240 and they are asking for more. I told them their nuts as I am not going to kill myself for really you have to stand there every minute of the day working on those bolts. Without taking tax and all, my pay was close to $69.00 but after taking out taxes, the money they left me was $53.00.

Same old story with your mother. She asked Mrs. Odell to make a blind date for her with an acquaintance of Odell. George Shane said you're lucky in being in the Army as he is getting gray. As he puts it "from the damned old woman." One girl in my dept. was sick and went to surgery where they told her she should go home as she had a temperature of 102. When George tried to give her a pass, she refused and worked till midnight. We all thought she was nuts and I had to laugh when George told me. Well darling, I guess that's all for now. Keep smiling and I'll keep thinking of you. Also, I am praying for better luck for the both of us. Say how about that Air Corp. Please let me know. Good night and God bless you,

Ever faithfully,

Maryanne

Thursday, November 18, 1943

My Dearest Darling,

Sorry I couldn't write yesterday but over a day late. I hope you enjoyed yourself yesterday, "Happy Birthday." I know it will be late but I want you to know that I am always thinking of you. Only I wish that I could have fun with you to celebrate your birthday. Don't feel any older do you? At least you look the same. Boy after being out in the field over these two days, I feel like a man of sixty. I am really all wore out.

Boy I am catching it now. It gets harder and harder in the field. Also, much colder. I wish I could be back with you to keep me warm. Remember while you were here? I don't know honey, but I think that if this doesn't end soon, I'll go nuts as I don't believe in being so far away from you. Just think of the fellows back home who are able to stay out of the Army. Don't know why I am always the unlucky one.

So honey, will close as I am writing this letter before falling out in the morning. So lots of love and best wishes for the next year. I hope you get all you pray for. So until tonight's letter I'll close.

Forever yours,

Ed

Friday, November 19, 1943

In Italy... In the east, the last German forces withdraw north of the Sangro River. Although the British 8th Army has also crossed the Sangro, it will prove necessary to mount a prepared assault to expand their foothold.[57]

My Dearest Darling,

You know I always think that your birthday was always on the 17th but it seems that it is on the 14th. Got some bad news for you. No furlough until April at the earliest. Can get a three day pass but not a furlough. Leaving next month for Texas. Will probably spend Christmas there. We were out all week. Had today in. Company going out tomorrow coming back Sunday and out again Monday. So you see honey, that I was right in having you come here when you did. As it may be a long time before I see you again.

I'll try and have a picture taken as soon as I go to town. You know how I dread taking them but will do so as soon as I can. Honey, I never take any thing wrong when you write about having fun with the fellows. As I trust you and know that I am the only one you care for. But don't ever do anything to make me lose that trust that I have in you as that is something that keeps a marriage solid. As when a man or woman can't trust each other then they may as well quit. As they'll always find fault in each other. And you know that I love you and believe in you. I may sound strange at times but don't mind that as I always mix things up when I try to write my feelings.

So honey, whenever you think you are slipping, remember that I am keeping true and clean as I have a wife who I love. And wouldn't do anything to chance ruining myself so that I couldn't be the husband I should. As it is very easy to go wrong in the Army and by doing that, you ruin your own life and also your wives if she doesn't know your troubles. So you see honey, no matter how hard it is for you, it is that much harder for me.

Your Faithful Husband,

Ed

Sunday, November 21, 1943

My Dearest,

Well we are in for a few hours as we go out in the morning. Just got cleaned up and feel like a new man as I really was dirty. It was dusty and cold most of the time. It's a good thing you can't see me when I come back from these doings as I really am dirty and look terrible. I'll bet you'd change your mind quick. Had it rough these few days as had the Company Commander in my tank. Also, had a radio which you call any station around by pushing these different channel buttons. Well coming in he had taken the tank over and he rode in the peep. Boy did I have a time. Had to answer all calls from the big shots. Also, answer any question they would ask. Of course, first I would call the peep and find out what he wanted to tell them. But even so, the radio is awful hard to understand especially in a tank.

Honey, you make me feel good now that I was able to convince you of my love. As I am sure that you know I love you. You did have me a little worried but no more as your latest letters tell me what I wanted to know. Honey, never worry about me not loving you as I always will no matter what happens.

Honey, I'll close for now but will write tomorrow or rather Tuesday as soon as I come back. So lots of love and kisses. Forever and ever yours,

Always,

Ed

Monday November 22, 1943

In Italy... Elements of the British 8th Army have established a bridgehead over the Sangro River that is five miles wide and nearly 2000 yards deep. Supplying the bridgehead is tenuous because of the swollen state of the river which makes bridge building or crossings difficult.[58]

Wednesday, November 24, 1943

My Dearest Darling,

Well here it is Wednesday morning. I have a few minutes before we fall out so am starting this letter. We came in from the field last night and it was after eleven before we got thru so that we could go to bed. I feel sleepy as a dunce right now. It gets pretty bad in the field. Mostly the weather is the hardest factor and it really gets cold.

We are suppose to get tomorrow afternoon off but as yet we are not sure. It really will be a treat if we do as we haven't had any time off in some time. Will go to the dentist this morning. I hope to get a couple of teeth fixed.

Well honey, here it is noon. Came back from the dentist. I have had 8 teeth filled and have a few more to be taken care of this afternoon.

Well, I just notice on the board that we have the afternoon off tomorrow. I guess it was a good thing when I had you come down as things seem to be getting worse here. Always in the field and usually on weekends. Then we are going to Texas next month for at least 15 days. Boy that is going to be hard to take. After that, we are suppose to go on maneuvers but not sure. I can't tell what may happen. But don't worry until the time comes.

Well honey, tomorrow is Thanksgiving but can't see anything to be thankful for. If I could only spend the day with you, I wouldn't ask for anything else. And I can't have you so why should I be thankful? I may as well be across the ocean then there's a chance of coming home even if in pieces but still home. I know I am talking out of my head but forgive me. Honey, I will close before it gets the best of me. Love you and don't want you to feel blue as better times are coming. I guess the holidays nearing are on my mind. Closing with love.

Forever,

Ed

"October and November were months of alternating exercises and maintenance in preparation for the important "D" Series scheduled for December. Most of November days and nights were spent in the field, but Thanksgiving was a holiday and the mess crews pulled all stops to give the men turkey with all the trimmings."[59]

Friday, November 26, 1943

My Dearest Darling,

Here it is a day after Thanksgiving and I don't feel any better than the other day. Stayed out all day yesterday. Altho the fellows say they had a swell dinner but I didn't care to stay. As I have had to many Army meals to enjoy one even if they have all the trimmings. Was thinking of you the whole day. Saw two shows and had two meals in town. Only wish you were here to spend the day with me.

Honey, I suppose you may wonder why I don't write as often as I use to. Well I shouldn't make up excuses but one reason is that we are in the field more and more. And another is that I have been down in the dumps ever since you left. And once I am in a very down cast mood, I hate to write in such a state. As I don't want you to know just how lonely it can be here. And I know that by writing more often, I am sure to do so and that would make you unhappy. So why should both of us feel blue? Don't worry honey, I will be alright as soon as the holidays are over. As I believe that the holidays are what is keeping me in such a state.

You may know by now that I won't be home for a long time, which makes me feel very sad. As I was very set on being home before the year is up but now it looks like I won't be seeing you for a long time. Can get a three-day pass but don't know if I should take it. I am afraid that it would be a little too much. Will stop until noon.

Saturday, November 27, 1943

My Dearest Darling,

Well here it is Saturday and I am on guard. Also, I have to work tomorrow, which means no time to enjoy myself. I guess it is a good thing I am able to save money for a month. Will go to town tomorrow night and see a show if possible. Wish it was you I could be seeing instead of going out alone.

Oh yes, I finally turned that application in to the Office. I don't know what will become of it as there are about 80 applicants in the Co. and as yet they haven't turned them in as yet. So can't tell what will happen as it will be kind of hard for the C.O. to explain why so many fellows want to get out. Myself, I always wanted to but will he believe that? He may even try and take it out on me in training but I am willing to take that chance.

Well honey, will close for a time. Will write soon. Loving you with all my heart. Honey, pray that I get to go to the Air Corps.

Loving you forever,

Ed

Sunday, November 28, 1943

In Italy... The British 8th Army launches an offensive across the Sangro River. The assault begins with an air and artillery bombardment. A new bridgehead is established and the 8th Indian Division penetrates as far as Mozzogrogna. The defending German 65th Division is badly shaken by the offensive but German reserves have assembled behind it.[60]

DECEMBER

In Italy... The US 5th Army becomes more active as preparations for a resumption of its offensive proceed. Diversionary attacks in support of the British 8th Army offensive continue.[61]

In Italy... Elements of the US 5th Army launch an attack on Monte Camino. The British 10th Corps and the newly arrived US 2nd Corps (General Keyes) lead the assault. The US 6th Corps advances to right. In the east, the British 8th Army captures Lanciano and Castelfrentano in its advance. During the night (December 2-3) German bombers raid Bari. An ammunition ship in the harbor is hit and explodes, sinking 18 transports of 70,000 tons and 38,000 tons of supplies.[62]

Saturday 7:00 A.M., December 4, 1943

My Dearest Darling,

It is Saturday and we are out for another two days of rest from work. Yesterday I received your letter with the jokes and clippings. Read them over and thought they were cute so I took them to the shop. You know, they got a great kick out of them but I always lose the jokes as someone keeps them. And once they're gone it's no use asking for them.

Some of the girls took over at the shop and thought they would run the place as they feel like. So Coffee and Cutler got hold of them and gave them a good bawling out. No I wasn't one of them.

I also received the gov't check which puts me to over a $100.00 savings money. That 5 cents raise I received certainly makes my pay look good. I'll never make as much as you used to but still I never made this much before.

You said you'd like to prove in some way to me in how much you love me. Well darling, you may not know it but you already have. As you don't go out with the others guys which is the biggest proof and you don't go out to get drunk because you want to please me. So you see, I have all the proof I want. When I'm near you it seems you can't ever stop hugging and kissing me which I added up to very much love. However, sometimes I think you love me too much and it scares me. **As** maybe I'm not worth it or maybe not good enough for you. I do love you very much and always dream about you at work and everywhere I'm at. Many times I talk to you saying something like, "Oh Ed, someday we'll be together. I just can't wait. You're such a darling. I hope I'm good to you. Wish we can keep our life always like this." After that comes a sigh and a goofy look in my eyes as I stare dreamt eyed into space. Creedon caught me at one of those moments and teased me for being in love. I didn't deny it and told him I was thinking of you. Oh yes, he also told me that your old boss, I think he was—I forgot his name, but he lives around that curve off Deerfield hill. Remember the white house which you wanted to visit after----well anyway, he's back on 4-1 shift working on a machine. Well, must close as nothing more to write and I have run out of this paper. So love and good night.

Love,

Maryanne

Sunday, December 5, 1943

My Dearest Darling,

Excuse the paper but I ran short so I had to borrow some. Well, here it is Sunday morning. I have been thinking of you and the big doings today. You don't realize how much I want to be with you. Pickell and I are going to town this afternoon. We will see a show or two. As next Sunday we will be on our way. Boy I hate to think of going but I guess it is bound to come sooner or later. Just stopped to help a fellow eat some of his food from his package he received. He's an Italian fellow and he got a lot of their food from sausages to nuts. Some of the fellows really get all kinds of food. By the way, how about that cake? I hope you can find a few minutes to bake one.

Honey, I went to the P.X. and they had some sweaters and different kinds of clothes. I was going to get you one but didn't know the size but gave it up as it would be foolish to get some thing and it wouldn't fit.

Gee honey, you surely are making money. Boy your income tax is really going to be big isn't it? Well now you can get a lot of things you wanted so long ago. Don't be afraid to get anything you need. As money isn't any good unless you spend it.

Well hon, will stop for present but will write again as soon as the unit comes in. Sorry that I don't write more often but you understand how it is. Thanks a million for writing as often as you do. You can't realize how good it feels to get mail. As then I know that you're not to tired or busy to think of me. So long and until I write tonight. Love and kisses and many of them.

Forever,

Ed

Monday 7:00 A.M., December 6, 1943

My Dearest Darling,

Sorry I didn't write last night as I promised, but I didn't come in from town until rather late. Seen two shows again. It seems we are going to catch up on some entertainment before we go out into the field. As when we get into the field, it may be some time before we'll be able to enjoy ourselves. All the fellows are getting gifts for the holiday's. As yet I haven't done any shopping and when I do, it's going to be very slight. Got a Christmas card from your folks yesterday. Honey, I am getting you some thing. I hope you'll like it. I know it isn't much. But it is something to make the holiday spirit right. I wish I was home to give you a Christmas the right way but by the looks of things, it will be quite some time before I'll even see you again.

This morning is a wet morning as we had rain last night. Altho, it is nice and warm in comparison to the weather we have been having. Well honey, it is now dinner time. I had pork chops, gravy, mashed potatoes, salad, beets diced, and butter. Also, a lemon pie or rather it was suppose to be but they made it in a large pan. It was pretty good but I rather have your cooking and baking. It can't be to long before I may be there to have some again.

I asked the 1st Sgt. for a pass and may get it Wednesday. I would like to get one so I can do some shopping. Pickell and I asked for them. I was refused over the weekend for a three day pass. My eye has been causing me a little trouble so I have been wearing the glasses more frequently but still can't get use to them. Pickell and I intend to go to town tonight if we can get away. At present, we are getting ready for a big inspection for three. By us winning last week, it leaves only two of us to get ready for that inspection as the other three are on pass. Will write more tonight.

6:00 P.M.

Well, I have shaved and showered and put on that lotion. Smelling pretty good if I say so myself. Wish you were here to enjoy it. Have to wait for Pickell as his platoon has to G. I barracks. In other words scrub them. Boy what a mess as we are trying to get ready for the field. Now we may go out a few days early. So can't say how I'll manage to write. By the way, your letters have stopped all of a sudden. Nothing wrong is there?

Well honey, I will close for present. I hope to hear from you tomorrow.

Forever yours,

Ed

Wednesday, December 8, 1943

In Italy... Free French troops begin to come into the Allied line. The first unit is the 2nd Moroccan Infantry Division. Italian troops are also being mobilized. Meanwhile, veteran units are being withdrawn to Britain in preparation for Operation Overlord -- the invasion of western Europe (D-Day). The US 5th Army continues attacking but little progress is achieved. To the east, the British 8th Army operations continue as well. The Canadian 1st Division begins attacking over the Moro River, a few miles from the east coast.[63]

Saturday, December 11, 1943

Dearest,

Another day and another dollar the old Army saying. Did all my Christmas shopping last night. It really is a disgrace the way they rob the soldiers here. I hope that what I got will answer with you approval. Pickell and I got about the same things. It's funny but we seem to go for the same things.

While in town last night or rather on the way back, a couple of drunks got in a scrap on the bus. It all ended up with one of them cutting the front tire on the bus. So I had to wait for another bus with Pickell. But Pickell and I got a ride on a jeep. It was breezy but we got back to camp.

Honey, I am going to send all the gifts in one package. I want you to give them out. Won't send it until the last of the week.

Well honey, I apologize for saying you don't write as today I got three of your letters and one from mother. The only thing I can't understand is they were written Wednesday, Thursday, and Saturday but all mailed on the 4th and they all got here at the same time. As you had me worried as I didn't get mail from you but forgive me honey. As you know how much I love you. As for not being good enough for me, well that is far from being right. If any one isn't good enough, it would be me. As you know, I am an old Army man and you have seen enough of Army men to know what they are like. But honey, I have told you all about myself and all I have said, is the truth. As you are the one and only one for me, now and forever.

Well some more news. I heard a rumor today **that** I am in for a Sgt's rating. Not sure but hope so as the money can really come in handy. Well dear, will stop for now and write another tomorrow. But never get an idea that there is someone else as you know better. So honey will close with a clean conscience and may you always believe in me.

Faithful forever,

Ed

"The famed "D" Series field exercises, described by veterans as the 'most rugged hardships the State of Texas and the weatherman could devise,' took place between 11 and 28 December. The various problems gave the troops a chance to put to practical use the basic and unit training they had previously undergone and at the same time provided excellent training in preparation for full scale maneuvers soon to follow. The "D" Series were the initial problems of this type for an armored division, and the 8th Armored had been selected to test the validity of the problems. The Division maneuver area was located in eastern Texas and ranged from Hemphill in the north to Newton in the south."

"The first problem involved gaining contact with the enemy and maintaining it until intelligence concerning enemy activities could be had."

"The division was in bivouac in the vicinity of Geneva, Texas, when the second problem got underway. As the Division moved from the bivouac area a meeting engagement with the enemy ensued with the 8th successfully carrying through an attack."

"Problem three began on 21 December 1943 with the 53rd Armored Engineer battalion being used primarily to insure Division mobility. The efforts of the entire Battalion went toward building bypasses, breaching minefields, and constructing bridges. As the problem continued and the enemy forced the Division to retreat from newly won ground and take up a delayed action, the engineers put down minefields, blew up bridges, and built obstacles to slow the enemy advance."

"Christmas Day, 1943, found the 8th still in the field. A convoy from the maneuver area moved into Camp Polk on 24 December to permit those men with families quartered in the Leesville vicinity to spend Christmas there. On Christmas Day Lieutenant Colonel Vaughn MacArthur, Division Chaplain, visited several unit bivouac areas and put forth his best efforts to dispel the general gloom. Christmas in bivouac was a bitter contrast to the tradition Yule!"

"The final "D" Series problem consisted of breaching a minefield and pouring tank and armored units through the gap to establish a base for another thrust into the heart of the enemy. Following this coordinated attack came the order to cease all action and the "D" Series officially ended."

"During January, 1944 The Division remained in the field preparing for the maneuvers to follow. Pursuant to General Grimes' instructions, 10% of the men in each unit were given leave during the break period, and this policy was continued with respect to passes throughout the maneuvers." [64]

Saturday, December 12, 1943

Dearest Darling

Here I am writing and it is way past my bed time. We came in off the field at 4:00 this afternoon but have to get up the same time and be ready to leave motor park by six. Yes tomorrow is Sunday but we work all the time now as they are trying to get us out of here quick. Don't know but what we may spend two more days out in the field. Some of the fellows are having a hard time seeing their wives and going out in the field.

Well, we had two of the tests and so far we got 84 and 92 which isn't bad. We had a pretty bad accident. This fellows foot got crushed in the tank. They took him to the hospital. Boy the ground felt pretty hard last night. And then I think of the nice bed you have at home and how half of it is empty.

Honey, do you know that I have only got two letters from you so far so I don't know which of mine you have received as yet. I hope all that I have sent. Well honey, here I go closing again. So pleasant dreams and keep the other half of the bed warm. I'll be there soon. Love and kisses.

Forever,

Ed

Tuesday 7:15 A.M., December 14, 1943

My Dearest,

Yesterday came your beautiful Christmas card and a letter telling me you are about ready to start on your journey. Last night when I walked into the shop, in our room it seemed like a morgue. As there were only a few fellows scattered here and there and the rest of the drill presses all cleaned up and standing idle. I knew then that this only meant one thing; most of the boys were transferred to "B" gun or other dept.'s. Before the night was over, ¾ of the girls were told they were laid off for good. No your wrong. Just one girl besides me are to stay a little while longer. We don't know just how long they are going to let us work but gosh darned it, I'm going to put in plenty of hours and get all I can right now. Wouldn't it be funny if I was lucky enough to stay on right thru till they start up again? But rumors (as I don't listen to much of them) go that night shift is to be discontinued entirely and everyone is talking crazy of how the war must be close to an end. Of all attitudes to take, this is the worse yet as they will not listen much about finding another job. All the boys seemed to be concerned and feel glad that I can stay a little while yet. They told me this to my face.

Say darling, those little clippings you sent are quite funny. I do get a big kick out of them. Your not that big a wolf though only when you are kidding. I'm talking about work but I didn't tell you that I'm back on bolts instead of on sporting goods. Although if I stay without a lay off, I go back to sporting goods you can bet on that. I don't care, anything as long as some money comes in. I'm waiting to hear from you again to see if you really are Sgt. Brodowski. If you are happy to receive such a rating, then I'm glad for you too. I love you my dear and all I care is that you keep happy and stay as you are. Now that's enough for me. Even though you'd only be a private, you're still the tops with me. On the radio right now they are singing that new song "They're Either Too Young or to Old." Have you heard it? It's really good and take the meaning of it and you. You won't have to worry your head over your wife falling for someone else.

I think it's time I went to bed as I am tired after working like a horse on my first night of the week. Goodnight darling. I hope you like the cake. Till tomorrow good luck and be careful.

Love,

Maryanne

Bette Davis was approached to do a song called "*They're Either Too Young or Too Old*," which described the plight of a woman whose beau is in the army. She had never done a musical number and was petrified to try it. Frank Loesser wrote the lyrics, and Arthur Schwartz the music. This song, "*They're Either Too Young or Too Old*, " was Frank Loesser's first big hit. It was the top song on the "*Lucky Strike Hit Parade*," a very famous radio show of the time in 1943, for almost a year.

They're either too young, or too old,
They're either too gray or too grassy green,
The pickings are poor and the crop is lean.
What's good is in the army,
What's left will never harm me.

I'm either their first breath of spring,
Or else, I'm their last little fling.
I either get a fossil or an adolescent pup,
I either have to hold him off,
Or have to hold him up.
The battle is on, but the fortress will hold,
They're either too young or too old.[65]

Wednesday, December 15, 1943

My Dearest Sweetheart,

Today brings in another day and with it some good news. Our sister-in-law Mary had her baby Monday night at 11 o'clock. Of course mom and dad didn't hear of it till I broke the news to them on my way to work, as Pop Putney didn't deliver the message. Your mother happened to stop in at his place late last night with Harry and that was when he told her. So now we have a little boy name of (don't know which is first) Thomas Stanley.

About me and my work comes quite a sad part. All the fellows have been transferred except about a handful or a couple more. Another girl and I have been left to finish up for this week. We may be getting thru Friday unless I'm lucky enough to be transferred. I even hate to go in tonight to think of working in an empty place as the girls I was chummy with have been laid off permanently. The fellows are now on "B" gun so you can imagine how bad it is. They have even said no more nights for "A" gun but I'll let you know about this more definitely next week.

Creedon was out for 3 days sick with a bad cold and lost some weight. He shows it right away. Talking about weight, I still stay at 119 lbs. Can't lose it and at the rate of my appetite, I'll be getting fat. I'll check it somehow though but I don't believe, rather hope, never to see you weighing 200 lbs. It isn't becoming to you at all as you look much better at 160 to 165 lbs.

I've been at my mothers and had breakfast there this morning, as I wanted to get all the information on Mary. I will have to visit her over the weekend. Golly, I still haven't done any Christmas shopping. I now will sign Christmas Cards and send them out.

Will close with lots of love and kisses. Hope all's well with you and best wishes on being Sgt. I'd give anything to spend Christmas with you but as the song goes, "I'll be home for Christmas, if only in my dreams," so I will imagine you with me. Good morning darling. I remain,

Ever faithfully yours,

Maryanne

Friday, December 17, 1943

Dearest Ed:

Haven't anything to write about but yet here I'm jotting a few lines. All the news that's around here I've already told you. Didn't receive any mail from you for 2 days so now I'm wondering if you have begun your long journey of maneuvers. I am still eating breakfast but would like to have mother mail this letter so am writing while eating. Tonight, I will know the verdict if any of what happens at work. If I stay and they begin "A" gun, over which they said they wouldn't, or get kicked out. I'm hoping for a transfer if there won't be anymore A gun but I don't think I'll be that lucky. Tomorrow I will visit Mary and our new nephew at St. Lukes Hospital. Have received Christmas cards from about every member of the family. In return, I sent them one.

As yet the package you said you sent out hasn't reached here but am still waiting for it to come. I heard some bad news last night as they broadcast that 1,000 of our merchant men were either killed or injured. That includes both and it happened while we were off guard and had no plans to protect our ships. They say this is the 2nd biggest tragedy since Pearl Harbor. It happened somewhere in the Mediterranean on an island which name I have forgotten. I'm glad tonight's my last night of the week to be working cause my hands are so bad that I'm ashamed to even look at them myself. On top of breaking out from the soda water at work, they chapped and I don't believe I saw anyone's hands as bad as these are. You'd think I didn't wash for over a year but I keep saying someday they'll be nice again.

The weather here now is real winter with snow on the ground and freezing zero weather. Well dear, this all seems nonsense but it's a letter anyway. I'm also getting fatter and don't know what I'm doing to gain those pounds but darn it, I'm always hungry any hour and so I eat. Closing with best of love and luck. Hope I get mail from you today but till then, I'll be going to bed and must say adieu-

Yours ever,

Maryanne

Saturday, December 18, 1943

In Italy... The US 5th Army captures Monte Lungo, threatening the German position at San Pietro. German forces launch counterattacks. San Pietro falls to the US 36th Division (part of 2nd Corps, 5th Army). The 6th Corps advances as the German forces withdraw.[66]

My Dearest Darling,

Well honey, here we are again getting our tank fixed again. Now we are going to get a new motor. It seems the enemy for this maneuver are only about three miles away from us. We are eating field rations again as we are away from our Company. It's no telling when it will be before we get there again. I only got two letters from you while I was with the Company. Now it will be some time again before you'll get any mail from me again.

It seems a shame that we are here in the states and still it is hard to get mail to one another. But I guess that's the Army for you. Feeling in the dumps again. I have seen "Pickell" for a few minutes. Boy he really looks rough. In fact we all do. In checking myself honey,

I am afraid that you wouldn't want me the way I am now. I look like a bum and feel twice as bad. I hope that you'll never feel that way but honest honey, this field life real makes us look bad.

By now I hope you received my package. Also, I hope you like it. Let me know as soon as possible. Honey, I don't know what else to say now as I am stopped for lack of time. I will continue as soon as I can. Honey, love you and think of you all the time. So closing with thoughts of you and home. I remain,

Your devoted husband,

Ed

Monday, December 20, 1943

Over Germany... Allied aircraft drop about 2000 tons of bombs on Frankfurt, Mannheim and other cities in southern Germany. There are also raids on the V-1 ramps in France.[67]

Tuesday, December 21, 1943

In Italy... The British 8th Army engages in heavy fighting on the approaches to Ortona; the US 5th Army is heavily engaged near Monte Sammucro.[68]

Wednesday, December 22, 1943

To Sgt. Edward Brodowski

My Dear Sweetheart:

Haven't received any mail from you and I do understand your predicament. Also, want you to know I am patient and I know I will hear from you soon, maybe today. But will you please forgive me for missing two days as Monday I went to town and was busy sewing. Then I found it was time to go to work. Well when I reached there, I worked two hours on bolts and Shoes breaks the news to me that I am transferred to 109 on inspection. What am I to do but obey orders but before I went, I told him I didn't like the idea and he shouldn't be surprised if he didn't find me in sometime. He promised that if and when work starts picking up, he will call us back, all that were transferred. 3 other fellows went with me, they were from 4-1 shift. They also have Creedon all over the shop in "A" gun Dept. You see I was so disappointed and blue that Tuesday morning when I came home, I didn't, rather couldn't, get myself to write to you. So I put it off till evening. I finished my sewing and went to bed at nine o'clock. Early in the afternoon, mother had company and of all places, she brought them into the parlor and those fools were having the grandest time laughing and talking. They woke me up and I just was to tired to get up and say something and yet maybe embarrass both sides. So all I could do was endure it till they left. Another thing I forgot to pull out the stem so the alarm would ring at 5 o'clock. So here that time past and at 6:15 your mother woke me up saying I'm sleeping overtime. I got up and dressed and washed my dishes. Then I went to work. Felt lousy for a long time at work, with a headache but about 3 A.M. I began to feel a little better. And now here I am writing to you. Received a good number of cards for Christmas and sent out a few myself. It is quite cold here today and we expect more snow altho it isn't deep but it snows quite frequently.

Darling I'm wondering how is everything with you? Is this Texas business the real maneuvers or are you still to face that? Are you well and are you gaining anymore weight? It's very lonesome without you and hope this war finishes soon. Christmas is hard to think of but anyway I'll think of you every second. I love you and I am behaving myself more so now than ever before. I used to have fun with the fellows teasing them once in a while altho I stayed within my boundary line. I could be trusted as you yourself know. Now I'm not interested, in fact I am very serious and care not to laugh very often. I am proud of you and best of luck in everything and your rating. Closing with love.

Yours ever

(wife) Maryanne

Wednesday, December 22, 1943

My Dearest Darling,

By the time this letter reaches you it will be after Christmas. All I can say is I hope you have a happy and enjoyable Christmas. I know the gifts are few. Then again the time will come soon we all hope which will be many times better then any gift can be. That is, as you know, when we all can be together again. Resuming the life, which we had to stop.

We had a funny and then again a bad mistake made. One of the fellows, I believe I mentioned something about him in one of my letters, how he was under a peep and was pulled out in time. Well anyway, it seems that the same night another fellow was hurt. Altho the fellow died. They made a mistake and sent the telegram to the other fellows folks from our Co. It wasn't until his family wired back wanting to know how the body would come that the department saw their mistake. I can almost see his folks faces when they got the other wire telling them of their son still living. While on the subject, we are losing at the rate of one man a day not counting the sick and injured. But don't worry I am still well but very unhappy.

With you saying the work is slack, I almost was going to suggest for you to come here but it is a foolish thought as we won't be in Camp long before we move again. It won't be until April at the latest that we may be staying in one place. I am also hoping on that time off to come through so I may be able to come home and see you soon.

Darling, I miss you. I guess I needn't keep repeating this but I want you to know that I am always thinking of you and may we be together again soon. I hope you enjoy yourself over the holidays. Have a good time. Sorry I can't join you but my thoughts will be with you. So will close with best wishes and Merry Christmas.

Forever yours,

Ed

Friday 8:30 P.M., December 24, 1943

My Dearest Darling,

Well honey, here it is Christmas Eve. It really feels like it as we have had rain for two days now. I thought I froze yesterday. Stood up in that rain and cold for eight hours never getting in till late last night. Cold and weary and wet. Had to make a tent and fire. I didn't think I would ever thaw out. Today it has been cold and rainy. All the fellows are sleeping right now. I am sitting alone and wondering just what you are doing. If you could only see me writing this letter sitting on a blanket with a flash light stuck in my underwear so that I can see in order to write. I suppose all at home are having a glorious time. More power to them. All I can say, I hope I'll never have to spend another Christmas like this. Mud and rain is all we see. We hope that by this time next week we will be back in Camp.

Darling, I'll finish this letter in the morning. Just wanted to start it tonight as I am thinking of you. Honey, will say good night for now and also Merry Christmas. Only wishing I was home to tell you so until the morning I stop.

Here it is Christmas morning. Raining as it has for the last two days. Didn't get up until 9:00 this morning. Also have found out I am on guard this afternoon so was unable to go to church. Honest honey, every one is in the dumps. Two of the fellows went to Jasper, Texas as some family there. One was able to take 8 fellows from our Battalion. So that only makes two to a Company. I am sure they will enjoy themselves. Pickell and I are here at my tent writing. It doesn't seem possible that this is a holiday. Muddy shoes, dirty clothes, looking like a bum. Altho, I have clean ones but why put them on when I will only get them all muddy again.

Remember at home how every thing had to be just so, clothes and shoes. Couldn't sleep very well last night wondering how you were taking it. In fact, the same thing was bothering me all night. I couldn't figure just what, but you were always coming up. Wondering how you felt or did you sleep well.

Honey, we all are wondering where we will be a year from now. My driver is a Polish lad John H. and we were telling each other what we do on Christmas Eve which brought back memories. Talking about my crew, I have quite a combination. Two Polish, one Indian, one Irish, and one Scotch fellow. Quite a combination don't you think?

Honey, I'll close this letter. I want you to know I am in a good health even tho the field life is rather hard. Perhaps not happy but then again I am doing the best I know how with what I have. So don't worry about me as it takes more than an Army to hurt me. After this is over, you'll have me around to pester you. Then you'll get tired of me hanging around. I hope with all my heart that you are having a nice Christmas. And try not to think to much of us being apart as I know how I feel when I do. Perhaps next Christmas we will all be happy and together. So will close for now. I hope I get a letter from you today then everything will be perfect. Lots of love and kisses. I am thinking of you.

Always and forever yours,

Ed

Sunday, December 26, 1943

In Italy... The US 5th Army clears Monte Sammucro and the surrounding hills of German forces.[69]

Monday, December 27, 1943

My Dearest,

Well honey, the holiday is all over and we are all set to move again. Now I hope the last stop will be back to Camp but you can be sure that we will be all over the place before the week is up. Altho, we are suppose to be in camp by Friday. But nothing is certain yet. As soon as we do, I'll write you. As I know the mail isn't very good out here. I also know that some of the letters I and the fellows write never go out for three or four days. So don't be to disappointed if a few days go by with out mail. As you'll get them all at once. I am sure some of your mail is on the way. It seems at last we ate all of our candy and extra food we had. Now we are hurting. It really is a shame as to all the candy we ate. We spend at least $18.00 dollars on them alone.

Hon, I am going to try and get a pass to go to Shreveport next month. You don't mind do you? I have been thinking of asking you to come down but I know better. I will have to wait until they give out furlough again. I suppose I needn't say how much I miss you but really honey, it gets worse all the time. Tell me did you get many gifts this year? I hope you did. Have been waiting to here about your job. I suppose it is on the way, I mean the letter.

Now hon, I don't know what the score is going to be from now until we get back to camp. So if you don't receive any mail for a few days, don't worry. Tell me, have you any plans for New Years Eve. You better go out as it would be a shame to see you stay in on New years Eve. You know honey, this having our own children idea seems alright. At least you would have something to occupy your mind. Now don't think I am getting any ideas about having children as I'm not. Only think, the people with children don't have to worry as to where they will go on New Years Eve as they have a reason to stay at home.

Well darling, the space on this paper is getting short, so will sign off for now. Enjoy yourself over New Years Eve. As I will be thinking of you even tho I'll be in camp or the field. So until next letter, love and kisses.

Have a good time.

Ed

P.S. All kidding aside, please have a good time on New Years Eve. Make believe I'm with you. That should help. I don't believe I'll be able to go any place as it is probable I won't be able to. So there is no reason you should suffer also. Ed

Wednesday, December 29, 1943

My Dearest,

Honey, we are back in camp after a few of the hardest days I have seen yet. That rain of the last week has made the roads almost impossible. In fact, it took us 16 hrs. to go 9 miles. That is pulling one another out one at a time. It took three tanks to pull one out at one time. Our food has been short and we have missed quite a few meals in the past few days. But now we are back to garrison for a while. Yes, we have still the big maneuvers ahead of us as this was only an example to what is to come. Personally, I wish it was all over as it isn't any fun in the field. I wish I could tell you everything about it, but then letters are suppose to bring cheer and happiness. And if I went into detail of what these past few weeks have been, I am afraid you wouldn't think much of the Army.

Honey, that job in the inspection department isn't to bad. In fact, better than nothing. It is a little money coming in on weekends. Well dear, this barracks really is a mess as a lot of the fellows just threw their equipment just any place and took off. Pickell went to town but I stayed in as I have quite a bit of work to do. So I will stop this letter now but I'll write again tomorrow. I hope you have been getting my letters as I have written quite a few. Loads of love and kisses until next letter.

Forever yours,

Ed

Thursday, December 30, 1943

My Dearest Darling,

My dear, I got your long letter for which I have been waiting. I am sorry to hear that Christmas didn't come out to good. Let's hope that next year we will be together again. Tomorrow night is New Years Eve. I hope to go out unless I have to do something. As we are on alert. Our turn comes Saturday night until Sunday so you can see what a weekend I am going to spend. Also honey, I am going to ask you to send me at least $10.00 as we aren't getting paid until next month. As by being out in the field, every thing has been screwed up. So our pay won't come until the last of the next month.

Also, another late rumor is that we may leaveon maneuvers before the month is over. If so, it will be April or maybe longer before we come back here. Or maybe we won't come back here. Nothing certain but I guess we may see California during maneuvers before long.

Darling, you say how you felt over the holiday. Well I feel the same way and much worse. I would give anything to be with you again. It seems I am having quite a job sewing my stripes on my uniform. I wish you were here to do it for me. Gee darling, I can't seem to think of anything to write. Everything here is about the same.

Oh yes, they keep telling me what a good job I do on my tank. Always proving me. Sometimes I am thinking that they are building up to something. I hope not. **As all I do is my job**. Well dear, keep your nose to the grind stone and I am sure that you'll be back on bolts soon. So love and kisses until next letter.

Forever yours,

Ed

P.S. Send money by telegram as soon as you can.

December 31, 1943

In Italy... Both the US 5th Army and the British 8th Army continue their offensive operation without significant success.[70]

Chapter Three

JANUARY-JUNE 1944

"During January, 1944 The Division remained in the field preparing for the maneuvers to follow. Pursuant to General Grimes' instructions, 10% of the men in each unit were given leave during the break period, and this policy was continued with respect to passes throughout the maneuvers."

Sometime after January 1, 1944 Ed Brodowski left camp Polk on a 15 day furlough.

"During January, 1944, the Division remained in the field preparing for the maneuvers to follow. Training in small unit tactics (which was decentralized to battalion and separate companies for control purposes) went forward along with the duties of equipment maintenance. Training Memorandum Number 61, Headquarters, 8th Armored Division, dated 31 December 1943, specifically stated the January objective: "— to prepare for Louisiana Maneuvers and/or overseas service."

1st Phase (Flag Exercises)	7 February---17 February
2nd Phase	21February---24 February
3rd Phase	28 February---1 March
4th Phase	6 March--- 9 March
5th Phase	13 March---19 March
6th Phase	24 March---27 March
7th Phase	1 April-----3 April

The problem was drawn to illustrate a movement to contact in a meeting engagement stressing aggressive action by both sides, a withdrawal of the smaller (Red) force, the arrival of Red reinforcements, and a large scale counterattack by the reinforced Red unit. The Blue Force, as part of the U.S. XVIII Corps, consisted of the 75th and the 92nd Infantry Divisions. The Red Force, Provisional Red Corps, consisted of the 44th Infantry Division and the 8th Armored (which was to play the role of the Red Reinforcements during the latter phases of the maneuver action).

For maneuvers with an armored unit, the weather was foul. Constant rain restricted tank movement to roadways; deploying was virtually impossible. The meeting engagement resulted in complete "bog down" for all units except the engineers. During the next week the 53rd Armored Engineer Battalion utilized bulldozers and corduroy bridges to prepare the area for the 8th's entry into the contest.

The final days of February saw a coordinated attack by the Blue Forces. The maneuvers continued throughout March with the 8th Armored Division often employed as a flanking force or in direct support. There were two river crossing problems which necessitated establishing bridgeheads from which an armored attack could be launched.[71]."

Saturday, January 1, 1944 New Years Day

Dearest Darling;

Will begin for once with a wish of good luck, good health, and good cheer. All is quite well here at home altho one thing is missing and you already know that I mean you. We went to see my brother's wife Mary and little son Tommy but didn't find them home so we went to my other brother's and altho he was home, his wife wasn't because she took their daughter and my little brother to a show. We didn't visit very long and went to the Oneida theater to the movies. My sisters and I made up the group. It brought back memories of when you and I used to go there. Gosh it's kind of hard to ever go up that way knowing that our best part, even tho it was only a short time, was spent up that way. You know darling but I think I will nickname that our "honeymoon paradise." Maybe a crazy name but you must admit it has a meaning. Some rich buggers go away for that long on a honeymoon and it was paradise to us wasn't it. I long to have you back so much to hold you close and follow you around even if I did ask crazy questions or wouldn't answer yours. This morning of course was a Holy day of obligation so off to church and so we'll go tomorrow as it being Sunday. We were at St. Anthony's Church for 9 o'clock mass. Was over at mom's and dad's and they gave me some of those stuffed cabbage leaves that you don't care for and I sure do crave so much.

It seems funny but I just couldn't wait before having to go to work. It used to make me so happy. When my hour came, I'd even start out before 7:30 many times and talk to the workers. But now that they've slacked down and had transferred so many of us, it don't seem like home and I don't care if I do go in or not. Even though I've been taken off inspecting and am to operate again, all that matters is that I have money coming in for our future. I go thru my routine like a mechanical toy, do my work, and come home just to go to bed. Gee I used to feel swell to wake up and take in a show in the afternoon but now I go to bed late in the morning, sleep till five, and almost curse that I have to get up. I was wishing they'd transfer me on days but it didn't work.

I'm getting kind of tired now so I believe I will retire. My sisters and I made some fudge and boy did it come out rotten. We used Hershey's Cocoa and it tastes like bitter sweet altho I put in a lot of sugar. It did get hard, to hard to suit me as it is all in crumbs. Oh well, I see I can't graduate as a cook as yet. It only takes to have you around to guide me and then things turn out O.K. It's high time I quit jabbering and say so long. Good night my darling and pleasant dreams. Please pray for this war to end and I'll be darned if only you tell me when. I'll be in St. Louis to meet you half way to ride home with you. God Bless you and I remain loving you.

Maryanne

P.S. Did you think I'll forget to say "I love you"?

Maryanne left on a train and met Ed in St. Louis during his 15 day furlough. They then traveled together on a train home back to Utica, NY. Ed spent some time at home with his wife and then returned back to Camp Polk, La.

Tuesday, January 11, 1944

Over Germany... The US 8th Air Force carries out a fighter escorted daylight raid on Oschersleben. A quarter of the 238 bombers are lost. The attrition effect on the defending German fighters is not reflected in this loss.

In Washington... President Roosevelt asks Congress for a new national service law to prevent damaging strikes and to mobilize the entire adult population for war.[72]

Friday, January 14, 1944

In the United States... The union representing railroad workers accepts contract terms suggested by President Roosevelt, avoiding a major strike action [73]

My Dearest Darling

Was going to write last night but lights went out account of the rain. As it has been raining for a couple of days and freezing which makes every thing bad. We are suppose to take the tank out this morning but don't know what they will do as it is raining.

Made the trip O.K. I got off at Hope Arkansas. Then into Shreveport. From there by bus. Got in camp about four in the afternoon which was good for me as had quite a bit of work to do to get ready for today. The camp is the same. Muddy when I left and just as bad when I came back.

Oh yes, I got those packages. Also, your letters which made me homesick. Almost wishing I could turn around and start back. As this life is getting me down. Now that have been home twice, it seems all the more reason to want to go back.

Honey, I am sending mothers registration back as I found it in my pocket. By the way, did she get my car started? So honey, it doesn't seem possible that I am back to Camp Polk and the old grind. And it seems that in the near future it will be hard as it is getting colder and miserable in the field.

You may wonder about those apples. They were rotten but otherwise, the package was O.K. How about your work? Are you still working or did they lay you off? Also, how is the work? Is it the same or harder? One of the fellows got a discharge while I was home. How fortunate for him. It makes it nice since he has a wife and a small child. But the reason for the discharge is he was having trouble with his stomach.

Well honey, will stop for now but will write again tonight. So until then. Love and kisses.

Forever Yours,

Ed

Friday, January 14 1944

My Dearest Darling,

Here I am keeping my promise that I would write, to begin with we did go out this morning and we did get wet and cold. I thought that I would freeze to death but we finally came back about noon due to the fact it was raining so very hard and we couldn't see the target at about 50 ft. Of course I had to go out and am I glad I came in yesterday early as I did, as that gave me a chance to get ready for today.

Every thing here is a big mess. It seems that we have a lot of exams coming up. Also, we have to prepare to leave La. for good. When, I don't know but all of our personal equipment and odds and ends must go back home as we won't have any place to carry them. Now don't take anything for granted as no one seems to know just what the score is.

You know honey, I just signed a payroll and the 29th of this month I'll have three years in the army. Honey, I am going to send all the pictures I have as they get ruined if I take them with me. Also, from now on I won't be able to save any more letters as there won't be any place to put them not that I don't want to save them but you'll understand.

I am writing this letter by candle light as we haven't had any lights since last night due to the rain freezing on the wires. It seems strange to be in the dark so much. Honey, I wish now I had bought some of the things I was going to while at home as it really has changed here from what it was when I left.

Well honey, how does it feel to work again? Well honey, may be now you'll be able to save a little as it will be some time before I'll be able to come home and I know you won't be able to visit me for a while anyway. Gee honey, I miss you. I was almost tempted to stay home a few more days. You really don't know how hard it was to leave. I may not have shown it but it really was. Well darling, will let you know from day to day what happens. Until next letter. Love and kisses.

Faithfully,

Ed

Saturday, January 15, 1944

In Italy... The forces of US 2nd Corps (Keyes) capture Monte Trocchio. This completes the US 5th Army advance to the German defenses of the Gustav Line. In part, the operations serve to keep engaged German forces that might otherwise be available to respond to the planned landing at Anzio (January 22).[74]

Sunday, January 16, 1944

My Dearest Darling,

Didn't write to you last night as I got a ride into town with Sgt. Keaton and didn't come back until very late. Also, lights were still out so unable to write and I am trying to make up for it now. Seen a picture by "Deanna Durbin," which wasn't too bad. Went to a place and seen a girl take two guys for a ride. Boy were they drunk and she knew her business. I am afraid the boys woke up broke today. Boy the way some of these girls can work, it is almost a shame to watch them take the fellows to the cleaners.

I went to DeRidder today. Seen another picture. I know I never cared for movies and even now I'm not to crazy about them. Only it is something to do and it also gives me a place to get away to from camp. We now can use a toilet. They dug a hole in the back of the barracks and put a canvas around it. That is what we use for a toilet.

Tonight the lights are on so it is much better but still we do not have any water. Oh yes honey, I am eating your cake while I am writing this letter. It still is good and not hard at all.

Gee honey, now that I haven't anything to look forward to, it seems like a jail. As now I have no furlough to look forward to. Only dreaded months of field life which isn't any fun. But darling, I know I have you at home. That is one thing I look forward to dear. The day I can come home and say, "well honey, I am here to stay." I know that will be our happiest moments and lets hope and pray that they aren't far off. So

darling, I am going to close because we have to go out early tomorrow. So good night and pleasant dreams.

Yours,

Ed

Thursday, January 20, 1944

In Italy... The US 2nd Corps (part of 5th Army) begins attacks across the Rapido River toward the Liri valley and Monte Cassino. German forces successfully hold. To the south, the British 10th

Corps (also part of 5th Army) captures Tufo in its continuing attacks.[75]

Saturday, January 22, 1944

In Italy... Allied forces establish a beachhead at Anzio. The assaulting forces are drawn from the US 6th Corps (Lucas). To the north of the town the US 3rd Division lands. Naval support is provided by forces under the command of Admiral Lowry. To south, the British 1st Division comes ashore. Naval support in the south is provided by forces commanded by Admiral Troubridge. The landings meet light resistance. By the end of the day, 36,000 troops have been deployed and only 13 are killed. The port of Anzio is captured intact. The German commander in chief in Italy, Field Marshal Kesselring requests reserves from OKW while organizing a defensive cordon around the beachhead with improvised units.[76]

Sunday, January 23, 1944

In Italy... There are now about 50,000 Allied troops concentrated in the Anzio beachhead. General Lucas commands. German resistance is light but the Allied forces advance slowly. Meanwhile, Kesselring believes it is possible to maintain the Gustav Line defenses at the same time as containing the Anzio landings. The commander of the German 10th Army, von Vietinghoff favors a withdrawal from the southern defensive line. [77]

Tuesday, January 25, 1944

My Dearest Darling,

Here it is another late evening and just got thru working. Well, at last we finished all the exams. I didn't do very good today either. 60 of 72. My average for the six tests was 65% which isn't passing but then again, I wasn't the only one who didn't pass. The test today was my fault as I did all I could but the gunner happen to have an off day.

The furlough boys came back last night. My driver came back and I gave him those letters from that girl. He can write if he wants to. That is up to him. You know honey, this outfit is getting tough as heck. A person is even afraid to say anything as he don't know if some one will take a poke at him or not. Honey, I am to stop for tonight. Will write more in the morning.

Well here it is 6:05 A.M. and we are ready to go out to see land mines. We are suppose to have school on it for the next five days. It seems there is no rest for us. On the go all the time. I have a small package I would like to send but haven't had time as yet. I will send it as soon as I get time.

Gee honey, the weather has been pretty nice for the last few days. Only yesterday it rained in the morning but it stopped before dinner. Honey, I hope that after maneuvers we go to some camp. Then perhaps we can be together again. Boy that would be swell. If we do go to some camp, you'll be staying with me until I leave here. As far as the money, well we can't take it with us so we may as well enjoy ourselves while we can.

Well dear, am going to close for now. Just about now you are getting breakfast, as you are one hour ahead of us so pretty soon you'll be going to bed. So good morning and good night. Love and kisses.

Only yours,

Ed

Wednesday, January 26, 1944

My Dearest Darling,

Well honey for once I got an evening off. I had an easy day. I went to that mine school and had a lot of fun planting them as well as looking for them. Also, had a chance to plant booby traps with some with five crackers on them. For the whole day only three fellows got hurt. One required stitches where one exploded while another got three fingers burned. Otherwise, I had fun. Came back at 4:30 to find out that I was suppose to go out for the next three days to Alexandria so I started to make a big fuss and got off. And am I glad that I did as I hate to go out where we only have so little time to get ready to leave for the field.

You know it seems that something funny is up. A lot of fellows are getting transferred to other outfits. I just can't see how we can go into the field with so few men. The latest is that we only will stay out a few days and then go to some camp. Gee, I hope so because I don't care to much for that out door life.

You know sweetheart but your mail doesn't come very often. Is there any reason why that is? I am wondering if I have said or done anything while I was home or in my letters that would come between us. It is so hard when people in love have to live so far apart. Well Hon, I hope to get a letter from you tomorrow so until then, I will close.

Love and Kisses,

Ed

Thursday, January 27, 1944

Dearest Darling,

There seems to be something wrong as I have always received letters at least every other day. But here it is four days and still no mail. I know that you work nights and are tired in the morning but at least you can take a few minutes and drop a line. I've tried to keep mail going your way. You can't possibly see under what conditions some of your letters are written, but still you get at least a line telling you all is well. Is there some problem between us?

Honey, I worry to heck when I don't get any mail from you as I wonder why you haven't wrote. Then I picture a lot of things that could happen while working in the shop. Now honey, don't get mad at me but I think you'll agree with me that I am right when I ask for mail from you. I hope nothing is wrong at home. If there is let me know at once as I believe I should be the first to know so what do you say. Am I going to hear from you soon?

Honey, we are busy as been trying to get ready to leave by Sunday. Everything is a mess all over. The Sgt. in charge of our platoon got into a fight with a Pvt., so I broke them up but the whole company is keyed up to the point that they fight at the least word.

Now honey, how about you? It seems like a life time since I have seen you. Gee I wish I could be back with you again but it looks like a long time before I do. As the rumors are going around which don't sound too promising. But don't worry hon until the time comes. So honey, here I am coming to a close with another letter. I hope I'll hear from you tomorrow. Loads of love and kisses. Don't forget and keep the home fires burning as I'll be back soon.

Love Forever,

Ed

Saturday, January 29, 1944

My Dearest Darling,

I suppose I could start with Hon, or "snuggles puss" but the way I start my letters seems the best. Talk about your rain well we are having another rainy spell. The worst part is that we have to vacate the barracks in the morning and go in the field. That mud really isn't any pleasure especially sleeping in it. We're suppose to have a parade this morning after getting dress and while we were waiting they called it off. I had to work in the motor park all morning. We are now spending the afternoon packing our own equipment and that is some mess. You don't realize the stuff you have until after you start packing. I can just imagine if you go to move then you will have a job.

I still don't know what will happen to us. As the days go by the rumors get worse. But as long as we don't go to P.O.E. (Port of Embarkation) then we're O.K. But if that happens that'll be the end. Hon, here I am writing again as we had to go to motor park again and work until supper. I then was all dress to go to town for the last time when I got called for a detail to the motor park again. When I finished it was to late to go to town.

Honey, remember my driver writing a letter to that girl? Well he got her picture. I guess now he is going to start writing to her. I guess everyone can't be as lucky as I. It seems I got all a man could ever want in one package. As a lot of fellows go looking for other women so they must not have all they want in one. Now take you for instance, you have everything. A man can't ask for more. The only thing is that we aren't together. I have been in the dumps in the last few days. I guess I ate something, which didn't agree with me.

Sitting here on my foot looker for the last time. I think back of the evenings at home in the parlor listening to the radio. Makes one feel homesick. I guess I shouldn't of had that last furlough as I haven't been myself since. Can't wait to get to camp so that I can have you near me. But I guess we can't have everything.

Honey, I have a slight favor to ask of you. If you have time you can send me a package every now and then. Perhaps candy, cookies, or cake but not all at once. But every so often as the field duty will be hard and that will be something to break up the monotony of it all So honey, I will close for now and if I have time I will write tomorrow. Loving you forever.

Always,

Ed

P.S. Honey, today I finished three years in the Army. I happen to think of it while writing to you. You know, I feel right now as I did when I was in Panama. Just like a caged animal not being able to do or go where I wanted to.

Sunday, January 30, 1944

In Italy... At Anzio the Allied offensive begins. There are heavy losses and no gains against the German defenses. To the south, along the German-held Gustav Line, the US 5th Army continues attacking. The British 5th Division (part of 10th Corps) breaks through the line and captures Monte Natale. Around Monte Cassino, the US 34th Division (part of 2nd Corps) holds its bridgehead on the west bank of the Rapido River.[78]

FEBRUARY

Wednesday, February 2, 1944

In Italy... Allied attacks around Anzio end. They have suffered high losses without significant success. Defending German forces, however, have had to postpone counterattacks planned to begin today because of their own losses.[79]

Friday, February 4, 1944

My dearest Darling,

I am writing as I don't know if we will be able to find the time next week so will try and keep the letters going until we leave for the problem. Everything is about the same here. The only change is my assistant driver "Smith" the Indian fellow, well he went for a physical examination last night as he is up for overseas duty and he'll be in the next group that leaves. Boy that really hit me hard as one man is going to school and now Smith is ready to go over there. That'll leave me with only two fellows to keep my tank going. It seems now that we'll all go the same way. One at a time.

Oh yes, had news that some guy is up for some bust. It seems he didn't do something or other. No kidding. Getting the rating is easy compared to the job of holding on to it. Went to town again last night, seen "Gloria Jean" in, "Moonlight over Vermont", pretty good. They are showing a good movie Saturday but won't be able to see it as we will be restricted by then.

Boy it was cold last night. Wish I had you around so that I could have some one to get close to keep me warm.

Gee honey, that picture of you was swell. I have showed it to everyone by now. The only handicap is that I can't be near you. As that picture made me lonesome for you. Now I hope that your hand is better from that injury at work. Let me know what is the outcome as I am worried about it. I have seen many things happen while I was working at Savage Arms.

You know I can't get used to sleeping on the ground. If I go to bed early then I am awake by midnight or shortly after. Then I just lay around until morning. I hope that during the next week I can get more sleep but won't as it will be tactical and that means no fire. Have a small one right now which I made to heat some water for shaving.

You may not hear from me in a few days as we are going to start a maneuver problem tomorrow so don't worry as I'll write the first break I'll get. Miss you and wish I could find some way to be near you. Sometimes I am tempted to forget the army and come home but then if I was caught, I would never get home. So honey, will forget it and only wish it will be over soon.

Honey, it is now dark using a flashlight to finish this letter. Just finish washing up and wish you were here to wash my back. No kidding honey, we are talking about girls and wives and do I get lonesome. Honey, I miss you something terrible. Wish I could bring you here again but in a few days we are going to start maneuvers and then it's no telling where we will end up. But don't worry honey, I will take care of myself. Honey, after this war I am going to come home and the Army can go to H. as far as I'm concerned.

Honey, will close with loads of love and kisses. Good night love until tomorrow.

Loving you forever,

Ed.

February 6, 1944

Honey it's dinner time and I got a letter and card from you and one from Stark. Haven't much to add only that it's rather warm and the work is coming to a finish as we are all ready to move out anytime. I believe tomorrow is the last day to write until we get out in the field.

Honey, I am glad you told me about going out with Howard. Of course I don't mind, as I know it must be rather hard working nights and not having any time to go to the shows. So of course you can go out. But that deal with that guy in the shop that you work with, well I guess you better not go out with him as I sure would be mad if I find out you did. Honey, use your own judgment on all of that. I want you to enjoy yourself. So have a good time. Wish I could be there to have fun with you. Honey, closing again for now.

Loving you,

Ed

Monday, February 7, 1944

My Dearest Darling Wife,

We are waiting to move out so have found time to scribble a few lines. As that is all my waiting amounts to. I believe I told you of going tactical last night. Well we're suppose to move out at 13:00 or 1 o'clock but now have heard that we may not move again until tomorrow. And anyway, if we do move it will be in this vicinity. After these series of problems or ones which will take something like ten days. Then I believe we will go around Texas or in other words almost the same places as in December.

We have been losing men every day, such as going to other places, hospital, etc. Before these maneuvers are over, we will lose all our men. Wish they would pick me out for some extra duty of the same sort. Got some late news. Pickell is now my tank driver. They took John H. and made him a tank commander in another tank. It seems they are changing a lot of fellows around. Altho I have asked them to take my crew away. As I am not very happy as is. You can't realize the job it is running around trying to see that all the little things are done. If not, then you are to blame. I always have some sort of headache. I know you'll say that I am only fooling, but don't be surprised if you will be writing to a Pvt. one of these days.

At the present time I am in the turret of the tank waiting for any news over the radio. I wish I had a camera with me so I could take pictures of how we are existing in the field. I am sure you'd enjoy seeing them. I know you'd disown me if you did see them. At the present time, I have a short hair cut, not to clean of face and hands, and the outer clothing is such that, well I would be ashamed to be seen with them.

Remember how many times you wanted to go to other cities to spend a few days as more or less a vacation. Now that it is to late, I think it is a good idea. I will try and make that up to you when I get back. There are a number of things I must make up to you. And I will try hard when I get home. Gee honey, I miss you. Hope the people at home don't make it hard for us when we get back. I hope the men leave our women alone as it will be hard for them if they don't. But I am not worried (much) as I know you'll be faithful to me. Honey, what ever you do is O.K. by me. I ask only that you write as often as possible as that is all I wait for. Let me know if everything is O.K. at home. No matter what happens, write and let me know. Will close for now and I will write as soon as possible. Loving you always. Loads of love and kisses.

Your faithful husband,

Ed

Thursday, February 10, 1944

My Dearest Darling,

This waiting has us all down in the dumps because as yet we haven't moved. They give us notice one minute and the next minute we stay where we are. I wouldn't mind it to much if I had a fire but they aren't allowed at a tactical situation so I have to do without. The weather has changed again and now we are having a cold spell. Nearly froze last night as there was a rather cold night. I just had the Colonel stop by the tank. A good thing he didn't see me because he asked the crew some questions and I may not have been able to answer them.

Today's mail came in and I had a letter from you mailed on the third so you can see why I haven't heard from you. Glad to hear that your hand is better because I was very worried about it. Now about you moving. to another place, well that is up to you as I know how much you dread the place. So if you find a place that suits you, then go ahead and move.

Now about where I am, well we are still in good old La. and as I have said in previous letters, we will remain here for some time. I hope that by the time we finish these so called maneuvers, the war will be over. Altho it will be somewhere around April before there will be any change. I would like to spend a few days at home again in the summer but I can't be sure of that as a ruling came out that you have to wait six months before you're entitled to another furlough. But if we should get stationed somewhere near by then don't worry because I'll call for you as to come as soon as possible.

You say in your letter to be careful. Now you know I'll take care of myself and if something should happen, then you'll know that it was unavoidable. As for heroism, well I don't think much of that. All I want is to come back to you. Let the other fellows take the medals as I don't want them. Even these stripes I have. If I have to be in good to keep them, well, they can have them as I don't believe in that. I do my work to the best of my knowledge and that is all but I won't go and be nice to the officers just to keep them.

Well honey, here it is evening again and as yet nothing is happening. I did stop writing for a time as we had classes. So will close for today. Love and kisses.

Your loving husband,

Ed

"In Italy... At the Anzio beachhead, German attacks force the British 1st Division to fall back. Meanwhile, to the south, the forces of US 5th Army continue offensive operations. The US 34th Division gains ground near Point 593 and Point 445 as well as attacking Colle Sant'Angelo.

In Italy... At the Anzio beachhead, there are new attacks on the British 1st Division by German forces. The Germans aim for the village of Aprilia and "The Factory" nearby. Meanwhile, the British 56th Division and the US 45th Division arrive at Anzio.

In Italy... At the Anzio beachhead, German forces capture Aprilia from the British 1st Division which continues to hold "The Factory".

In Italy... At the Anzio beachhead, German forces capture "The Factory" from the British 1st Division. Meanwhile forces of the US 5th Army continue to engage German defenders around Cassino. The US 34th Division makes an unsuccessful attempt to approach the Cassino monastery from the north.

In Italy... Forces of the US 5th Army are redeployed. The New Zealand Corps replaces the US 2nd Corps opposite Cassino. At Anzio, there is a lull in the battle. The British 1st Division is withdrawn from the line because of heavy losses. American

General Lucas, commanding Allied forces on the beachhead, organizes an inner defensive perimeter

In Italy... Allied aircraft bomb the historic monastery on the crest of Monte Cassino. German forces, which have not occupied the position previously, move into the ruins of the monastery. The New Zealand Corps (part of US 5th Army) follows-up the bombing with an assault which fails.

In Italy... German forces begin a new attack on the Allied forces on the Anzio beachhead. The US 45th Division and the British 56th Division are engaged by elements of 5 German divisions. There is no decisive breakthrough. The *Luftwaffe* provides close air support for the offensive as well as attacking shipping off shore. The ammunition ship *Elihu Yale* blows up after a German air strike. To the south, around Cassino, forces of New Zealand Corps (part of US 5th Army) continue attacking.

In Italy... German forces continue attacks on the Anzio beachhead. The US 45th Division barely contains the German attack. Heavy losses are sustained by both sides. Offshore, the British cruiser *Penelope* is damaged by a torpedo attack. To the south, near Cassino, German forces recover Point 593 after losing possession briefly to the British 4th Indian Division (part of the US 5th Army).

In Italy... At Anzio, heavy fighting takes place on the Anzio-Campoleone road (the "Flyover"). German armored reserves (26th Panzer Div. and 29th Panzer Grenadier Div.) are committed to the attack. Allied artillery prevents significant gains. Offshore, the cruiser *Penelope* is hit again and sinks. Meanwhile, around Cassino, further attacks by Indian, New Zealand forces of the US 5th Army fail to hold the gains made in attacks from the hills north of the monastery and over the Rapido River.

In Italy... The Anzio beachhead becomes stabilized. Neither sides plans significant attacks at this time. To the south, there is a lull in the fighting along the Gustav Line."[80]

Friday, February 25, 1944

Over Germany... In the climax of the "Big Week" bombing campaign, aircraft of the US 8th Air Force (830 bombers) and the US 15th Air Force (150 bombers), with fighter escorts, conduct a daylight raid of the Messerschmitt works at Regensburg and Augsburg. Losses are reported at 30 and 35 bombers, of the 8th and 15th Air Forces respectively, as well as 8 escort fighters. The Americans claim to shoot down 142 German fighters as well as destroying 1000 German fighters on the assembly lines and 1000 more lost to the disruption of production. During the night, RAF Bomber Command attacks Augsburg in a two waves.[81]

Monday, February 28, 1944

My Dearest Darling,

Remember a year ago today? If not, then perhaps you'll recall that I went for my blood test for the Army which came on a Sunday. Now do you remember? Now looking back at it, it seems like only a short time but then when you stop and think about what you have done and where you have been, it then seems like years. Here I have been home only last month but it seems like such a long time. In fact, I am all ready for my next one and that is so far away. July at the earliest. I just can't wait until we get into some sort of camp so that I can send for you. What about your side of that situation? Can you come when the time comes and what about the job you have?

There has been no change here as yet. We will probably move again tomorrow and finish this maneuver. Then Wednesday we'll get a couple of days break. During this break they are going to give out 24 hour passes. They will be given to the best four of each platoon. I am hoping I can get in there someplace. As I can use a few leisure hours in town. At least I will be able to clean up.

Honey, have you got any more new clothes lately as don't you be afraid to get some any time you wish. How about your heating oil? Has that been holding out? Also, if my car gets to be a problem then sell it. It may do you better if it was out of your hands. Anyway honey, all I am planning now is that we get stationed someplace so that I can send for you. As we all know the time is drawing near to the time that I will have to go across the ocean. We hate to admit it, but it is time. After all, the government isn't training men and then not using them. I am wishing we don't go over but remain behind and teach others what we have learned. So I believe it will be better if you should come when ever we get stationed at some camp. What do you think? But honey, no matter what should happen, I will always love you. I don't have to say "honey, wait for me" as I know you will. I only hope that I can come back as good a man as I left, I mean physically. That would be the only thing I think I would dread to do. To come home to you handicapped in one way or another. I know you'll say that regardless of how I came, it wouldn't matter but that wouldn't be the best way.

One thing I want most is to be able to come back and start where we left off. I think you'll agree with me. So honey, I guess I better stop for now as I intend to write a short letter. I hope you don't have any trouble understanding my letters as I sometimes write with out knowing what I do write. So honey, until next letter, I will close with love and kisses. XXXXXXXXX

Wish I could have those real kisses instead of cross marks.

Forever yours,

Ed

MARCH

Friday, March 3, 1944

In Italy... On the Anzio beachhead, German forces attack the line held by the US 3rd Division, near Ponte Ricco, but fail to penetrate. The German 14th Army goes over to the defensive after this failure.[82]

Monday, March 6, 1944

Over Germany... US heavy bombers raid Berlin for the first time. A force of 660 bombers is sent and 69 are lost.[83]

Tuesday, March 7, 1944

My Dearest Darling,

It seems that the days go by pretty fast now that your letters come in regularly. I have been getting them almost every day for some time. As usually, all I can say is that everything is the same here. I expect to move out some time today. Probably I will have Thursday off. It doesn't seem possible that they let us stay in one place as long as they have but it seems that our tanks aren't any good around here. All we do is march up and down the road and that is no way to fight a war. That rumor I wrote to you about seems to be a sure thing. I do hope so, so that maybe we can find a place around the camp for you to stay. I wish there were someway to bring my car down because then we wouldn't have to worry about going to and from camp. If you only could drive then I could have you bring it down as it would be cheaper than the train. But then the question comes up as to how long will we stay there so you can see that it is impossible to do anything. Sometimes I think it is useless trying to keep the car until after the war. As you keep saying that it looks like a long one. But then if you did bring the car down and I stayed there only a month or two, the question would come up as to how to get it back home, so there you are. Anyway you look at it, you get stuck.

So I guess the only thing we can do is have you come by train and hope that the transportation is the best. Honey, I must close this letter in a hurry as a message just came and I believe we are going to move out. So until the next letter I remain.

Yours forever,

Ed.

Wednesday, March 8, 1944

Over Germany... USAAF heavy bombers raid Berlin for a second time. About 10 percent of the force of 580 bombers is lost despite the escort of 800 fighters.[84]

My Dearest Darling,

In the last letter from you, you are wondering how I feel when I read of you losing your job. I am afraid it really doesn't matter to much. I use to worry about your health working nights. Also, that job isn't quite the type for a woman. So don't be to anxious to go back to work. So as I said in one of the letters, I am rather glad because now you can get plenty of rest in case you should get the chance to come down here. And I am pretty sure you will if it becomes possible. Also, I wish I could arrange to have my car but I am afraid it wouldn't be worth the trouble. What is your opinion? Another thing, I was thinking that wouldn't it be better if we took the money and had it in the bank in an checking account because then you wouldn't have to worry after you came down here especially if something happened and you had to have money. Just an idea to think about however you do as you think is best. But you can almost be sure of coming down so be prepared in a small way. Such as putting some of your things away such as your fur coat. Because honey, even if I don't get to see you only a couple of times a week, it will be better than not at all, right? And we know in our hearts that I may not be around to long so we might as well make the best of what time we have left. I don't know how I am going to be able to stand it if I go overseas as I am lost now without seeing you. I guess by now you don't have any doubt in your mind as to my love for you. Remember what you once said to me, that you weren't sure that I loved you. If you only knew how much I do. So let's hope and pray that all these rumors are correct and I can have you come sometime in April. Maybe even Easter together.

Yours forever,
Ed

Friday, March 10, 1944

My Dearest Darling,

I am going to write a hurried letter as it is getting dark and at present we can't use the lights. Everything is fine here. Now we are just waiting to go back into camp. Just had the Captain tell me what a good job I have been doing out here. Which doesn't make me feel any better.

Gee Hon, sorry that all the bills are coming in now but they are bound to come in sometime. I believe that the idea of a checking account is a good one if you should come down here. Also, as you definitely plan to move, you should do it now because I know I will call for you sometime next month and it will be the early part of the month. And if you intend on moving out of that place, then do it now. Then when the time comes, all you will have to do is leave. Don't forget the things in the attic and all the odds and ends we have around. And if you have some one to bring the car down, then do so. Then put in the car all the things you may need down here. But as for how long you will stay, I don't know. I don't think I have to tell you what to do as you have said time and again, you are not helpless.

Really honey, I must close but will write the first chance I get. So until the next letter.

Love and kisses.

Ed

P.S. Can't wait until I am able to send for you and hold you in my arms again.

Wednesaday, March 15, 1944

In Italy... Forces of the US 5th Army launches new attacks on Cassino. A preliminary bombardment consisting of 14,000 tons of bombs and 190,000 shells is directed on the town. The New Zealand 2nd Division then attacks with the 4th Indian Division to follow up against the monastery. Armored support is hampered by the rubble created during the bombardment. The German 1st Paratroop Division offers strong resistance. Allied forces make some gains at Castle Hill and Hangman's Hill.[85]

Saturday, March 18, 1944

The 392nd conducted a heavy bombing campaign over Friedrichshafen suffering heavy losses of aircraft and aircrew.

Sunday, March 19, 1944

My Dearest Darling,

I got your letter and also the car registration. I will go to town tomorrow and send it out. Honey, I don't feel very good tonight but will try and answer all the questions. I should feel pretty good now that you haven't sold my car as it may be for the best if we should keep it. Honey, that tire inspection paper is in the car in the dash compartment. So if you can get the car running, do so and be ready to come as soon as I call for you. Another thing, if you bring the car, keep the tool box as they are my tools and I may need them. Honey, I think you will find all the things you need in that compartment in the dash. But have everything ready to come around the first two weeks in April. As we are moving Tuesday to Texas and by the 4th of April we are suppose to be ready to move to Bowie.

Honey, everything is a mess here so do as you think is right because I can't help to much. But I hope that you can bring my car. I will wait for tomorrow's mail, as I believe you have all the information I need. So honey, I will close until tomorrow's mail.

So good night, until then.

Ed

Monday, March 20, 1944

In Italy... British General Alexander, Supreme Allied Command in the Mediterranean, agrees to the request of New Zealand Corps commander General Freyberg to halt attacks on Cassino because of heavy losses, unless substantial progress is achieved within the next two days.[86]

My Dearest,

I am enclosing the car registration in this letter. I have signed it and all I left out is the date. So fill that in yourself. If you should use it, you better see about that insurance as if you don't, there is bound to be something that will happen. Now about coming down here, hold fast and as soon as I can I'll send for you. So be ready. Now whether you'll come with the car or not, that is hard to say. But look around and see what you can do. As all they tell us is that we won't have much time off but I know that even if it is only once or twice, you'll rather be here with me than at home. Now honey, they say that we'll be there only six weeks so tell me if you think that it would be worth having the car here or not. I'll leave that up to you. If things should go from bad to worse, take the car to my mothers, as it would be as well off there as if we gave it to some one to take care of. As they'll be hard to get after the war. So until I hear from you I'll leave it as is.

Now about ourselves or rather myself, everything is as good as can be expected. Nothing certain. I hope that you can bear it a little longer and I am sure you'll be better off next month. Just put everything away that you don't need and after we leave Texas perhaps you can follow me.

Honey, I'll close for now as I am getting ready to go to town. As that is the only way I can send this letter out. So until I can find out for sure. I close,

Your Loving Husband,

Ed

Tuesday, March 21, 1944

My Dearest Darling,

No, there is no reason why you shouldn't call me all those names. As I have no reason to be mad or think that you had done anything wrong. I was the one who told you to sell my car. I realize now what a headache it must have been to you. I hope that now it frees you up and gives you a chance to go and do as you please. Did you get cash for it as I can't think it would have not been good other wise? Honey, the rest of the things that are in the car be sure that you clean out everything. But leave the jack and the wrench to change a tire. Otherwise, that tool box that is in there is MINE. Also, clean out the compartment in the dash. Also, I believe I have that lock for the tires in there. If you find it, I believe who ever bought the car will know how to use it. You know, when I think about it, it seems hard to take. I am rather glad I'm not home and getting rid of the car, as I don't think I would have been able to.

I never heard about the checking account that I mentioned to you. Did you forget about it or what? Now the only problem left is bringing you here and that will have to wait until I get down to Bowie. I hope the rooms will be easy to get. I also heard that they have taxis in and out of the post. That will make it a little easier. What is your opinion of coming down? As I believe I told you about not being able to see you all the time. Our chances will be about once or twice a week. Personally, I believe that it will be worth it. How about you? As I miss you and don't care what the cost will be as long as I have you here.

Honey, it looks like I must close for now as we are suppose to move at 5:00 and it is now 4:00. So you see that I haven't to much time. Closing for now.

Love,

Ed

Wednesday, March 22, 1944

In Italy... The forces of the New Zealand Corps (part of US 5th Army) makes a final attack on German-held Cassino. It fails. General Freyberg, commanding the corps, then calls off the attack. Allied troops are withdrawn from the most advance positions and the remainder consolidate recent gains.[87]

Thursday, March 23, 1944

My Dearest Darling,

Well it seems that I lost out on that trip to Bowie as they are only sending one officer per company and I guess that's one position I couldn't take. Well anyway, we expect to leave around the fourth of next month. So I guess you'll have to wait a week or more before you'll be able to come here. I'll send for you as soon as I am able.

Now about my car, I am waiting to hear that he has taken it as I am anxious to know how it ran. I guess he started it up before buying it to see if it did run. Gee, I am sorry to see it go but I guess it was for the best. Now no one will have any worries about it.

Well, getting the $100.00 for the car will make us that much richer. I suppose you'll have quite a bit of trouble getting moved out of that place. But now that we have gone so far, I can see that it is for the best.

Honey, I will make this one a short one again. I will try to get more time in the next letter. Hope that everything has turned out O.K. at home. Until tomorrow's letter I will close with love and kisses.

Yours,

Ed

Friday, March 24, 1944

Over Germany... During the night a thousand plane raid on Berlin is carried out by Bomber Command. Heavy damage is reported in Berlin but many bombers are blown off course and more than 50 are shot down by German Flak defenses. A total of 73 bombers are lost in all operations (including a diversionary attack on Kiel).

Flight Sergeant Alkemade jumps, without a parachute, from a burning RAF Lancaster bomber at 5486 meters above western Germany and lands safely in a snow drift.[88]

My Dearest Darling,

I was waiting to hear from you today but I received no mail. So I guess I will receive one tomorrow. I am wondering if the car is gone as yet. As I would like to know just what is the score? Also, what about your moving the furniture? Everything here is about the same, as by now you know that I am in Texas. About the same place as I was in the December series. As in other letters that I have written, we won't be in Bowie until the first or second week in April. So I guess you'll have to wait for a couple of weeks longer than you expected. But I'll send for you as soon as I possibly can.

Wish I could be with you right now as you must be having a hard time moving and all. But after you once move you'll be free to go and do as you please. Well that hundred dollars is better than nothing. Get yourself an Easter outfit with it. Well Honey, have to go. Closing again and hope that I can find more time to write next time. So until then, I am,

Yours,

Ed

Thursday, March 30, 1944

Over Germany... RAF Bomber Command raids Nuremberg with 795 bombers. The force loses 96 aircraft, representing the single highest nightly loss of the entire war. It is apparent that on clear nights the growing technical skill of the German night-fighter controllers and the new Lichtenstein airborne radar units combine with the German ability to track RAF H2S and IFF transmissions in inflicting unacceptable loss rates on the attacking force.[89]

My Dearest Darling,

You'd be surprised if you knew just where this letter is being written. Well, this morning I picked up the (old man) Company Commander and after a fashion we started for that payroll. It so happens that we had to travel about a hundred miles one way. We got there and then started back around noon. Well about halfway back the rear end on the peep mind you went to heck. That was around two thirty and it is now six o'clock. I am still waiting for some one to come for me and this peep. The Company Commander got a ride back with one of the other peeps. I hope I won't have to wait to long as I am getting hungry. One fellow stopped and I got a drink but now I am waiting for some one to take this darn peep back.

Well, so much for that. Now this is for sure that we are going back to Camp Polk. It is expected to be on the seventh but I am not sure. Also, we may live just outside of camp for a few weeks. Now the question is do you want to come to Leesville for a few weeks and then on to the next place or would you rather wait until we get some definite place? One thing, it may be some time before we leave Camp Polk. Tell you what, if you are willing to come to Leesville and then move on with me then send me a letter to that effect and as soon as we get back to camp, I'll look for a place. Then when I find one, I'll send for you O.K. ? So I'll wait until I hear from you that you'll come to Leesville. Then I will do my darnedest to find a place.

Honey, I will stop for now and finish when I get back to the Company.

APRIL

The Seventh Period of Louisiana Maneuvers closed on 3 April 1944. From 3 to 24 April the Division was billeted in administrative bivouac and time was devoted to maintenance, polishing up small unit tactics, correcting mistakes, and utilizing lessons learned on maneuvers.

Saturday, April 8, 1944

My Dearest,

Here it is Saturday night. I am thinking of you and how I wish I was able to be home for tomorrow, Easter Sunday. So I hope that you had enjoyed yourself, as I want you to be happy. We are allowed week end passes but there isn't any place to go so I am staying in.

We had that big parade only it rained a little which dampened the whole works. Otherwise everything turned out O.K. Boy there is really a big bunch of guys going home on furlough.

All we can do is wait until we find out for sure just what is going to happen. As I hate to think of you coming to Leesville and finding me gone or not finding a place to stay. So all we can do is wait and pray for the best. Well honey, will close for now. I will write tomorrow.

Loving you always,

Ed

P.S. Just a couple more months and it will be three years. (of marriage) Doesn't seem so, does it?

Sunday, April 9, 1944

My Dearest,

Today is Easter Sunday. Guess what, I went to church this morning. They had a choir of girls, which really lightened the atmosphere, as they were dressed in their best Sunday clothes. It really reminded me of home on such a Sunday. Could of gone to town this afternoon but I decided against it. So instead I washed clothes and took a bath. Also, I got a good sun burn. It really is a nice day with lots of wind and sun.

Tell me what are you doing today? Did you enjoy yourself today? What about the clothes you wore, did you get a new outfit?

Sgt. Miller is looking for a place for me and as soon as he finds one, I am sending for you regardless if we move or not. So keep your fingers crossed and hope that he can find a place.

This field life is not so hot as it is hard to go to town. Also, it is harder to come back. Then again the clothes always stay dirty.

We are suppose to have a road march tomorrow. I hope it isn't a long one. Gee honey, I miss you and I was thinking of you all day. Just wondering what you are doing. I hope you are making out O.K. You can be sure that as soon as I can, I'll send for you. The future looks very bad on my part so I want to have you around me for as long as possible. I intend to be near you. Here is hoping that the 8th Armored Division isn't needed overseas then we'll be together for some time. Honey, I will close for now. Until tomorrow's letter, I remain,

Yours,

Ed

Thursday, April 13, 1944

My Dearest Darling(and I am meaning just that) I mean Darling Wife,

It seems that our letters are leading us astray. And it seems that it is over a few lines in my letters where I say something about your short letters. I realize now that I should have reread those letters. I suppose it would be useless to say how sorry I am, as it wasn't meant the way you took it. Also, this darn place is driving me screwy. I must have been in one of those moods where I got hell all day and then I tried to write a decent letter. But let's stop this foolishness right now as it may cause us to be sorry later on. As for my feelings toward you, even the time and distance couldn't change it. As I have been doing everything possible to bring you here. Yes, you're right in saying that if we could be together for just a few minutes then I believe I could just explain everything. You don't realize what goes on here. As all of my letters have been saying that nothing is certain. If things were uncertain before, then you should see them now. No one knows as to what, where and when we are going to do anything. I intend to have you stay where you are and as soon as we find out for sure what we are doing, you are coming down. So don't get hot headed and look for other jobs or rooms. It may be a few weeks perhaps longer but I assure you as soon as it is definite where we will stay, you will come.

It seems every thing is so slow in getting here. Take these two letters that I got today for example. The airmail was sent out on the 7th and the plain on the 9th, however, I got them today. Your sister sent one on the 7th with plain postage and I got it yesterday. So you can see why we are getting at each other. I swear I tried for two days to get a place. I tried everywhere. You probably know what it is like as you have been here before.

We came back last night and found out all passes have been cancelled. So you see, even if I had sent for you, I couldn't meet you. I don't believe I can express myself when I say that things change from one hour to the next. I do want you to get that idea out of your head that I have lost interest in you. As the way it reads, you now believe that I have found someone else and that hurts because you are the only one I care for and always will be no matter where I may be. I hope that in the answer to this letter you'll say that you believe that I love you and that nothing will ever stand in between us. I hope that this letter so far will explain everything. If I could some possible way phone you, I believe I could make you understand just what is what.

Honey, I want you to be happy so if my letters have hurt you in any way, please forgive me. As I didn't mean any thing by it. So what do you say? Am I forgiven? I will worry until I hear from you. I must close and I will write again tonight.

Your Lonesome husband,

Ed

Monday, April 17, 1944

In the English Channel and North Sea... The British Royal Navy and Bomber Command begin intensive mining of the approaches to the English Channel and as far north as the Danish coast. This operation is intended to prevent German interference with the D-Day invasion fleet. (It continues until June 5th by which time 7000 mines are laid. An estimated 100 light warships and other vessels are sunk by the mines.)[90]

Tuesday, April 18, 1944

Over Britain... The last of the "Little Blitz" air raids on London is conducted by 125 aircraft (14 are lost on the mission). A total of 53 tons of bombs are dropped and a hospital is among the buildings hit.

Over Germany... American B-17 and B-24 bombers attack the Heinkel works at Oranienburg and other targets near Berlin. British Mosquito bombers strike Berlin.

Over Occupied France... RAF Bomber Command drops a record 4000 tons of bombs on marshalling yards and railway workshops at Juvisy, Noisy-le-Sec, Rouen and Tergnier.

In London... The British government bans all coded radio and telegraph transmissions from London and elsewhere on the British Isles. Diplomatic bags are to be subject to censorship and diplomats are forbidden to leave the country. The only exemptions are for the USA, USSR and the Polish government in exile, in London. These measures are intended to maintain the secrecy of the preparations for D-Day. In addition, incitement to strike is made a punishable offense.[91]

Over Occupied Europe... British bombers drop a total of 4500 tons of bombs on four rail junctions: Cologne, La Chappelle (Paris), Lens and Ottignies (Brussels).

Over Germany... The US 8th Air Force raids factories and airfields in Friedrichshafen, near Munich. A total of 55 planes are lost, including 14 which land or crash in Switzerland. During the night, 250 RAF Lancaster bombers scatter "Flying Meteor" methane-petrol incendiary bombs over Munich causing devastation in the area between Central Station and the Isar River.

In Britain... The *Luftwaffe* carries out the first of a series of nighttime raids on shipping at Portsmouth and Plymouth-Devonport.

In the English Channel... During the night (April 25-26), the British cruiser *Black Prince* and 3 Canadian destroyers engage German warships: *T-29* is sunk (136 killed), *T-24* and *T-27* are damaged.

In Britain... During the night (April 27-28), 3 American LST landing craft, conducting an invasion exercise (Exercise "Tiger"), are torpedoed by German E-boats in Lyme Bay. A total of 638 troops are killed. This incident is kept secret for fear of damaging Anglo-American relations.

In the English Channel... During a nighttime sortie, the Canadian destroyer HMCS *Athabaskan* is sunk by the German *Elbing* class destroyer *T-24* in the early morning hours. Her Captain, John Stubbs and 128 men were lost, 83 taken prisoner and 44 rescued.

MAY

"**1 May**: The 339th Infantry regiment is assigned the combat area northwest of Minturno, centered around the village of Tremensuoli and the seaside villa of Scauri, held at that time by the 338th Infantry, 85th Infantry Division. The unit is facing the outer defenses of the "Gustav Line" held in this sector by the German 94th Infantry Division.

3 May: 339th Infantry relieves the 338th Infantry in line from Minturno to Scauri, and assumes responsibility for guarding Garigliano River Bridge on Highway 7.

11 May: "The Big Push". Operation DIADEM begins at 2300 hours. The 339th Infantry attacks promptly at H-Hour, with the 1st Battalion containing Scauri and enemy held Domenico Ridge east of the town. The 2nd Battalion advances into the area between Tremensuoli and Scauri, objectives of Hills 58, 79, and Intermediate Ridge. The 3rd Battalion crosses Capo di Acqua and assaults Hills 69 and 66. Casualties are heavy within first few hours."[92]

"The Minturno Breakout began at 11 p.m., 11 May 1944, uphill, against a well-entrenched and fortified German Army. 1LT Harry Rudolph (Rudy) Albright , Company A, 337th Infantry, 85th Division , was assigned to lead his platoon in taking Colle San Martino, or Hill #69. His body was found, with a heavy artillery wound in his right thigh, a few days later. His death was estimated to have occurred 12 May 1944."[93]

From copies of 337th Regiment Operations Reports from the National Archives in College Park, Maryland**,** the following records are on file:

"Although no troops of the Regiment participated in the initial attacks it was not, long before our organizations were engaged. Company "A" moved out at 0400 to bolster the 337th Infantry. This Regiment had run into bitter opposition as they attempted to take Hills 68, 69, one 79. At 0430 Company *K* moved to assist the 3rd Battalion, 339th Infantry. The company suffered heavy casualties, but managed to -get a slim hold on Hill 69. Company "I" rejoined the 3rd Battalion and Companies "I" and "L", in defensive positions, were used to back up the 339th Infantry line. "[94]

"13 May: Battle along front line continues. 1st Battalion, 337th Infantry relieves 3rd Battalion, 339th Infantry at Hill 69 after nightfall and continues attack on Hill 66, which is repulsed. Remnant of F Company surrounded on Intermediate Ridge finally capitulates at dusk. G Company holds Hill 79 against continued counterattacks with no relief."[95]

"In the meantime, the rest of the 1rst Battalion moved out to join the 339th Infantry, closing into the Tremensuoli area at 0930, sustaining some casualties on the march. The battalion was ordered to pass to the left of Company K on Hill 69 and to capture Hill 66. At 1100, as the commander, and Captain Hugh R. Ballantine. company :B" commander. The Battalion Executive Officer. Major Arnold L. Sanders, immediately assumed command. The Battalion, without its heavy weapons company, crossed the Cappo d'Aqua at 1400 and competed the capture of Hill 69 by 1500. At 1630 Hill 66 was attacked, but our troops found this hill heavily defended with reinforced bunkers, and they were forced off the hill and back to Hill 69, Another attack was organized with strong artillery support, and scheduled to 'begin at 1830, Every yard was bitterly contested by the Germens and after much close combat and ferreting the enemy out of dug-outs, Companies "A" and "C" took Hill 66. During the operation casualties were great from enemy mines, artillery and automatic weapons. The hill in their hands;. the 1rst Battalion organized a reverse slope defense and prepared for the counterattacks they knew would come at daylight."[96]

15 May: First signs of German withdrawal. 1st Battalion moves onto Domenico Ridge. Hill 79 is secured by G Company, 2nd Battalion. 3rd Battalion reorganized and moved back to front line near Tremensuoli."[97]

> The 8th Armored Division ended almost six months of continuous life under field conditions on 28 April 1944 when the unit moved into South Camp Polk Maryanne finally moved to Leesville Louisiana to be with Ed. She stayed at a rooming house next door to Gretchen Brewer from Maine, wife of PFC Frederick Allen Brewer nickname Buggy. He was in the 7th B Company of the armored infantry battalion, 8th armored division. It was at that time that began a life long friendship between Maryanne and Gretchen. Gretchen writes: Maryanne had the room next to ours at the rooming house. Mrs. Underwood was the woman who owned the rooming house, she was a nice old lady at that time. Our husbands were allowed to come into Leesville from Camp Polk and spend the nights. Then they took the bus back to camp in the morning. All the wives had pass cards that gave us permission to go into Camp and see our husbands, incase they couldn't leave the base. Most of us wives stayed there in Leesville up to the same day the guys left October 25, 1944

AC122 ©MWM
DON'T LET DISTANCE MAKE YOUR
HEART GROW FONDER ——
FOR SOMEBODY ELSE !!

GAS RATIONING
CAN'T STOP ME
NO
GAS
TODAY
WHEN I'M ON
MANEUVERS!
AC129 ©MWM

July, 1944

Image:M4A4 cutaway.png

From Wikipedia, the free encyclopedia

- Image
- File history
- File links

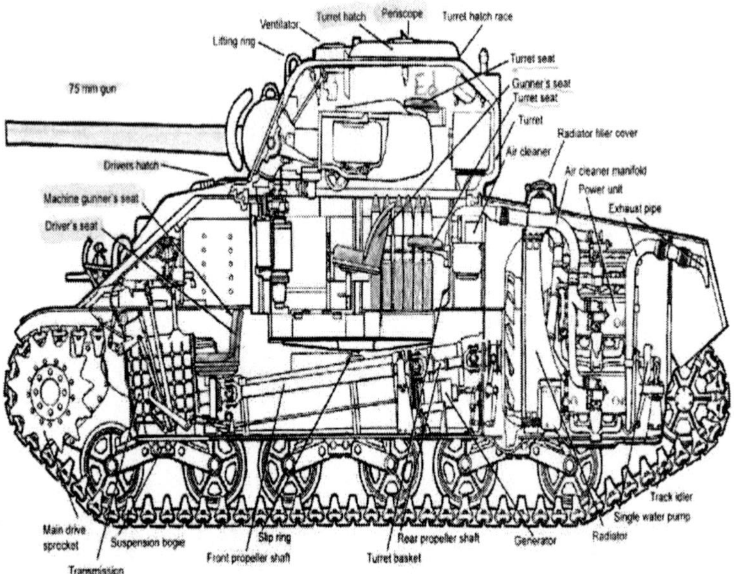

Eddie, Johnnie, Windy, and Kenny in Germany

"Ward", Johnnie Helinski, Ed Brodowski, Ken Ritkopky, Earl"Windy" Coffman on guard in Germany

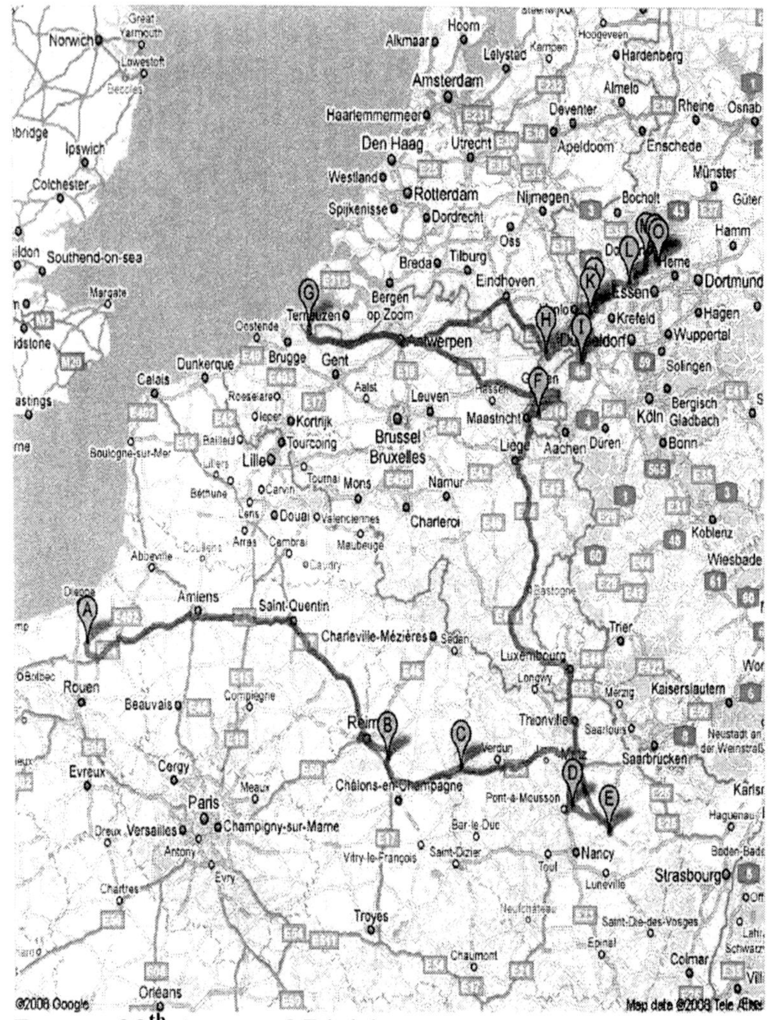

Route of 8th Armored Division

LEGEND

A. Cressy, Seine-Maritime, Haute-Normandie, France
B. Sept. Saulx, France
C. Les Islettes, France
D. Morville Sur Seille ,France
E. Vic Sur Seille , France
F. Vilt, Holland
G. Aardenburg Sluis, Zeeland, The Netherlands
H. Maasbracht, Holland
I. Roermond, Holland
J. Tuschenbroich, Germany
K. Wall, 47669 Wachtendonk, Kleve, Nordrhein-Westfalen, Germany
L. Grefrath, Germany
M. Lobberich Nettetal, Viersen, Nordrhein-Westfalen, Germany
N. Bruckhausen Duisburg, Duisburg, Nordrhein-Westfalen, Germany
O. Kirchhellen Bottrop, Bottrop, Nordrhein-Westfalen, Germany
P. Scholven Gelsenkirchen, Gelsenkirchen, Nordrhein-Westfalen, Germany
Q. Buer, Germany

JUNE

> "D Day in Europe was big news for the Division early in June 1944. 8th men had sober expressions as they listened to the broadcasts originating off the coast of France. Their thoughts went either to those marching with the invasion forces or to the future when they also would be facing enemy fire.

6 June 1944 Normandy - D-Day "The 506th Airborne PIR took off for their first combat jump at 0100hrs, 6 June 1944. In the predawn hours of D-Day a combination of low clouds, and enemy anti-aircraft fire caused the break-up of the troop carrier formations. The scattering of the air armada was such that only nine of the eighty-one planes scheduled to drop their men on the Drop Zone (DZ) found their mark. Consequently, the sporadic jump patterns caused most of the troopers to land far afield of their designated DZ. Some of the sticks landed as far away as 20 miles from the designated area. Only the 3rd Battalion landed in close proximity to their designated DZ. However, the area had long been recognized by the Germans as a likely spot for a parachute assault. The Germans set a strategic trap and in less than 10 minutes managed to kill the battalion commander, Lt Col Wolverton, his executive officer Maj George Grant and a large portion of the battalion.

The only part of the battalion that survived were those who were dropped in the wrong DZ. These two planeloads of troopers under the leadership of Capt Charles Shettle managed to accomplish the battalion's objective of capturing the two bridges over the Douve River. The men of the remaining battalions fought valiantly in small groups, and as others joined them, they moved towards their objectives. Just prior to the landing of seaborne forces, the high ground overlooking the beaches was seized and held by the men of the 506th Parachute Infantry Regiment. "[98]

"CPL Franklin Maynard ("Bud") Elliott of Company A, 741st Tank Battalion was on Omaha Beach 6 June, 1944 . His assignment was as a gunner in a Sherman 'Wader' Tank, landing at 0630 as part of the "initial assault wave" which was to pave the way on the Easy Red sector of Omaha for the entry of other troops and supplies. His unit was attached that day to the First Infantry. His tank was hit in shallow water and diabled, however, he and the other 4 crew members did get to the beach. One was wounded and had to be evacuated. Bud continued to fight in the tragic and bloody confusion on that beach until some time that afternoon, when, near the bluff, just as he and some others were about to get off the beach, he stepped on a land mine and was killed."[99]

During the remainder of June the infantry and tank battalions of the 8th armored division fired the light and heavy .30 caliber machine guns for record on various ranges. A large detachment from the Division departed for two weeks firing on the Anti-Aircraft Ranges at Camp Dona Anna, Texas. July ushered in the second phase of post-maneuver training. The objective of this phase was "to perfect the tactical and technical proficiency of units from the platoon to the reinforced battalion." Assault of fortified areas, indirect fire of tank, anti-aircraft, and air-ground training were all included. The training schedules of the Division units reflected a directive that 50% of all training would take place at night. Many a sore-footed Herder could testify that the division hiked! A favorite device of battalion commanders, the twenty-five mile hike came around at least once a month. Many units, in efforts to escape the heat of the day, marched into camp on Friday evening after a week in the field."[100]

JANUARY-JUNE 1944

Chapter Four

AUGUST-DECEMBER 1944

August 1, 1944:

In Occupied Poland... In Warsaw, the Polish Home Army initiates an uprising against the German occupation. These forces are formally under the direction of the Polish government in exile located in London. The timing of this action is intended to liberate Warsaw, by Polish forces, prior to the arrival of Soviet forces (which is, however, expected to take place shortly).

On the Western Front... The US 3rd Army (General Patton) becomes operational on the right flank and is tasked with clearing Brittany. American forces are now organized under US 12th Army Group (Bradley) and include US 1st Army (Hodges) as well as 3rd Army. The British 21st Army Group (Montgomery) command British 2nd Army (Dempsey) and Canadian 1st Army (Crerar). Field Marshal Montgomery retains overall command of Allied ground forces and General

Eisenhower remains Commander in Chief of the Allied Expeditionary Forces.[101]

August 7, 1944:

On the Western Front... German forces begin a significant counterattack from east of Mortain, opposite US 1st Army (between US 7th and 14th Corps). Elements of German 2nd and 116th Panzer Divisions spearhead the offensive. Mortain is recaptured. Heavy Allied air attacks prevent more significant advances by the German forces. Meanwhile, in Brittany, the US 8th Corps (part of US 1st Army) attacks the German garrisoned ports of Brest, St. Malo and Lorient. During the night, Canadian forces (part of British 21st Army Group) launch attacks southwest of Caen after a preparatory bombardment involving over 1000 RAF heavy bombers dropping more than 3000 tons of bombs on German positions.

August 10, 1944:

On the Western Front... British elements of the 1st Canadian Army capture Vimont, south of Caen. Meanwhile, the US 3rd Army continues attacking. The US 8th Corps, in Brittany, has cleared St. Malo and Dinard of their German garrisons. The US 20th Corps captures Nantes and reaches the Loire River near Nantes. The US 15th Corps advances toward Alencon from Le Mans. German forces around Mortain pull back because of pressure from US 1st Army and the growing threat of encirclement from the converging Canadian and American armies.

August 15, 1944:

On the Western Front... Elements of British 8th Corps (part of British 2nd Army) enter Tinchebray from the north. Allied forces of Canadian 1st Army are attacking along a line from Tinchebray to Falaise. From south of Tinchebray to Argentan the US 7th and 5th Corps (elements of US 1st Army) are attacking northward.

Most of the German 7th Army as well as elements of 15th Panzer Army and Panzer Group Eberbach are now threatened with encirclement. These forces now begin a withdrawal eastward. Field Marshal Kluge is touring the front during the day. Allied aircraft are heavily engaged in ground attacks throughout the day.[102]

August 25, 1944:

On the Western Front... The French 4th Armored Division (General Leclerc) enter Paris. German garrison commander, General Chollitz, disobeys orders to the contrary and surrenders the city. To the northwest of Paris, forces of British 21st Army Group capture Vernon, Louviers and Elbeuf on the approach to the Seine River line. In Brittany, the US 8th Corps launches an attack on Brest were the German garrison continues to resist. The HMS *Warspite* shells the town.[103]

SEPTEMBER

September 1, 1944:

On the Western Front... General Eisenhower establishes his headquarters in France as Commander in Chief of the Allied Expeditionary Forces. Canadian forces of British 21st Army Group capture Dieppe. Inland, British forces take Arras in the advance north of the Somme River. The forces of US 12th Army Group continue as well. US 1st Army approaches St. Quentin and Cambrai. The US 3rd Army captures Verdun and Comercy.[104]

September 10, 1944:

On the Western Front... Canadian elements of British 21st Army Group attack German-held positions near Zeebrugge. Troops of the US 1st Army (part of US 12th Army Group) enter Luxembourg. Along the English Channel coast, the battleship HMS *Warspite* and monitor *Erebus*, shell Le Havre. General Eisenhower, commanding the AEF, accepts a proposal by Field Marshal Montgomery (commanding British 21st Army Group) to conduct a series of airborne assaults to capture bridges in Holland and allow a rapid advance to the Rhine River (Operation Market Garden).[105]12 September, 1944

> "*On the Western Front...* The German garrison of Le Harve, about 12,000 men, surrenders under pressure of attacks by British 1st Corps (part of Canadian 1st Army, British 21st Army Group). Forces of US 1st Army (part of US 12th Army Group) reach the German border between Aachen and Trier."[106]

September 17, 1944:

On the Western Front... Operation Market Garden begins. The Allied intention is to secure key bridges over a series of rivers and canals in Holland to achieve a rapid advance onto the north German plain. On the first day, the US 101st Airborne Division secures bridges at Veghel and Zon. The US 82nd Airborne Division secures the bridge at Grave but not the one at Nijmegen. The British 1st Airborne Division, dropped near Arnhem, fails to secure the bridge there because of unexpected German resistance. Unknown to Allied planners, the 9th SS *Hohenstaufen* and 10th SS *Frundsberg* Panzer Divisions are located in Arnhem for rest and refit from combat on the Eastern Front. Meanwhile, the British 30th Corps (part of British 2nd Army) attacks northward toward Eindhoven to relieve the paratroopers. To the west, Canadian forces, also part of British 21st Army Group, launch an attack on Boulogne after a preparatory bombing by the RAF.[107]

September 25, 1944:

On the Western Front... Operation Market Garden ends. The remnants of the British 1st Airborne Division are evacuated from the north bank of the Rhine. During the night, 2400 of the 10,000 men are removed. About 1100 have been killed and 6400 captured by German forces. A few are sheltered by Dutch families. Meanwhile, other elements of British 2nd Army capture Helmond and Deurne, a few miles east of Eindhoven. On the Channel coast, the Canadian 3rd Division (an element of Canadian 1st Army) attacks the German garrison trapped in Calais[108]

September 26, 1944:

On the Western Front... Allied forces continue to attack in Belgium and Holland. Forces of the British 2nd Army capture Turnhout,

OCTOBER

> "During the first week in October, the 26th Infantry Division was ordered from Normandy to the 3rd Army front in Lorraine. The 26th Division went into the line on the right flank of XII Corps, Third Army and Twelfth Army Group, relieving the 4th Armored Division which has spearheaded General Patton's drive across France. There in the hills and forests of Lorraine between Nancy and the German border, the Division took up the fight, just east of the Toulon sector where it had fought in 1918. During the month of October 1944, the 26th Infantry Division underwent its baptism of fire as it pushed towards Germany."[109]

The month of October was the official alert for movement to the Port of Embarkation. Naming train commanders, picking kitchen car details, and preparing loading plans consumed the time between 18 October and 27 October. On the 27th, the Division boarded troop trains, which would stop in Camp Kilmer, New Jersey. On 30 October 1944, the winding, devious route of the troop trains ended in the railroad sidings of Camp Kilmer. The long hard months of training in the humid heat and damp chill of Camp Polk, Louisiana, were over. The 8th Armored Division was ready to complete processing and embark for the European Theater of Operations. Members of the Division whose homes were near camp Kilmer had time for one more hurried farewell. Others were given the opportunity to visit New York or Philadelphia."

Temporary Pass for the USO, Leesville. LA.

Military Wives Club,

Mrs. Edward Brodowski, 300 Pine St., Leesville, LA

NOT GOOD AFTER October 13, 1944.

Certified by Charlotte Ressegieu, Director

Maryanne went home after October 13, 1944.

> 14 October 1944 PVT William E. Adams of the 9th I.D. 15th Engineer Bn. Co. C was part of the battles in Forest, Zweifall, Germany

William E. Adams was assigned to the "Old Reliables" of the Army's 9th Division, who became known as "Hitler's Nemesis." On 6 October 1944 the 39th and the 60th Infantry Regiments, along with the Engineers, began their first attacks on Schmidt. William was officially K.I.A. 14 October 1944[110]

"Hürtgen. If a single word can cause a U.S. Army veteran of the European theater to shudder, it would be that. The foreboding image of dark forests, steep hills, voracious mud, pillboxes, constant rain and shells bursting in treetops immediately comes to mind. The battlefield was where soldiers walked a few feet from their foxholes and was never seen again. What little has been written on Hürtgen has often focused on the November 1944 battles involving the 28th Infantry Division and has ignored the horrible prelude to the "Bloody Bucket's" mauling, which occurred over 10 days in October.

The struggle for the 50 square miles of heavily wooded and hilly terrain south of Aachen actually began in mid-September. With their supply line stretched to the breaking point, the Allies' rapid advance through France had finally slowed down at the Siegfried Line, the formidable defensive belt that blocked Germany's western border and guarded the entrance to the Ruhr Valley. Hoping to seize Aachen and establish a firm breach in the Siegfried Line before winter's onset, Maj. Gen. J. Lawton Collins, commanding VII Corps, ordered Maj. Gen. Louis A. Craig's 9th Infantry Division to seize the villages of Hürtgen and Kleinhau. After some initial progress, the American drive stalled when two of Craig's regiments were diverted north to assist the 3rd Armored Division, which was embroiled in a brutal battle at the Aachen suburb of Stolberg. In early October, Craig was ordered to resume his attack in the Hürtgen Forest. Now, however, he would have to do so minus his 47th Infantry Regiment, which remained in support of the 3rd Armored, and with understrength units sent from the fighting around Aachen

By the time major combat operations in the area finally ceased, six U.S. divisions and some 33,000 soldiers had become casualties without achieving a breach in the Siegfried Line. According to the U.S. Army's official history, "The real winner appeared to be the vast, undulating blackish-green sea that virtually negated American superiority in air, artillery, and armor to reduce warfare to its lowest common denominator." Given the terrible cost, it seems clear that Maj. Gen. James Gavin might have been more correct when he said, "For us the Hürtgen was one of the most costly, most unproductive, and most ill-advised battles that our army has ever fought."[111]

Friday October 20th, 1944

My Dearest Darling;

At last I got a letter from you now I feel better. Please forgive me for what I wrote yesterday as I was really mad as it has been quite a few days since I hear from you but now my mind is at rest. Happy to hear that everything is well at home. I am afraid I can't say the same here. As I have said in previous letters, things are a mess and continue to be more so as the days go by. Now they broke my crew up after I spent all this time getting them to work the way I wanted them. The "old man" wants us to keep on the boys to do more work as we have to get out by Monday. That means take everything and I don't think it is possible to do so as we have so much equipment to take.

Honey, it seems things are coming to a head. Now we are going with the Fourth Army. We all believe it will be overseas soon. I guess it is bound to come sooner or later so we might as well face it. I hope that nothing will change our feelings for one another when and if I do go. As you know, war is no game and a lot of things may happen. Honey, I hope our love will never die. As it wouldn't be worth the trouble of coming back.

Honey, there are a lot of things I want to say but I don't know just how. All I can say is that I'll always love you and don't ever let me down as I'm fighting for you and you alone. As I want to come back and take up where we left off. Have a happy home and family. Yes, I know, I always said I didn't want any children but I would give anything to have our own. But then again, it seems almost impossible to do so with the way everything is. No sense having you carry the whole load with out help. Darling, no matter what happens, remember I always love you and think of you no matter where I am or what I do. Thinking of you.

Love,

Ed.

P.S. Honey, sorry I am in such a depressed mood. I just don't want to have to leave you. I love you so very much. I could take a walk out of this army and head for home any day.

Ed.

"22 October 1944 PVT Fred C. Farris of the 120th Regiment, 30th Infantry Division ("Workhorse of the Western Front"), 3rd Army was in Germany when, according to his Commanding Officer, Col. Branner P. Purdue, "his platoon, which had been assigned to the right sector of the company zone had successfully accomplished its mission of clearing enemy troops and had captured 40 German soldiers. During the closing phase of this patrol, the platoon was ambushed, resulting in his death."[112]

NOVEMBER

Training is over. It is time to go!

Conrad Church was a rifleman in the 49th Armored Infantry Battalion in the 8th Armored Division. In his memoirs he recounts the departure from Camp Polk to board the ship for the trip overseas. "The entire division left Camp Polk in a troop train that meandered through the country and finally arrived at Camp Kilmer, New Jersey, our Port of Embarkation Center. Our entire group was relatively quiet and reserved during this train trip, envisioning what our futures might be as we realized we were headed toward the shooting a long way off. Arriving at Camp Kilmer, we went through a series of final inoculations, or shots, and did some very little training, including climbing down rope netting from a simulated ship to lifeboats with full gear. We had a final show-down inspection and lost or replaced unserviceable equipment, followed by boat drills, censorship instruction, gas mask drills, personnel lectures, security lectures, and other miscellaneous instructional lectures and movies.

"On the 6th of November, orders came through to move out, and we took the train to New York with box lunches, passing through the Erie railroad station in Jersey City in the early evening. It was a short hike to the ferry, and from it, after crossing the river, to the dock where His Majesty's ship "SAMARIA" was waiting to take on about 9,000 soldiers. The Red Cross was there handing out coffee and doughnuts. We walked up in single file to the gangplank, carrying our musette and duffel bags, weighing about 150 pounds, it seemed. An officer at the gang plank called out "Church", and I answered, "Conrad F., 42177187 and went on board. This procedure was repeated for each man boarding.

> "As troops were methodically loaded into the darkened hulls of the waiting ships on the night of 6 November 1944, many a man, poised on the threshold of the unknown, honestly and humbly wondered what his own reactions to the

> holocaust of modern war would be. But no one questioned the ability of his platoon, company, or battalion to meet the test of combat. It was infinitely reassuring to know that the man who led this team, Brigadier General John M. Devine, had already proved himself a capable combat commander.
>
> On the morning of 7 November 1944 as many Americans went to the polls to cast ballots for the next president of the United States, the men who belonged to the 8th Armored Division turned their eyes to the New York skyline as their ships eased out of Pier 45, Staten Island Docks, and headed to sea."[113]

Aboard the ship we were packed in like sardines. The ship had an odor that almost made you vomit, probably from too much use over the many years. I never did get used to it in the three weeks we were aboard. It was a large ship, rising some 20 or 30 feet above the water, it seemed. Because there were so many men on board, it was necessary for 1/3 of them to sleep for 8 hours with all others on deck or in the stairways for shelter. Then, another 1/3 went below to sleep etc. etc. Sleeping quarters were crowded. We slept under, on and above (in hammocks) the tables upon which we ate, if we ate., which seemed not very often. Actually, we had two "meals" a day, which consisted mostly of bread and coffee. For a table of ten, only a couple of loaves of bread were served, and every man could have eaten both loaf at any time. If you were on the opposite side from the server at the table, you could end up with little or nothing for that meal! Everyone was always hungry.

We suspected that the English ship crew members were taking a lot of our food, since they offered to sell us sandwiches at any time for $2.00 and up to $3.00 each. Since no one had any, or at least not much money, not many took them up on their offer, but we were always hungry on this voyage. Cigarettes were plentiful, though: one could have all of these he wanted at 5 cents per pack from the PX, and some were distributed free.

We put out to sea on the night of November 6, 1944, joining in the outer harbor about 40 to 50 other ships that were to be a part of our convoy. There were three or four troop ships, oil tankers and other cargo ships, plus a small boat that had been converted to carry planes. This was our "aircraft carrier" escort. We were also escorted by three or four U.S. Destroyers.

At sea, within a few hours, almost everyone became seasick. Imagine 8,500 men all sick at the same time, and not in a delicate manner! Crossing the ocean, we had one big storm with lots of wind, rain and high, heavy waves".

> "Some Herders soon discovered that they were poor sailors. Seasick men lined the rails of the ships and many unfortunate accident occurred when a stricken man chanced to run to the windward side."[114]

November 7, 1944,

In the United States... Roosevelt is elected to an unprecedented fourth term as president, winning over Republican candidate Dewey with 36 states and 53 percent of the vote. The elections for the House of Representative result in 243 Democrats, 190 Republicans and 2 others. [115]

The November battle for Metz at Vigny

"At 0600 on 9 November, the 2nd Infantry began the 5th Division attack along the line of the Seille. crossing the river, now nearly two hundred yards wide, by footbridge and by assault craft. A squad and a half pushed into Cheminot, whose guns had held the southern Seille crossing sites in enfilade during September, but the Germans already had fled in order to escape the trap formed by the advance of the 80th Division. The 10th Infantry launched its assault conjointly with that of the 2d Infantry, but its 3d Battalion met real resistance as soon as it deployed on the east bank. Here, in a cluster of stone buildings called Hautonnerie Farm, a German company determined to make a fight for it. When the American infantry surrounded the farm the enemy captain sent out word that he intended to die for the Fuehrer-an exaggerated statement. Within a matter of hours he surrendered.

> 10 November, 1944, the second day of the attack the German troops still showed little sign of recovering their balance, and the left wing of the 17th *SS Panzer Grenadier Division* remained in a state of "collapse. The three battalions of the 2d Infantry advanced on a narrow front to the left and rear of CCB, 6th Armored, moving fast."[116] "PFC John William "Jack" Phelan of the 3rd Army, 5th Inf. Div., 2nd Inf. Rgt., 2nd Bn., Co. "G" was at a small village named Vigny near the city of Metz, when his platoon had stopped to regroup. He and three other soldiers were standing about 10 yards from their commanding lieutenant when a shell landed and exploded nearby, killing John and the other three soldiers instantly while wounding the lieutenant."[117]

"12 November,1944 PVT Ova Wendell Ratliff of Company C, 110th Infantry, 28th Division was on Oschenkopf Hill in the Huertgen Forest southwest of the small village of Simonskall, Germany. Private Ova W. Ratliff, was killed in action on a cold, muddy, battle scarred hillside in the Huertgen Forest of Germany, a few hundred yards southwest of the small village of Simonskall On November 7, just after arriving in an abandoned village near the Huertgen Forest, he wrote two letters home, one in the afternoon and one in the evening. In one of those letters he wrote, "This kind of life is rough but it may be rougher. We can't move much more for the front lines are Close Now. I can hear the guns

Now". He was placed with Company C, 110th Infantry, 28th Division as a replacement soldier on November 8th. ."[118]

> 13 November, 1944 2LT David Baird Finch of the 17th Infantry, 7th Division was on Leyete, Philippines. After the initial landing on Leyete, Philippine Islands, he was sent on a mission in the foot hills west of Guinarona to determine the location and strength of enemy positions. The patrol had to cover ground thick with tall grass and bamboo thickets. Approaching a high ridge, they were suddenly hit by deadly machine gun and mortar fire at close range. The enemy was strongly entrenched and well concealed by the thick brush. Realizing that he was greatly out numbered and his position extremely perilous, he started withdrawing his men to safety. To do this, he had to expose himself to enemy fire. Hit by sniper fire, he died almost instantly.

Thursday, November 16, 1944:

On the Western Front... Allied air strikes support offensives of US 9th and 1st Armies; about 10,000 tons of bombs are dropped by some 1200 US 8th Air Force planes and 1100 RAF bombers with the goal of obliterating the fortified towns of Duren, Julich and Heinsberg as well as the German defensive position west of Duren.. The US 9th Army advances toward Geilenkirchen and Eschweiler with the objective of reaching the Roer River. To the right, the US 1st Army attacks toward Duren, east of Aachen.[119]

Friday, November 17, 1944

Dear Maryanne,

Well honey, after ten days at sea I feel I can write as up to now I have been helping in the feeding of the fish. I am afraid that at this time there isn't much to write about. We have managed to see a few movies. The usual thing happening from day to day on card games, and they really have some good ones.

Tonight had a few fellows box. At present, finding most in bed, where I'll be in no time.

I hope this letter will be able to be read as it will be one of the first of this type. Let me know if you can read it. I hope that the letters in near future will be longer and more interesting. As it has been some time since I have been writing.

Love,

Ed

Disembarking at Plymouth and Southampton on 19 November the Herders were welcomed by the Red Cross, again on hand with hot coffee and doughnuts. The British troop trains which would carry the Division to Tidworth Barracks near Salisbury were standing ready in the train shed on the pier as the men disembarked. Arriving at Tidworth, England, after a two-hour train ride, the Divisional units which were to remain in the town marched through a torrential downpour to Tidworth Barracks, which had been designed by Kaiser Wilhelm of Germany for the purpose of housing Queen Victoria's troops. Upon arrival most of the Division units received a hot meal which had been prepared by elements of the 11th Armored Division.

During the stay of the 8th in the Tidsworth mud, preparations for a cross-Channel move went forward with heretofore unknown urgency."[120]

Sunday 19 Nov. 44: Ed Brodowski arrived at Newport, England 0030. (Ship named USS Ocean Mail – Shipment No. was 2881 – K) Disembarked 1250. Boarded train for Tidworth England. Arrived 1920

Conrad writes, "We arrived at Southampton, England and disembarked on the 19th. Again the Red Cross was there with coffee and doughnuts. We boarded an English train waiting at the dock with the smaller English style coaches, holding about eight men. We traveled through the English countryside, through many small and to us quant English Villages on the Salisbury Plain, finally arriving at Tidsworth. Tidsworth, was and is, a permanent English Army Base, with brick barracks in the village. Arriving again at 7 o'clock in cold and rain, we found a hot turkey dinner awaiting us, courtesy of some members of the 11th Armored division.Monday, November 20, 1944

Dear Maryanne,

Have finally reached land safe and sound. Now that I have been able to get my feet on solid ground, I feel like a million. At this present moment, am sitting near a fire and wondering just how Leo's wedding came off. I suppose every one really enjoyed themselves.

Have seen a little of the country side and have come to the conclusion that no matter where you go, you find the country looks alike. At present, can't say much as haven't seen anything of the place I am in. One thing, I am sleeping in a bunk and have a roof over my head.

Hon, I am waiting for mail from you as to what has taken place from the time we last seen each other. Will close for present with love.

Thursday, November 23, 1944

My Dear,

I hope that this letter finds you in the best of health. As for myself, am feeling fine. Today being Thanksgiving Day, we had turkey with all the trimmings and for me, I got my fill. Also, to our surprise, we got the afternoon off, in which I spent most walking around and seeing the sights. Found the large Red Cross building in an old time castle. I guess, anyway, it really is something to see. It has a number of rooms. You can almost get lost in it. Spent a short time watching a foot ball game, a show later, and now am in the barracks waiting for some water to get hot so I can shave.

Now Sgt. Keaton has been given another job in the Co. He now is our mess Sgt. I have been promoted to Staff Sgt. and now have taken Sgt. Keatons place. I hope that I can do as good a job as he has done in the past.

Well honey, it seems there isn't much room left so until tomorrow.

Love

Ed

Saturday, November 25, 1944

My Dearest,

Have received only one letter from you since I have been here. It seems that it takes some time for regular mail as believe that V. mail will be much faster. I hope my letters reach you in short time. But don't worry if the mail takes some time to reach you. I hope you are feeling well. Also, let me know how you make out in your hunt for a flat

As for myself, am feeling as good as can be expected. At present, we aren't doing much, just taking life easy. Expect to get a pass to London in the near future. Will write you about it when I do. Trying to get use to this weather but am afraid it will be some time. Seen a movie last night but didn't look to see what was on and when I got in, I realized I had seen it before. I believe we seen it together. (The girl I left behind)

Johnny says hello. He kids me once in a while about the things we spoke about the time he went out with us. If you should ever want to send a cable, the address is

AMOTOW. The cable office can get full details. You know, could use a box of Fanny Farmers Candy, as they ration it.

Love,

Ed.

"26 November, 1944 T/SGT Johnnie H. Martin, Jr. of the 8th Air Force, 491st BG(H), 854th BS was on his fifteenth mission to the target that day of the Misburg Oil Refinery Minden, Germany when the 491st, Squadrons 853rd, 854th, and 855th, were attacked by German fighters. He could have stayed at Blackland Army Air Field in Waco, Texas, as an airplane mechanic for the duration of the war, but he volunteered to go overseas, because, in his own words, "I don't want someone else doing my fighting for me."" [121]

"Located some 16 miles east and north of the target was the town of Wittingen. A large number of enemy fighters appeared in the distance, southeast of the bombers. They made no move toward the Liberators but were "just playing around in the clouds" as if daring the Mustangs and Thunderbolts to come over and mix it up. The chance seemed too good to miss and the entire close fighter escort, consisting of 197 P-51s and 48 P-47s, went storming after the Germans, estimated at from 150 to 200 strong. In a matter of minutes they were fully engaged, leaving the B-24s on their own.

The 491st wheeled into the Big Turn and came out on the bomb run. Almost immediately a chance mishap occurred in the lead aircraft of the low squadron -- the nose gunner brushed against the bomb toggle switch with his shoulder. The entire squadron, as briefed, dropped on their leader and 30 tons went down into open fields 15 miles short of the target. In order to avoid further exposure to flak the low squadron veered away from the formation and angled for the rally point south of Hanover, bypassing the target.

With all fighter escort lured away, the stage was set for disaster. It came swiftly. Flak suddenly ceased and another, previously unseen hoard of 100 plus German fighters (nearly all FW 190s) struck the high squadron like a scythe. The second pass took out the two B-24s of the high right element. The fighters now swung southwest and turned their attention to the separated low squadron, pressing their attacks home with almost reckless determination. Meanwhile the lead squadron, having reached the target unmolested, bombed with good results. With at least some warning as to what was coming, they had tucked it in as tight as possible and the gunners were ready when the first wave of fighters hit."'[122]

"The Misburg Oil Refinery Mission became known as "Black Sunday" to the 491st Bomb Group, 8th Air Force. The 491st was flying "tail end Charlie". Johnnie Martin was the Engineer and Top Turret Gunner with First Lt. Robert W. Simons' crew on Grease Ball. 'Grease Ball caught a fusillade of 20 mm explosive shells that killed two gunners, knocked out all communications and most of the controls, and set fire to the bomb bay. The plane dropped like a rock with only three of the crew able to get out.'[123] Johnnie Martin was killed in action. Of the 28 B-24s on that mission, 16 did not return to North Pickenham base in England.[124]

Monday, November 27, 1944

My Dearest,

Was rereading your letter for as yet it is the only one I have received. Our days now are just a routine of chores.

Nothing new happens from day to day. I do manage to take in a few shows. Most of these are full. Of course church on Sunday. Johnny and I intend to go to confession this coming Sunday. I hope you wrote with out waiting for letters from me first as my letters may not get there regular. So keep them coming.

Love

Ed

Tuesday, November 28, 1944

My Dearest,

Just came in from seeing a movie "Lifeboat". Wasn't to bad. Some thing to do in the spare time. It really is a lovely night out. Clear with a large bright moon. But here it don't mean a thing, just another night.

Tried some of the English soft drink. There is something about it which doesn't taste like ours. Also went into the Y.M.C.A. Saw nut bread on the shelf so asked for some but it isn't called bread here, instead it is called Cake. Their pies have more crust than filling but still pie. The sandwiches are mostly SPAM, cheese & sardines. The best part of them is the bread. I really enjoy eating the bread.

Went to the P.X. with my ration card. Can get only a few bars of candy and one pack of gum a week. Soap is limited to one bar and so on. But manage to get along on what I get. Seems the space is taken up, so will close for now. Hope your letters will be many.

Love always,

Ed.

DECEMBER

Saturday, December 2, 1944

On the Western Front... Elements of the US 3rd Army reach Saarlautern. To the south, the US 7th Army advances to the Rhine river after the Germans have withdrawn across it at Kehl. The three available bridges are all demolished in the retreat.[125]

My Dearest,

Here it is Saturday night and nothing to do. For a moment I was thinking of how we use to spend our Saturday nights. Oh well, before you know it we will be doing it again. In last nights letter I mentioned going to a dance. Well it was just one of all dances at Army Corps. The girls were all English, most of them seem friendly. The girls aren't any different here than at home. Perhaps talk a little different but that is about all.

Johnny & I are going to confession tomorrow. So you can see there is a slight change in me. It looks like it is for the better and not worst. Dropping a little hint but a couple of fellows got Christmas packages. Well honey will stop for now.

Loving you always

Ed

Sunday December 3, 1944

My Dearest Maryanne,

I don't know just what to write tonight. I'm in one of those rotten moods. You know how I am when that way. Don't know what to do. Just moving around all day. Johnny and I went to church this morning, also went to confession.

You know I have been thinking that the last seven months were our happiest ones yet. Perhaps not the way we wanted to spend them but at least we were together. I hope we haven't waited too long to do the things we always hoped to do. Honey, I guess I better quit writing for tonight. Will write again tomorrow.

Always yours,

Ed

4 December, 1944

"1st Bn, of the 318th, with B Co. 702nd Tank Battalion in support, jumped off on schedule at 0730, preceded by a heavy artillery preparation lasting more than an hour. Continuous fire from the mortars of the 319th reserve company and all three of the 318th heavy weapons companies, direct fire from Co B, 808th TD Bn, and 15 .50 caliber MG's of the 319th was directed at the objectives until they were taken in order to give maximum protection to the advancing GI's. The high ground northeast of the town was the initial objective. Companies B and C attacked through the town against medium resistance. Their progress was at first impeded by the natural obstacles of muddy ground, the raised railroad bed running along the western side of the town, and flooded creek at its base. Company B of the 305th Engineering Bn quickly constructed a treadway bridge across the creek to permit passage of the motorized elements who were reported across at 1038. By 0900 the two rifle companies had gained the elevation north of the town known as the Schallberg while A Co, as the reserve company, moved along the sheltered western slope of hill 316, the Winterburg, overlooking the road, railroad, and the stream running northward through the valley toward Cocheren. No tanks or assault guns had been used to support the German defense, although artillery concentrations were fired on various locations in the regimental zone from a battery located south of Bousbach, about four miles NE of

Farebersviller, and a battery of three 150 mm howitzers near Diebling, about three miles due east. The 75 mm anti-tank guns of the 3rd and 4th Co.'s of the 17th SS AT Bn were all destroyed near Farebersviller, and two 150 mm howitzers and four AT guns manned by the 13th Co, 38th SS Panzergrenadier Regt. ran out of ammunition and were captured by the 2nd Bn near Theding.

By 1100, B and C Co.'s were crossing the road running from Cocheren to Theding through the valley SE of Cocheren and about two miles north of Farebersviller. By 1325 they had occupied their final objective, hill 342, a steep bluff northeast of Cocheren known locally as the "Herapel," overlooking the village below, and were digging in. A Co., advanced along the hillside parallel to the Farebersviller-Cocheren road to cover the road on their left and provide support to the advance of B and C Co.'s if called upon. The weapons platoon was deployed behind the rifle platoons in the usual manner. Russ Mitchell recalls setting up the gun on the slope to fire on a building at the base of the hill to clear it of German troops retreating from Farebersviller who had taken refuge inside. The company CP was then set up in the building, presumed to be le Moulin Bas, or, the Lower Mill. The rifle platoons moved up to the village and, meeting no organized resistance, cleared it of the scattered enemy troops that remained, taking 34 POW's, and established defensive positions there. The weapons platoon remained a short distance south of Cocheren where they set up an outpost in the vicinity of a cave-like opening - possibly a mine entrance - at the base of the bluff east of the road. Russ remembered returning to the CP for the night when the outpost was withdrawn after dark, and felt certain they passed no other buildings which seems to confirm le Moulin Bas as the location of the CP as it was the last building along the road south of the village of Cocheren. The "cave" opening he remembered as being a natural opening - "definitely not anything constructed" - that could be entered by stooping a little. The battery of four 88's north of the town, manned by the 2nd Battery, 17th SS AA Bn, and with only AA ammunition at their disposal, was overrun, with only one POW taken. Company commander, Capt. Otto Schultz was awarded the BSM for meritorious service at Cocheren."[126]

Tuesday, December 5, 1944

My Dearest,

Am on the rocks today. My cold doesn't seem to want to leave me. Have been using all kinds of pills but to no success. I am wondering how you are coming along. I hope that you are feeling well. Also, if things are the way we want them to be as to a baby, then there should be signs shouldn't there?

The last few days seem to drag along although the days themselves were nice. Tonight a couple of fellows are selling odds and ends. You'll probably get a box in a couple or three weeks. Also I got a pair of ear rings for mother. Knowing how she likes those odd ones. I hope that these are odd enough.

Honey will stop writing for tonight as not feeling up to par. Love and kisses.

Ed

My Dearest,

We had a fairly nice day today – the usual hike to make the day start off right. Still have that damn cold but it will go away before too long. How is everything at home? Let me know if you went to the doctor's during November, also if you made out any applications in regards to the Army sharing part of the expense. I believe I mentioned it to you on my last pass. If so, was it before the 22nd of November. Otherwise it is too late as the rating promotion cuts that out. As you (know) every little bit helps. Oh yes today I increased the allotment from 40 to 70 dollars. You should get it the first part of next month. As I am having it start this month.

Well, now, we are going to the Red Cross tonight. Will let you know what goes on there tomorrow.

Love,

Ed

Monday, December 11, 1944

My Dearest Darling,

Just came in from the Y.M.C.A. and it really is a swell night. Stars shining just like many nights that we have seen together. Only when I see them you are starting your afternoon. I hope that this letter finds you in the best of health. As for myself, I am finally getting rid of my cold. Am I glad as I could hardly talk and for a platoon Sgt. that is bad.

The boys are playing cards as usual. That seems to be the only thing they can find to do in their spare time. The only thing is that it cost money to play so that leaves me out.

Oh yes, I was reading in one of the Army papers that you had about seven inches of snow at home. How has the winter been so far?

Have been working the last few days and feel much better than loafing around. Who gets my car now, I suppose there was a slight misunderstanding over it or was there?

During my visit to London I was looking for some sort of gift to send to you but it was almost impossible to get anything worth while and the prices were way high. So I am sending the money instead. This letter should reach you just about Christmas so let's call it the gift. You can get something which you can use and I'll know it will be spent for something worth while.

Will shave, clean up and then off to bed. As I feel I can use some sleep so I'll say again "until tomorrows letters."

Loving you always,

Ed.

> " 11 December 1944, the 780th Bomb Squadron/465th Bomber Group, 15th Air Force, attacked one of the most dreaded targets of the war: the south ordnance depot at Vienna, Austria. At this point in the war Vienna was the second-most heavily fortified target, next to Berlin itself. At the mission briefing crews were told flak would be HIA, "heavy, intense and accurate." S/SGT George J. Le Comte was a replacement tail gunner on the Larson Crew, and for this mission they flew "Yellow O" or the "Mission Belle". It was his first mission with them, and his last. The flak was HIA, as predicted. Over the target and five minutes before bomb's away, Yellow O took a direct hit by a shell in the midsection and flight deck. The plane nosed up and to the left and then went into a complete roll. It then went into a flat spin. Six crew bailed out and were taken prisoner. Five crew were KIA. S/SGT Le Comte was seen slumped over in his turret. One crewmember stated, "I believe Le Comte was killed outright by flak, otherwise he would have made some attempt to leave his crew position as the plane began its dive."[127]

Tuesday, December 12, 1944

My Dearest Darling,

Well honey I finally received a V. Mail from you although I can't say it made me very happy. You seem to think that I haven't been writing but up to date I have wrote every day so you can see there must be a delay in the mail somewhere. If you wait and write only when you get a letter from me, I am afraid that I am in for very little mail. Also, I hope you change your attitude or we'll have the same thing happen which did happen about a year ago. Remember?

You also made a remark about the type of letters I have been writing. All I can say is you haven't started to get any so how can you judge from day one or day two? It's so darn hard to write as I have answered most of the questions in my previous letters. I hope that by the time this letter gets to you at home that you'll have changed your mind and realized that I have been doing my best trying to keep letters going all the time.

Have been thinking of you all the time. Also, I keep wishing I could be home with you more now than before now that you are pregnant. As I think that it is my place to be there but then who are we to do as we wish. I know that everything will be O.K. Are you going to have your sister stay with you? I wish you would then I'll know that you are not alone. As I always keep worrying as to what you are doing and also how you are making out.

Remember one time or should I say many times you have said, "that I can take care of myself?" I always have my doubts about that. Now don't get me wrong. Let me know as soon as anything happens. As it wouldn't be worth living if something should happen to you. Here we are going on our fourth year of married life. The old saying of that the longer you are married the more you care for one another is true. **Only it seems there is a war keeping us apart**. All I can say is keep praying and the day will come when we will be together again.

I guess that article I read about snow at home is true. Only I didn't realize you had that much at the present time. As for our weather, it is mostly damp and cold. I still have the cold. I can't seem to get rid of it.

Well honey, I would like to wait before mailing this letter as I believe that in my next letter from you it will be much different, but that may be days from now. Suppose you check dates on my mail and let me know if I am not right. So until tomorrow's letter, I'll close with all my love.

Your husband
Ed

" On 16 December 1944, General von Rundstedt started his last ditch offensive. Moving rapidly through the American lines, the Germans drove into Belgium. Bastogne was surrounded and cut off from all support except by air. General George S. Patton, Jr. Commander General of the Third Army, was ordered to move north to erase the "Bulge" created in the American lines. With this new development at the frontline, men of the 8th knew they would soon move to the Continent.

However, there was ample opportunity to visit the surrounding countryside. Most of the Division had the opportunity to spend 48 hours in London. Billeted at the Red Cross facilities in Albert Gate Mansions, the Herders visited Rainbow Corner, Trafalgar Square, Picadilly Circus, and many other historic spots in the British capitol."[128]

On the Western Front... The Battle of the Bulge begins. German forces of Army Group B (Model), under the overall command of Field Marshal Rundstedt, launch an offensive in the Ardennes Forest, between Monschau and Trier, aimed at recapturing Antwerp and splitting the British and American armies. The attacking force consists of the 6th SS Panzer Army (Dietrich) on the right and 5th Panzer Army (Manteuffel) on the left. On the right and left flanks are the German 15th and 7th Armies. Allied forces are taken by surprise. The initial assault targets the line held by US 5th and 7th Corps, parts of US 1st Army (Hodges), in the US 21st Army Group (Bradley) as part of the Allied Expeditionary Force (Eisenhower). A brief artillery barrage precedes that attack. On the first day, German forces successfully breach the American lines. English speaking German troops, wearing captured uniforms and using Allied equipment, infiltrate behind the American lines causing some confusion and uncertainty in the rear areas. Poor weather prevents Allied ground attack aircraft from operating against the German armored columns. Meanwhile, US 3rd Army continues operations along the Saar River until news of the German offensive is received.[129]

Sunday, December 17, 1944

On the Western Front... Eisenhower releases the US 82nd and 101st Airborne Divisions from AEF reserve to reinforce American troops in the Ardennes. Other infantry and armored forces from US 12th Army Group are also being redeployed to meet the German offensive. Meanwhile, German forces capture 9000 Americans at Echternach, on the extreme right flank of the attack. Soldiers of the 2nd SS Panzer Division *Das Reich* kill some 71 American POWs near Malmedy.[130]

Due to the new regulations as to the size of the mail to be sent home, letters have now become very short.

My Dearest Darling,

Here it is Sunday evening and no place to go. I have nothing to do. Johnny and I went to the movie and seen a couple of old pictures. So here we are tonight sitting around and wondering what to do. Johnny has written a letter to you tonight. You'll probably get it the same time you get this one.

Hate to think of next week and not having you here to enjoy Christmas Eve. Johnny and I intend to go to confession Saturday. Also, go to church Christmas Eve. You know Johnny is making me into a church going member.

The boys are trying to help me write but I guess I better not listen to them. It may get me in wrong. Well honey, I suppose you'll think this is a short letter but that's better than none. I want you to keep this in mind. I always am thinking of you.

Loving you always,

Ed

Tuesday, December 19, 1944

My Dearest Darling,

Have just finished rereading your letter and I believe I have answered all questions in last nights letter. Now that you have found a place I feel at ease as have been wondering if you would be able to get a place. I expect to hear all about it in the next letter. How is every one at home? I hope that this letter finds you in the best of health. What have you been doing lately as by now you are probably settling in your new place. I suppose sewing takes up most of your time or does it? Have you seen any good movies lately. Here we have seen most of them at one time or another.

Honey, haven't much to say on this end. Nothing of interest has happened as of yet. Some of the boys are lucky enough to see London again. Didn't even try to go. Probably wouldn't have been one of the lucky ones if I did. Well until next letter.

Your loving husband,
Ed

Wednesday, December 20, 1944

On the Western Front... Forces of 6th SS Panzer Army strike northward from around Stavelot but encounter heavy resistance from Allied defenders of British 21st Army Group. The 5th Panzer Army continues to advance to the south against forces of US 12th Army Group, but American defenders of the road junctions of St. Vith and Bastogne continue to hold their positions. Allied sources allege that in the area of Monschau the Germans have been shooting American prisoners with machineguns. Meanwhile, the US 3rd Army reports attacking from the Saarlautern bridgehead and having cleared 40 pillboxes and fortified houses.[131]

My Dearest Darling,

Today we got our Christmas tree as tonight the boys got together and made a few things to put on the tree. It reminded me of school days in drawing classes. We intend to put up the tree in the next few days. It will make it look like Christmas anyway. Are you having a time at home now?

Have you heard from your brothers Stan or Pete of late? If so, let me know where they are at. I am still trying to get rid of my cold. Any suggestions? As our medic tells us to drink plenty of water and keep our shoes greased. Well honey, I hope that I get a letter from you tomorrow.

Your loving husband

Ed.

Friday, December 22, 1944

On the Western Front... In the advance of German 5th Panzer Army, Bastogne is surrounded. An German demand to surrender, issued to the American defenders, is rejected by American General McAuliffe -- commanding the encircled troops. St. Vith is captured late in the day. However, the lack of substantial progress leads Model, commanding Army Group B, and Rundstedt, Commander in Chief West, to recommend an end to the offensive.[132]

My Dearest Darling,

Just a few more days and Christmas. Have been wondering just what and where you'll be. Here it will be just another day although we'll have church services and perhaps a big meal but still it won't be just the thing. The boys have been putting every spare minute making things for the tree. And I must say it really looks good. I wish there was some way I could get a picture of it but I guess that's impossible.

These evenings are really long and I don't know just what to do with myself. It usually ends up with a paper, a short letter or two, and then to bed. The shows are usually ones I had seen. Then again there is the old Army line. It seems that every time you decide to go to the movies, all the rest of the soldiers go. Honey, let me know what you do over the holidays. I know that this letter won't reach you until all the holidays are over. But will close thinking of you.

Your loving husband

Ed

Sunday, December 24, 1944

On the Western Front... The German Ardennes offensive is exhausted by the end of the day. The furthest advance has been achieved by elements of the German 5th Panzer Army. The 2nd Panzer Division has reached the outskirts of Dinant with the 116th Panzer Division on the right flank near Hotten and the Panzer *Lehr* Division on the left flank to the west of St. Hubert. American forces in Bastogne continue to resist; some 260 Allied transports drop supplies to the defenders. Allied fighter-bombers fly over 600 sorties in the Ardennes[133]

My Dearest Darling,

This morning I received two of your letters of the 14th and 15th and they were better than any gift I could get. As I have been hoping to hear from you. I have a few questions which I wish you would answer. First, you have a job in a store, what store is it? Also, let me know as soon as you are sure about when the baby will be born, as I want to know. As for the part about notifying me, that is a matter of routine. Also, don't let the expense worry you as things aren't that bad. Remember we planned ahead and we know just about what it would take. So I don't believe you need worry about that part.

Honey, don't put off going to the doctor's to long as you know what happened to with your sister Gene. Am thinking of you tonight wondering what you are doing. Will write a long letter tomorrow letting you know what I am doing. So for tonight. Love and Kisses, Your loving husband,

Ed

Sunday, December 24, 1944

Dear Mom and Dad,

I received your most welcomed letter this morning. I am in the best of health at the present time. It is impossible to find a place to go tonight as it seems that all the places are closed tonight for Christmas Eve. Not like at home where you'd find all places open doing a smashing business. So ended up in the barracks with the rest of the fellows feeling low and blue.

It makes me happy to know that Maryanne has been able to find a place to live. Also, it seems she has a job which I as of yet haven't been told the full details but am sure in the next letter she'll tell me all.

It would really be nice if Stan could get home for the holidays. I guess there is to be very few boys who'll be able to make it home this year. Tonight my thoughts go back just a few Christmas's ago when we all were having a swell time. I hope you are having a nice time tonight. I am thinking of all at home and hope that I can be one of the gang soon.

Your loving son-in law

Ed

"24 December, 1944 SGT Elmer A. Baker of Co. K., 262nd Infantry Regiment, 66th "Panther" Division shipped out for Southampton, England just days from his twenty-second birthday. On Christmas Eve morning, the 262nd & the 264th Regiments were ordered to leave Southampton on the converted Belgian liner, S.S. Leopoldville, even as they could smell the turkeys roasting for what would have been their traditional holiday meal. The orders came to ship out sooner than anyone had expected and the confusion that ensued was unbelievable - more than the ordinary SNAFU. Men were put on one ship, then taken off and put on the other. Regiments and companies were split up and there was no accurate listing of who was on which ship. Some were saved because of this, but others were doomed.

The S. S. Leopoldville was carrying more than 2,200 American soldiers from the 66th "Panther" Division, across the English channel as reinforcements to fight in the Battle of the Bulge. At about six o'clock in the evening, when they were only a little more than 5 miles from their destination, Cherbourg, France, a torpedo from a German U-486 submarine tore into the ship. Elmer was not seen again."[134]

Monday, December 25, 1944

On the Western Front... Allied forces surrounding the German-held bulge begin counterattacking. The US 4th Armored Division, an element of US 3rd Army, aims at relieving the Americans surrounded in Bastogne. Meanwhile, German attacks are halted by American armor at Celles, about 6 km east of the Meuse River, after having advanced about 80 km since the beginning of the offensive in mid-December.[135]

> On Christmas Day the 8th played host to a large number of British orphans. Opening his heart to these children, many a soldier found himself minus PX rations, but plus a warm glow in his heart at the close of the day."[136]

My Dearest Darling,

Just came back from a movie and it is a swell night with moon and all. Remember our little walk to the road and back after putting the car away. Keep wishing you and I could be together.

Honey, I went to pick up the children today. You should see them. I believe the oldest was about ten years. We had thirty eight in the back of the truck besides five persons who take care of the orphans. Had a little boy on my knee, and also another one. Both the kids just about driving you nut's. Well anyway, they had dinner and boy could they eat. After the meal, they had a movie and at four o'clock I picked them up and took them back. The children really enjoyed themselves. I only hope they don't get sick from eating too much.

Doing this made Christmas a little easier but nothing could make it perfect here. Honey, will close for now. Thinking of you always.

Forever yours,
Ed.

Tuesday, December 26, 1944

The spiritual warfare continues during the celebration of the birth of Christ.

On the Western Front... The US 4th Armored Division (an element of US 3rd Army) relieves the American forces in Bastogne. Meanwhile, British Bomber Command makes a daylight raid on the German held transportation hub of St. Vith. The Allies claim to have captured 13,273 German prisoners while the Germans claim over 30,000 Allied POWs and the destruction of 700 American tanks.[137]

My Dearest Darling,

No ill effects after the holidays. I guess the turkey agreed with me. I wonder how the children feel today. I'll bet some are sick. What about yourself. Did you have much for the holidays? How is everything at home? What is Leo doing or is he still hanging around.

Everything here is about the same. Managed to keep busy from day to day. Always can find something to do on the tank. Oh yes, we are calling it "Abner" again. It really was cold this morning and the grass was frozen hard. It is better that way then walking in a lot of mud.

I hope that packages come before long as I can use the things now. Also, your letters. I know there must be many on the way.

Honey, I hope you don't mind V-Mail. I know you can't write much in one but straight mail takes so darn long. So will write more often which will make that up. So honey, until tomorrow's letter.

Your lonesome husband

Ed

Wednesday, December 28, 1944

My Dearest Darling,

Well here it is almost the first of the year. Seems that I have been gone an awful long time. I hope that the time from now on goes by faster than what we have been through here. Remember our last New Years Eve. I guess I'll have a quiet eve. Probably stay in with the fellows. Took a shower today, the first one in a few days. I hope that my cold doesn't get worse because of it. We also were given our overshoes. I hope that now I can keep my feet dry and warm. As I really had a hard time keeping them warm.

Honey, let me know as soon as you get the bracelet as I want to know if it did get through the mail. Honey, had an opportunity to see a few cases of a so called (French foot) which is common when staying in wet & cold to long. They were awful looking. Toes and the bottom part of his foot were black and these parts were rotten away. The reason for us to see them is so that we could recognize it when we come in contact with it. I am wondering what you are doing. What ever it is, I wish I was there to help.

Loving you always

Ed

Friday, December 29, 1944

My Dearest,

Well at last I hit the jack pot. Three letters from you, one from my brother Leo, two cards and a box of hankies from your sister Gene. Remember the clipping of Leo's wedding, which you put in the V-Mail. Well it came as straight mail as they don't photo any enclosures in V-Mail. But the last letter from you was on the 20th so you see that it only takes nine days for it to come which isn't too bad.

I am glad to hear that you are finally caught up and able to find time to enjoy a few moments of rest. You asked me to return the boxes after I received them. Will do my best but you want to realize mail service isn't always available. Will do my best though.

Honey, you can send the rest of those gloves and a few hankies as will be able to use them. The weather at present is pretty cold and still have the three coldest months to come.

I showed Johnny that part of the letter which you asked what I wanted as far as a boy or girl. He says to tell you both. It would be funny wouldn't it?

Don't worry about me. I will take good care of myself. It wouldn't be too long and you'll have to put up with me. Have lost most of my cold. I guess I am getting use to the weather. It really has been cold in the last week. Also, a big moon every night. A heck of a place to be with a moon as big and bright as we have been having.

Oh yes, remember the fellow who was waiting to hear from his wife as to what the baby would be. Finally the news got here. He is the proud father of a baby girl.

Well honey, will stop for tonight. Thinking of you always.

Your loving husband,

Ed

Saturday, December 30, 1944

My Dearest Darling,

Am sitting here watching the others trying to write, so I am trying my hand at it. Some one said, that a lot of mail came in. I hope so. I also hope that I have some. Spent the afternoon washing clothes. Will have to work tomorrow as have a number of things which have to be done. One thing, I will get time off to go to church. That is something they'll let you do if possible.

Johnnie and I are going to the Y.M.C.A. for a cup of coffee and cake. Nothing else to do around here. Don't feel like going to the show. So will come back early.

A year ago tomorrow I was on my way home for a fifteen day furlough, remember? I guess this year will spend it in the barracks. Wish it was with you instead. Well honey, good night for now.

Always loving you,

Ed

Sunday, December 31, 1944

My Dearest Darling,

They say it is New Years Eve but it doesn't seem so. We worked most of the day and now at nine o'clock, I am ready to go to bed. We have been given little stoves so tonight made coffee in our barracks and it wasn't bad.

Was telling the boys about the flower I got for you the night we went to church for the New Years Eve party and how we had to search the city to find a place to buy something to drink. What are you doing tonight? I'll bet your sister is over and you two are staying in listening to the radio. Remember the night you and I listened to the radio. You with your knitting and of course me with my books. If only we could be doing that now.

Honey, Johnnie is playing some Polish tunes and it sound goods. You ought to hear him. The songs bring back memories. Oh well, will close for now. Until tomorrow.

Always loving you,
Ed

Chapter Five

JANUARY-MARCH 1945

January 1, 1945 On the Western Front... The German *Luftwaffe* makes a series of heavy attacks on Allied airfields in Belgium, Holland and northern France. They have assembled around 800 planes of all types for this effort by deploying every available machine and pilot. Many of the pilots have had so little training that they must fly special formations with an experienced pilot in the lead providing the navigation for the whole force. The Allies are surprised and lose many aircraft on the ground. Among the German aircraft losses for the day are a considerable number of planes shot down by German anti-aircraft fire. Allied losses amount to 300 planes opposed to about 200 German aircraft shot down. Meanwhile, the land battle in the Ardennes continues with the Allied counterattacks gathering force. The most notable gains are by the US 8th Corps. Farther south in Alsace the forces of German Army Group G begins an offensive in the Sarreguemines area (Operation *Nordwind*) towards Strasbourg. The US 7th Army retires before this attack on orders from Eisenhower.[138]

"Just before midnight Hitler began Operation Nordwind when eight German divisions attacked the US Seventh Army in northern Alsace. It was supposed to ease the pressure in the Ardennes, but had little effect. In addition Hitler's 'Greet Blow' was struck on 1 January 1945 when the Luftwaffe attacked Allied air bases, destroying 200 Allied aircraft and a cost of 300 Luftwaffe planes.

The full scale Allied counter offensive in the Ardennes was launch 3 January 1945 by two American armies and a British corps. The Germans, exhausted and short of fuel, were pushed back, suffering heavy loses in the process because Hitler wouldn't sanction a withdrawal. But by 8 January 1945, he was left with no choice and reluctantly ordered troops to be withdrawn from the rapidly shrinking Bulge. On 16 January, the Allies had won back all the territory lost in the offensive.

The Germans had inflicted 81,000 casualties and tank losses of 800 on the Americans, but in return suffered 100,000 casualties themselves. As well as large quantities of half tracks and artillery, 500 irreplaceable panzers had been lost in Hitler's last great gamble. In a futile battle he had senselessly thrown away the armored reserves."[139]

The expected order finally came to the 8th Armored Division on New Year's Day. The urgency of the current situation on the Continent demanded rapid movement. Between 2 and 4 January the advance units with the Divisional equipment cleared the Tidworth area, bound for Le Havre and Rouen. Disembarking at the ruined cities of Le Havre and Rouen, the 8th Armored Division got its first idea of the destruction on the Continent. The division was grouped into units and moved to the vicinity of Bacqueville, located north of Rouen, France.[140]

January 2, 1945 *On Western Front...* Battle of the Bulge-In the Ardennes, US 3rd Army troops take Bonnerue, Hubertmont and Remagne. In Alsace, the German pressure and the US 7th Army withdrawals continue. [141]

January 3, 1945 *On the Western Front...* In the Ardennes there are German attacks on the narrow corridor leading to Bastogne which succeed in disrupting the timetable of the planned American attacks but fail to achieve any advance. Forces of the US 3rd Army and US 1st Army are attacking toward Houffalize from the south and the north, respectively. In Alsace, the German attacks and the American retreat continue. The US 6th Corps (part of US 7th Army) is being pressed particularly hard in the area around Bitche. Farther south, there is also fighting near Strasbourg.[142]

January 4,1945 *On the Western Front...* The fighting in the Ardennes continues; a German counterattack near Bastogne is repulsed by troops of US 3rd Army. There are attacks by US 8th and 3rd Corps and by the British 30th Corps. Some of the units of the 6th SS Panzer Army (Dietrich) are withdrawn and sent to the Eastern Front. In Alsace, the German attacks in the Bitche area continue. [143]

05 Jan. 45: 80th Tank Battalion left Chickerell, England 0900 arrived Port of Embarkation Pottland, England 1015 departed 1530 destination Unknown

On the Western Front... In the Ardennes, the US 3rd Army reports reduced activity on its line while US 1st Army continues its attacks. There are German attacks just north of Strasbourg. Eisenhower's decision to divide command responsibility for the Allied defenses around the bulge between Montgomery in the north and Bradley in the south is made public. [144]

07 Jan. 45: 80th Tank Battalion arrived Rouen, France 1200. Disembarked 130 Convoyed to Cressy, France arrived 1500

Some time in January 1945

Dear Mom and Dad,

Haven't heard from you in some time so thought I would drop a line. I hope that this letter finds everyone at home in the best of health. I understand that you are having plenty of winter at home. I guess you haven't anything on me as I have been fighting the cold weather ever since I hit France. Doesn't seem to be anything I can do which will make me comfortable. I suppose the cold weather at home really hits the coal. As it must be a problem keeping the house warm.

I haven't seen anything worth while since I have been here. They can have France and England. Just give me good old Utica NY and I'll be satisfied.

Your son-in law

Ed

09 Jan. 45: 80th Tank Battalion left Cressy, France by convoy 2300

10 Jan. 45: 80th Tank Battalion arrived Sept. Saulx, France 2230.

"The Division was first assigned to the newly formed, then still secret, 15th Army and placed in Supreme Headquarters Allied Expeditionary Force(SHAEF) reserve. The 8th was ordered to move to the vicinity of the cathedral city of Rheims, with Division Headquarters to be located at Sept Saulx. After a 174.7 mile trip from Bacqueville to Rheims in a blinding snow storm, and near zero weather the Division closed at Rheims on 10 January 1945."[145]

On the Western Front... In the Ardennes, American forces are engaged near Laroche. The British 30th Corps is advancing on the town from the west, capturing Bure and Samree. German forces are withdrawing, in good order, from the western tip of the salient.

St. Hubert, 15 miles west of Bastogne, has been evacuated by the Germans under pressure from Allied forces.[146]

Thursday, January 11, 1945

My Dearest Darling,

It has been some time since I have had a chance to write. As we had left England and are now in France. There isn't much I can say about the trip only that I nearly froze as it has snowed here. I didn't think it could get that cold. So far we have been able to stay in a barn which isn't so bad but the ground gets pretty cold especially in the morning when you have to get out of your blankets.

So far the French people seem to be pretty nice, only so few of us can speak French that we have quite a time making civilians understand. We have been buying their bread which is very good when still warm but after a day or two the crust really gets hard. They would rather take cigarettes and candy for their goods than money.

Well honey I shall stop for now, will write more tomorrow. This letter is more or less letting you know that I am still well, from now on you may get few letters, so don't worry will write every possible chance.

Loving you always,

Ed

Ed's tank driver said that he heard Ed stomping his feet up in the turret to try to keep his feet warm.

"A movement order from Lieutenant General Leonard T. Gerow, Command General, 15th Army, dated 11 January 1945. relieved the 8th Armored Division from attachment to the 15th Army and attached it for administration and supply to the 3rd Army under General

George A. Patton. Still in SHAEF Reserve, the Division was directed to move on 12 January 1945 to the vicinity of Pont-a Mousson, France, in anticipation of a large-scale German counterattack aimed at the Metz seemingly brewing in the Saareguemines.

The German drive for the city of Strasbourg brought a hurried call for armor. The 8th, designated to answer the call, moved across France to Pont-a-Mousson in the midst of a blinding snowstorm. However the enemy had been halted before the 8th could be committed to action.

The 105 mile move from Rheims to Pont-a-Mouson was a nightmare for Division drivers. Fresh roads, poor even when in good repair in the summer, had become rutted and covered with ice and snow. Tanks and half-tracks kept sliding from the icy roads into ditches. The entire trip was a strenuous one, and it was only with the greatest determination and skill that the drivers were able to bring their vehicles safely to the new assembly area. It was said that you could trace the march of the tanks of the 8th across France by checking the skinned trees along the roadside, which in many cases kept the vehicles from falling off the road."[147]

> "The Germans had murdered the wounded men who cried out in pain and stripped the corpses of their watches and other valuables. Then their tanks rolled over the dying and crushing them to death. When Vaccaro and Shoemaker returned to the site the next morning, the carnage was horrible. Henry's body was straight as though he had died instantly. The others were all twisted from writhing in pain when they finally died. Tony Vaccaro took a photograph of Henry lying in the snow and over 4,000 images of his regiment. Tony was not a combat photographer. He was just a soldier with a camera. He later would become a world renown photo

journalist for LIFE and LOOK magazines. Tony entitled the photograph "White Death: Photo Requiem for a dead soldier, Private Henry I. Tannenbaum." Tony wanted the picture to be remembered as a beautiful death in the same fashion as a classical music requiem is beautiful. The photograph "White Death" has been on traveling exhibits throughout Europe for more than fifty years."[148]

13 Jan. 45 80th Tank Battalion left Les Islettes, France 0310, arrived Morville Sur Seille 0900

Sunday, January 14, 1945

My Dearest,

Again finding time so am writing a few lines. We have been moving around so that it has been impossible to find time for much writing. I think the letter I wrote during the last break is still around. Having finished shaving and washing feel like a new man. At last I am getting a taste of winter plenty of snow and cold. It really is an ordeal trying to get up in the morning. Like last night we have a barn to sleep in. There are times when we just lay on the snow.

Some of these towns are pretty well damaged but you can find people in all of them. Here the house and barn are together, that is they use one side as a house and the wall separating it from the barn. In one town a fellow came over and started talking Polish which got us a drink, and the fellows really enjoyed that. I don't have to tell you that everything is okay as at present time can't write much, perhaps in a few days will be able to say more. I hope you keep writing regardless of how my letters come. In this one place we have found dead Germans who must of laid there for some time. Well honey will close for now.

Loving you always,

Ed

Tuesday, January 15, 1945

My Dearest Darling:

Today I am a happy man as I received fifteen letters all but two from you. You asked me to write Air Mail as you say it gets to you quicker but here V-Mail is the quickest way as some of your letters are from the eighth of December. Oh yes, I also got your xmas card. At present there isn't anything that I need unless it would be candy & cookies, otherwise I have plenty of supplies

I mentioned dead Germans in one of my letters. It seems that these didn't run fast enough. Anyway, they are still on top of the ground.

At present time I am sitting in my tank "Abner", and writing. Johnny & another fellow are also here. Abner really gets cold on trips. I keep wishing I was back in the warm climate. It really is an effort to get up in the morning and then times are bad if nature calls during the night.

Oh yes, you said that if the baby is a boy you wouldn't name it Ed (Jr.). What's wrong with that? Just think he could name his (the third). I hope that every thing is alright with you and you better see the doctor before it may be too late.

Honey, from now on I can't promise as many letters but will write as often as possible and I hope that in due time yours & my prayers will be answered. So honey I close for now until tomorrow (if possible) I write again.

Loving you always,

Ed.

P.S. Honey I hope you don't mind the pencil as the ink is frozen.

My Dearest Darling,

Received five of your letters today and of those the one in which you told of the appointment with the doctor. Feel much better now that I know that you have seen him. As for the name for the baby, that is up to you. The one you mentioned isn't me. The boys got a laugh on the one which is Bruce Edward. They want to know why the Edward. Honey I wouldn't worry about having to save as the way things are now we have no or little money. Still think you should quit the job and take up knitting. It becomes you now. I hope that in the near future I can fill the empty years you mentioned.

Well honey still feel the same no change. Cold all day and slightly warmer at night. Still with "Abner" and on the move, he really gets mighty cold. During our stay in England we managed to get about ten lbs. of salt pork and you would be surprised how good it tastes during the day now.

Well honey it looks like I must close for today as am writing out in the open and the ink blots as only snow flakes on paper. So take good care of yourself and do what the doctor says. So until next letter.

Love and kisses,

Ed

January 16, 1945 *On the Western Front...* There are attacks by the British 13th Corps near Roermond aimed at eliminating the small German salient west of the Maas. In the Ardennes the US 1st and 3rd Armies link up at Houffalize. An Allied offensive aimed at eliminating the German bridgehead across the Rhine River, 8 miles north of Strasbourg, begins about 0200 hrs.[149]

"On 17 January 1945, the Division was assigned to XX Corps, 3rd Army, which was then commanded by Major Walton Walker. The mission of route reconnaissance was to continue, and the Division was to snow camouflage all vehicles and engage in training. In the Division area clearing of mines and removal of dead, both American and German, occupied much time. During January the Division conducted valuable combat training using the abandoned forts of the French Maginot Line and destroyed French villages as training areas.

At this time Supreme Headquarters, Allied Expeditionary Force, (SHAEF) was giving approval to a 3rd Army order which would implement the actual combat training of the Division pending complete committal as a unit. On 18 January 1945, Brigadier General Devine met with Major General Ray E. Porter, Deputy Commanding General of the 15th Army, and Brigadier General William A. Collier, Chief of Staff XX Corps, and plans for battle indoctrination of the 8th were outlined.

Confirmation of these plans followed in a message to General Devine from the Commanding General of the 15th Army:

"SHAEF has approved employment of elements of 8th Armored Division for combat training by Third Army in support of operations of 94th Division subject to the following restrictions.

(a) Not more than 1 normal combat command (CC) to be employed at a time.

(b) Combat employment of each CC to be limited to 2 days at a time.

(c) Subsequent CC's to be employed only after previous CC has closed in 8th Armored Division area. Only one CC may be away from Division area at any time.

'Units of your command subject to restrictions as listed above will be attached to Third U.S. Army for training as indicated above'"[150]

January 21, 1945 *On the Western Front...* Witlz falls to the US 3rd Corps in the Ardennes. German forces are making a general withdrawal to the Siegfried Line. [151]

> "23 January 1945 CPL William Kermit Jones of the 9th Air Force, 409th Bomb Group, 642nd Bomb Sqdn was on his 10th mission. He went as a gunner with a flight of six A-26 Invaders to bomb and strafe a German road convoy, supporting the American infantry as they pushed the Germans back across their own borders. The mission was described as a turkey shoot. A German historian reports that the road convoy was armed with a secret weapon that day...a Foenrockete...a ground to air missile. The experimental mission, meant to prove the versatility of the A-26 at low levels, was flown at less than 1000 feet over a road in Germany, between Dasburg and Arzfeld. It was a disaster. The plane crashed at Stolzembourg, Luxembourg,"[152]

Wednesday, January 24, 1945

My Dearest Darling;

Haven't written for a few days but as I have said, there may be days before I get a chance to write. Reason for not writing in the past few days is that the weather has been rather bad. So usually try to wait for a nice day or when able to keep warm inside in order to write.

Received one of your letters of the 5th of December. It must have gotten lost along the way. I am still waiting and hoping that your package comes thru.

Everything here is the same as in previous letters. Just following a daily routine and nothing else. Still trying to get used to the cold weather but I bet that'll be impossible. As it really gets cold. Have had it as cold as 12 below zero. I suppose the weather at home is much colder about now or is it?

I am trying a new system. Instead of wearing shoes inside of overshoes I am just wearing more socks, a little straw, and overshoes. I believe that my feet are much warmer this way.

Honey when you get this letter, let me know if you can read it or is the writing to small. I forget and keep writing small so let me know just how it comes out. Looks like the end of another day. So until next letter which I hope I can write soon.

Always yours,

Ed.

> "25 January 1945 PFC Rex Merrill Bowers Co. C, 134th Infantry Regiment, 35th Infantry Division was killed in action today at Weiswampach, northern Luxembourg Landing at LeHarve on New Year's Eve of 1944, he was transported by train and truck to the front line, joining General Patton's Third Army during the Battle of the Bulge as a rifleman and a BAR (Browning Automatic Rifle) man. On January 18, 1945, in his last letter home, he wrote, "It is really rough and I don't mean maybe. A lot of the time a guy goes on sheer guts. See you someday." Love Rex"

On January 25, 1945, units of the first battalion, which included Company C, of the 134th Infantry Regiment, of the 35th Division approached Weiswampach in northern Luxembourg at about 3:30

in the afternoon. They had jumped off before daylight that morning and had walked through waist deep snow all day.

The village sits on a high point, overlooking meadows and heavily wooded forests to the west. In 1945, the Germans had an excellent observation point from the steeple of the church at the edge of town. From that steeple and the church yard they could observe the Allied troop movement. In a final desperate move, this village became the perfect place for the Germans to hold up until they could get their men and equipment across the Our River into Germany. As the troops struggled through the deep snow, the fire got heavy and accurate. The battle lasted until 5:30 in the evening. Throughout the night, the people could hear cries from the soldiers in the field. Twelve men from Company C were killed that day, including Rex, PFC Bowers, 1st Lt. Larrieu, S.Sgt. Cooper, S.Sgt. Crider, Tec 5 Show, Tec 5 Stacey, Cpl. Polsen, and PFCs Jones, Kanapka, Palladine, Patrick and Scott. They came from across the United States Ñ from Mississippi to South Carolina, Pennsylvania to Kansas to Idaho."[153]

January 27, 1945 *On the Western Front...* Troops from US 3rd Army cross the Our River and take Oberhausen. The gains made by the German Ardennes offensive are now almost completely eliminated.[154]

Sunday, January 28, 1945

My Dearest Darling,

I believe your mail has finally caught up with me as today I received some way back in December. I hope that from now on our mail comes right thru. Today I am in a house writing as one of the fellows has made friends with a French family so we are able to use their house. Only thing, we can't understand a word they say. Only can nod our head and hope they don't get the wrong meaning. As yet your packages haven't arrived. But am hoping that they will arrive soon.

Oh yes honey, don't send any more gum as we can get plenty of gum. Only shortage is candy, especially for me. As I never can get enough of it.

Boy you should see some of the meals we have been getting lately. Chicken and the works also pie with whip cream. You know the type out of can milk and a little bit of flavoring but it still taste pretty good. Can't pick on the food as under these conditions we have been getting the best of food.

Well honey, I hope that you get this letter in the next few days. As it is pretty hard after getting a letter from a month before. You don't know just how to answer it as you may have answered the questions before.

Loving you always,

Ed.

30 Jan. 45: 80th Tank Battalion left Morville Sur Seille 0900 arrived Vic Sur Seille 1545

FEBRUARY

"Effective on 1 February and pursuant to instructions contained in SHAEF TWX SH GCT 31 2245, dated 1 February 1945, the Division was relieved from attachment to XX Corps, 3rd Army, and reassigned to the 9th Army. On the same date the 8th armored was attached to XVI Corps in accordance with instructions in 9th Army TWX Number 5M44. XVI Corps was at this time located far to the north in Holland."[155]

Thursday, February 1, 1945

My dearest Darling,

Well honey the weather has changed again. Today was a nice warm day. The snow is going away fast. I hope it continues this way as the cold and I don't get along. Oh yes, I believe I told you about raising a mustache. At present, I got it so you can see it. I know that you are going to say no kiss unless you shave it off. But I guess it'll be off before I ever start for home.

The boys are rather lucky tonight as we got five bottles of beer per man and right now they are feeling pretty good. It seems that our outfit, or in fact all outfits here, are trying to get clothes to keep us warm. Now we are going to get boots like the ones I got at home, which I use for hunting. Also, have a suit, which reminds me of a kids snowsuit. Even with all these clothes we get cold. But I guess it won't be long and spring will be around.

They even have trucks to take us for showers and I mean that is the deal. If you are lucky you even get a change of underwear and socks. They take your old ones or should I say dirty ones. Oh yes, another thing, we had a mobile Red Cross unit which served coffee and doughnuts and that was a treat.

Gee honey, it seems I forget asking about you. I hope that everything is well at home. Well honey, it looks like the end of the paper so will close for tonight.

Loving you always,

Lonesome Ed.

"At 0800, 2 February 1945, the 250-mile motor march to Holland began. The trip consumed almost three days, as the last units of the Division did not close in on the new bivouac area until the night of 4 February. The trip was another nightmare for Division drivers; icy roads, seemingly the usual lot of the 8th on long moves, continued until the border of Holland had been crossed."[156]

(i) 03 Feb. 45: 80th Tank Battalion left Vic Sur Seille 0300

Because of snow and ice conditions prevailing on 1 February, it was necessary to provide additional traction for medium tanks, as well as some means for preventing side slip. This was originally accomplished by tank maintenance crews welding small steel blocks on every fifth grauser of the track. This method was satisfactory until hard surfaced roads were encountered. Then the blocks wore out rapidly or broke off. Finally wedges were built up using either the wedge portions of two old wedges or suitable small blocks welded on top of the original wedge. This enabled the drivers of tracked vehicles to move over icy roads without sliding into ditches at every turn.

Halting only to refuel and to eat "C" or "K" rations, the Division moved northward. Ingenious individuals rigged up lights to read mail or play poker during the trip. Belgians greeted us at every stop in the dark with cake and cookies and got cigarettes in return."

Moving by battalion serials, each combat command of the 8th closed in on its respective tactical bivouac areas by the evening of February 4. The Division was located in the general vicinity of Maastrich, Holland.[157]

04 Feb. 45: 80th Tank Battalion arrived Vilt, Holland 1100

"Combat Command R(CCR), under Colonel Robert J. Wallace, had remained in the vicinity of Cadier-en Keer during this period, test firing and maintaining equipment. Enemy activity was restricted to occasional planes reported and V-1's seen or heard. Per instructions contained in TWX No. 1M018, 6 February 1945, 9th U.S. Army, 10th Armored Group, under command of colonel Fay Smith, was attached to Combat Command R. This integration formed three operating combat commands, each with a staff and a headquarters company to house and feed them. General Devine immediately set up three balanced combat commands, each with a permanently assigned infantry and tank battalion. CCR consisted of: Headquarters and Headquarters company, Combat Command Reserve; 58th armored Infantry Battalion; 80th Tank Battalion (authors note: which contained Ed Brodowski); 405th Armored Field Artillery Battalion; Company C, 53rd Armored Engineer Battalion; Troop C, 88th Cavalry Reconnaissance Squadron (Mechanized); Company C, 809th Tank Destroyer Battalion; Company C, 130th Ordnance Maintenance Battalion; Company C, 78th Medical Battalion Armored."[158]

"4 Feb, 1944 S/SGT Leroy Ernest "Babe" Leist of the 418th Squadron, 100th Bomber Group, 8th AF was declared MIA today over Walcheron Island, Holland. Leroy was flying on his 15th mission when his plane was lost to Erich Scheyda of the Luftwaffe JG26 Squadron. Because the aircraft was already weakened from a flak hit, the pilot, 22 year old Lt. William Green tried to dive through the undercast for cover. Unfortunately, Erich followed the crippled plane down through the clouds to issue the final blow and claim his kill."[159]

HOLLAND

Tuesday, February 6, 1945

My Dearest Darling,

It has been a few days since I have written, but you can see the reason. At present I am in Holland. Of course had to go thru Belgium. Looks like I'll see a lot of country before I get back. I will say that Holland is much nicer than either France or England. Luck is still with us, as we are still sleeping in barns.

We can now say where in France we were, so will tell you and you can perhaps check some map. We staged in at Morville Sur Seille. We were a short ways away from Metz. Another small place was Pont-a-Mousson.

Honey, I hope that you don't worry if the letters aren't regular as you can see why. So every chance I get I'll write. Also if possible, let you know where I have been. So now comes the close of this sheet. Will stop for tonight. Until tomorrow.

Always loving you,
Ed

Thursday, February 8, 1945

My Dearest Darling,

It has been ages since I have heard from you, but I know that in the next mail I am sure to get a letter. We have moved, and it causes a delay in mail. I told you a little about Holland in my last letter.

It is a nicer country than any of the others we have been in. The people are cleaner and keep their homes nice. They seem to go for colors. Their homes have a number of colors on them. Most of them speak a little American, as they take it up in school the same as we do French or any other language in school.

Honey, I am feeling swell at the time being. I believe by the time your cough drops come I won't have any cold. As I have lost it at the present time. We have hit some nice weather. The snow has disappeared, and it looks great with green grass all around. I suppose it is still cold at home. In fact, have read something about the trouble getting coal for heat. I hope you aren't having any trouble keeping warm.

Honey, the next package you send, how about some lead for a lead pencil. Well honey, will close for now until tomorrow when I'll again be

Loving you always,

Ed

SOMEWHERE IN HOLLAND

Saturday, February 10, 1945

My Dearest Darling,

Boy this damn mail service is really a mess. Yesterday I received a letter from you which you mailed the 25th and today two of the 17tth and 18th. So you can see what I have to put up with. I believe I told you of sending out to the laundry. You should see the mess we got in return. Now I wish I never even sent any. By the looks of it, it will take us all afternoon to sort it out. The days seem to go by fast. Here it is Saturday and tomorrow church. We do get the morning off.

Honey you asked about the money you should get. Seventy dollars beside the fifty. Let me know if they send you that thirty for January. As if not, I'll see why here. If you need any more just let me know as I have no need for any here. I can increase that allotment about ten more if you want me to.

I am in the horse barn again only tonight the boys have a little gas stove and it doesn't work so they are trying to fix it. Right now they have enough parts to make two stoves.

Now honey don't worry as everything is still fine here. I'll let you know if anything should happen. You know that it is impossible to write too much as to where and what I am doing. I wish I could tell you everything as I know it would set your mind at ease. I can tell you of the better things that happen such as the shower we took when we went to a town to a public bath house. Had a hot shower and then used an indoor swimming pool and it sure was swell. That was the first real bath since I left England. Honey I guess I better close for now so until tomorrow I sign off.

Always,

Ed

"Tornado"(the name given to the division) did not wait long for another trial in the crucible of combat. On 17 February General Devine received the new mission for the Division tersely summed up in XVI Corps Letter of Instruction Number 13:

8th Armored Division(AD) with attachments will relieve 7th Armored Division(British), attached 1 Commando Bde, in its present sector commencing 19 Feb. Details of relief will be arranged by direct communication between commanders concerned. Relief will be initiated by CC "R" 8th AD relieving 1 Commando Bde prior to 19 Feb, 45 2400.

Relief will be completed by 21 Feb.45 0700

Command of Div sector will pass from GOC 7th Armd Div(Br) to CG rth AD at a time to be mutually agreed upon between the commanders concerned, at which time the CG 8th AD will assume responsibility for defense of the sector.

The 8th Armored as an integral unit was to be committed to battle to relieve the "Desert Rats." This British Division was along the Roer River in the vicinity of Echt, holding a defensive line running generally from Posterholt to Roermond, Holland, with the First Commando Brigade (British) located in the vicinity of Posterholt. The enemy defenses between St. Odilrenberg and Vlodrop consisted of an elaborate system of trenches, dugouts, and concrete bunkers."[160]

"Combat Command R had been selected as the first unit to move into the line, so Colonel Wallace immediately issued a movement order. On 19 February CCR moved into defensive positions in the vicinity of Brackterbeek. From the 19th to the 23rd of February little enemy activity was noticed except for occasional fire of 75-mm or smaller caliber shells. The Germans were content to sit behind the many mine fields they had laid over the marshy terrain."[161]

19 Feb. 45: 80th Tank Battalion left Vilt, Holland 1040 arrived at Aandenberg, Holland 1400

Wednesday, February 21, 1945

My Dearest Darling,

Haven't written in a few days, so will try and write a long one to make up for it. In almost every letter you write, you ask if I received any of the packages you sent. As yet I have only received the one from mother. Everything here is at its best, nothing unusual has happened. As for me I am feeling fine and the weather so far has been grand. It has turn for the best. Warm and every now and then the sun comes out. Only thing that bothers most of us are the long dark nights. But one thing you always have the next daylight to look forward too.

Had a lucky day today, and got some extra rations which included a bottle of Coca-Cola. A treat don't you think? Tell me, do you need any soap? Boy the Army must think we are a dirty bunch. Every time you look around you get a cake of soap and here we don't use hardly any. It seems we don't do much washing. Once a day and then that is a treat to do that.

It looks like everyone seems to believe the baby will be a boy. I'll win tho as I believe it to be just the opposite. I think we should be a little different and wait until the time comes and then say that is just what we said it would be. Then you aren't wrong.

Honey will have to stop for now. But the next chance I'll write again. So until the next letter am thinking of you always.

Ed

Friday, February 23, 1945

My Dearest Darling,

I hope that by now you realize that if you don't hear from me as regular as other times that there is a reason for it. As I have been writing as often as I possibly could. Have been pretty busy of late doing one thing or another. All I have hope for is that before long we will be able to take that boat ride back again. I know I won't mind getting seasick at that time.

You know Easter is just around the corner. I guess it won't do you much good getting an outfit this year will it? I guess I won't get any either. Good old Army clothes for me. Altho wouldn't mind say a new suit, tie, white shirt and bag. Would I feel great. Oh well, it don't hurt to dream does it. Well honey, will close for now until the next letter.

Always thinking of you,

Ed

23 February, 1945 CPT Earl L. Jackson of the 84th Infantry Division, 334th Infantry Regiment, Co C was killed in action after crossing the Roer River into Germany. On 7 February,

the Division assumed responsibility for the Roer River zone, between Linnich and Himmerich, and trained for the river crossing. On 23 February 1945, the Division cut across the Roer, took Boisheim and Dulken."[162]

"On the nights of 24 and 25 February aggressive patrolling was conducted all along the front of CCR's zone. Patrols found almost no resistance on the right flank, light resistance in the center of the line, and a hornet's nest of small arms and automatic weapons fire on the left flank."[163]

Saturday, February 24, 1945

My Dearest Darling,

Today I hit the jackpot and rec'd five of your letters. I really wish I could share some of the times with you back in the parlor and of course the fudge. Boy I could really go for some fudge now. Now don't get me wrong of course I would rather be in the parlor. But you know the best way to a mans heart is through his stomach. Really honey, I miss you but I know it may be some time before I can be there. So what do you say and cheer up and before you know it we'll be together again and of course by then it will be there. No more of the cooking just enough for two, but three. Well honey, will have to stop now as I have a little job to do. Until next letter.

Loving you always,

Ed

"The Commanding General of the 9th Army, Lieutenant general Willian H. Simpson, had decided to launch an attack to reduce all enemy pockets of resistance on the west bank of the Roer River and to make the initial crossing of the Roer. The XVI Corps established its own bridgehead and raced for the Rhine River in the vicinity of Wesel. The mission of the 8th Armored division in the 9th Army

"Operation Grenade" was to clear the area on the west bank of the Roer and push north to the city of Roermond."[164]

'Patrols sent on tactical reconnaissance missions on the night of 24 February reported considerable enemy activity. Large groups of men and vehicles were moving both east and west along the Roermond-Elmpt road."[165]

"General Devine learned of the new enemy situation and received from XVI Corps TWX Number 2732, dated 25 February 1945, which read in part, "Ren in force S of Roermond by 8th AD," he decided to commit CCR in order to strike the enemy while they were in a state of movement. This operation, XVI Corps' "Plan B," was to send a combat command on a reconnaissance in force to determine the extent to which the Germans had reinforced their lines and to clear the enemy from the Roermond-Linne-St. Oldilienberg triangle. The decision to utilize "Plan B" was received by the combat commanders at 1615 hours on 25 February."[166]

25 Feb. 45: 80th Tank Battalion left Aandenberg, Holland 1000 arrived Maasbracht, Holland 1400

26 Feb. 45: 80th Tank Battalion left Maasbracht, Holland 0430

"The attack jumped off at 0600 on 26 February. Major George Artman's 58th Armored Infantry Battalion crossed the line of departure with companies A, B, C abreast. The attack was met by intense mortar and small arms fire. Roadblocks and mines slowed the advance of Major Austin E. Walker, 80th Tank Battalion, whose unit was supporting the attack. These roadblocks were heavily defended and surrounded by an immense amount of "concertino" barbed wire entanglements. Working under small arms and mortar fire, Company C, 53rd Armored Engineer Battalion, managed to clear the Linne-Roermond Highway."[167]

> "27 February, 1945 PVT Vincent Leo Crough of Co. C, 83rd Armd Rcn Bn, 32nd Armd Regt, 3rd Armd Div., 1st Army was also killed in action today near Grouven, Germany Vincent was the gunner in an M24 "Chaffee" light tank, part of a reconnaissance unit in the storied Third Armored "Spearhead" Division of the First Army. He participated in the Allied counteroffensive in the "Battle of the Bulge," and was killed as his tank burned after being hit as the push to Cologne began.

On that fateful day, the 83rd Reconnaissance Battalion was operating in two Battle Groups. Vincent's platoon of tanks was in a column with A Company infantry. Combat interviews with officers of the 83rd contain this report: "Meanwhile, the attack was being organized on the town of Grouven (2060). It was launched at 1100, with A company moving in open formation across the field on both sides of the road to Grouven. It hit very heavy opposition and lost three of its five tanks to enemy AT fire."[168]

The Battle of Linne and Heide Woods

Pasquale Pepe was a combat infantryman in Co-A 58th Armored Infantry Battalion , anti tank platoon. In a letter he wrote: On February 26, Co-A was advancing toward the German lines. Co-B engaged the enemy in a wooded area which was the Heide Woods. Co-C fought along the railroad tracks into an area where some buildings were located. The 80th tank battalion was the tank support for the 58th Armored Infantry Battalion. Co-A was pinned down in an open field by enemy fire. The 80th tanks came onto the field behind us and proceeded to shell the German lines. We then was able to withdraw to the safety of an embankment to our rear.

N 45

SECRET

SHEET 37 S(E)

ROERMOND

Hammer

Roodeberg

Herten

Offerkamp

Merum

Steinhuis

Joosterhof

Armerhof

Schonder

Heide

Zwarte Water

Hoverenberg

Spielmanshof

St. Odilienberg

Breeweg

Struik

Shooting Range

TRACK

TANK X

Lino

C Co.

B Co.

A Co.

89

88

87

86

85

90

Conrad Church wrote in his memoirs:

We were facing the Germans near Roermond, Holland, which was held by their forces, and which, eventually became our objective in the offensive we launched later. Our squad was billeted nearby the corner in the village of Unne, (a mile or so from our advance battle line) and we pulled duty each day or night on that corner, directing whatever traffic came along. The corner was within easy artillery range of the Germans--their mortars fortunately reached about 200 yards short. We dug a foxhole in the middle of the road at the corner, and stayed in it as far as possible. Also, German patrols would sometimes infiltrate the area, so one had to be continually on the alert.

Our squad had as a billet a house in Linne which was intact. It had no furniture left in it except for a large dining table. We drew straws, and I won the right to sleep on the table, rather than under it or on the floor, as the others did. I spread my sleeping bag on it, and bunked down. The house had a barn attached, as did many of the Dutch residences in that area, but there was nothing in it, not even hay or straw. Across the street from this house, was a church and large courtyard, where, each evening, our mess truck appeared with the one hot meal a day we were getting at that time. This truck also brought up our mail.

Preparing to share a cake that I received with my squad mates, we noticed a group of Dutch children, probably 5 or 6 years old, watching us hungrily. We did not eat the cake, but gave it to these children. One night the sky again was blanketed with allied bombers heading for their target in Germany. About an hour or two later, we saw in the distance one of these planes, disabled and appearing to be on fire, trying desperately to reach our lines. Probably thousands of our soldiers witnessed this struggle by this plane's pilot since the land was so flat one could see in the sky for miles. Normally flying very high, this plane was no more than two thousand feet or so above the ground. The Germans were firing everything they had at it, hoping to down it before it reached our lines, to no avail. The plane came over our forward line, the crew parachuted to safety, (to loud cheers and jubilance from us, and. I am sure by our soldiers for miles along this line). The plane flew on to crash at an unknown distant destination. The crew were scattered although all landed within our lines. We picked up one of these men and took him to the rear in one of our jeeps.

At about 3:00 A.M., on the morning of February 23, we were awakened by the roar of our massed artillery, some of which was stationed very near our house. The house quivered and shook with the explosions, as all of our guns opened up on the German lines ahead. When asked what was going on, I said it was the beginning of the Roer offensive. We were attacking with the objective of crossing the Roer River and taking the village of Roermond located on the opposite bank.

Opposing us were the Panzer Leer Division, the 17th Panzer division, and elements of four paratrooper regiments, plus some other attached units. The morning was cloudy, with a sullen sky spitting out occasional bursts of mixed ice pellets and cold rain drops. As the morning grew older, this assault from the sky stopped, and we had a dull, cold, cloudy day with the temperature probably in the low 40's.

My Counter Intelligence and POW squad moved up the Linne - Roermond highway to the front, accompanying the 58th Armored Infantry Battalion for the attack on the Heide woods located on a small hill on our right, and a factory on the left side of the highway.. Running parallel to this highway was a railroad, which was elevated about eight or ten feet above the totally level land on either side. Company A of the 58th was attacking on the left side of the railroad along the highway, and other elements of the 58th were attacking on the right side of the railroad towards the Heide woods.

A large anti-tank ditch some 20 feet wide and 15 feet deep, perhaps, was facing all the American units on both sides of the railroad . There was an underpass so that one could move from one side of the railroad to the other without having to climb the railroad grade. The road to and through the underpass was at right angles to the Roermond highway and had three houses close together thereon, very close to that highway.

These houses and this road, at right angles to the Roermond highway, was the point of departure for our attack. The anti tank ditch was about 200 feet from these houses, and to get the tanks of the 80th Tank Battalion into action, our 53rd Engineers constructed under fire a bridge over which they soon passed. Once across, they joined with the troops of the 58th Armored Infantry Battalion for the attack on the Heide woods on our right, and the factory on the left.

A lieutenant stepped on a mine at this bridge, and the explosion blew off his right leg at the knee. Soon he was being carried out on a stretcher on a jeep by our medics with a tourniquet on his leg. I saw him, as he passed by give us a slight wave of encouragement with his right hand.

On the railroad elevation about 300 yards ahead there was sniper fire, which was doing damage to our engineers and infantry's comfort and health level. Everyone was firing everything they could at this sniper's position. Later we found two dead Germans in their foxhole there, hit by a direct mortar round, it appeared. One looked about fourteen years old and the another perhaps eighteen years of age..

Brad and 1, to have a better view of the battle, and not having any duty at the moment, climbed to the third story of the middle of the three houses on the line of departure, peering out the window on the side towards the action. It was a sight to see if one didn't know people were being killed and wounded in front of our eyes. From the Heide woods, there was the continual flash of gunfire and tracers directed towards our lines. In the fields on our side of the railroad were hundreds of haystacks, now all on fire, and here and there a burning vehicle contributed to the scene. Our troops were visible moving towards the enemy lines, up and running, then down and firing, and repeating the process over and again. Enemy troops were not visible, but their firing was, and the effect of their firing was apparent and horrible.

Tanks from our 80th Tank Battalion had now crossed the bridge over the anti- tank ditch, and were in the open field beyond, firing on the Heidi woods and the factory defenders' positions. Suddenly, two Tiger tanks appeared, from the woods, opening up on our tanks with their superior 88mm guns. Our tanks, armed with 75's were no match in fire power, and were in great danger. One could see our tanks' shells hit the Tigers, and bounce off like bb's hitting a brick wall. When an 88mm hit, it knocked out anything that was its target, including our Sherman tanks.

Suddenly two P-47 planes were over our lines, with their rockets firing on the Tigers. Immediately, the Tigers turned tail and ran back into the safety of the Heide woods. The Germans had a great fear of these planes with good reason. Brad and I stood in the house for a time watching until suddenly tracers started to come directly at us from the Heide wood area. We left in a hurry, figuring an artillery observer had spotted us. Sure enough, we had hardly reached the ground when an 88mm shell went through that very window.

Company A of the 58th AIB was involved in very heavy fighting, and were pinned down by the intense defense fire from the factory and the area around it. Company A of the- 7th Armored Infantry Battalion, which had been in reserve, came up the road from Linne to help, splendid looking troops in all respects. As they reached the point of departure, they were a wonderful sight to see--in single file on each side of the road facing towards Roermond, with a distance of about 15 feet between each man, laughing and joking between them all, with the usual question asked over and over, "What do you want to do--live forever?" With this help from these reserve troops, the 58th finally overcame resistance, and took the factory. The 7th AIB returned to reserve.

Monday, February 26, 1945

Bronze Star – for meritorious achievement.

Sgt. Brodowski displayed outstanding courage moving his tank up under intense enemy fire and dismounting to evacuate wounded. He was later assigned the mission of attacking an enemy network of trenches. In carrying out the mission, he exposed himself continually to enemy fire to man the machine gun on his tank. He continued his advance despite the fact his tank was struck once by anti-tank fire. His action enabled the pinned down infantry to resume their advance.

Witnesses have said that Ed had his tank come in at high speed with the 50 caliber machine gun blazing out hot lead. He purposely exposed his tank in order to draw enemy fire away from the infantryman.

"Combat Command R had withdrawn from forward positions in the Heide Woods during the day of 27 February after being relieved by elements of the 15th Cavalry Group (Mechanized). At 1800 on 27th Colonel Wallace had received instructions to move to the vicinity of Wegberg. At that point

Combat Command was to turn northeast and close in on the area east of the town of Aldekerk.

Arriving in the designated area on the 28th CCR moved rapidly through the towns of Richelrath, Duken, Boisheim, Flothend, and Lobberich. At that point the Corps' restriction on the use of the road net also hampered CCR's activities. Cross country movement was infeasible, as the terrain was not suitable for tank maneuver. Since the Corps order had directed that the Division use only one lateral road between Wegberg and Lobberich, movement was seriously restricted. [169]

"Colonel Wallace, employing all means possible to move forward, contacted the adjacent 84th Infantry Division, commanded by Major General A. R. Bolling, for permission to move through its area. This permission was flatly refused. Colonel Wallace could do nothing but sit and wait during the entire day of 1 March. Finally during the afternoon of the following day Colonel Wallace received instructions ordering him to move forward. CCR was to make an all-out dash for the Rhine River. General Devine, acting on orders received in XVI Corps Letter of Instructions Number 23, dated 1 March, 1945, ordered CCR to capture the towns of Grefrath and Moers and to secure intact, if possible, the railroad bridge over the Rhine in the vicinity of Moers. Contact was to be maintained with the 84th Infantry Division moving forward in its zone on the left flank of CCR.

Colonel Wallace divided his Command into two task forces to complete the mission. Task Force Artman, under the command of Major George Artman, CO, 58th AIB and Task Force Walker, Major A. E. Walker, CO, 80th Tank Battalion."

Task force Artman contained Company C, 80th Tank Battalion. Task force Walker contained the 80th Tank Battalion less Company C of which contained Ed Brodowski in Company A Third Platoon Tank 14 "Abner".[170]

"28 February 1945 Tech 5 Annon I. Bozeman of Cannon Company, 121st Infantry Regiment, 8th Infantry Division experienced enemy artillery fire which fell on his unit at Blatzheim, Germany. Here Annon along with Dymitry Sabot, Reuben A. White, Rex E. Chritchfield, William N. Cramer, Harold Roberts, Edward R. Ennis and Louis V. Connolly, were killed."[171]

MARCH

01 Mar. 45: 80th Tank Battalion arrived Tuschenbroich, Germany 0330

"GERMANY"

Thursday, March 1, 1945
My Dearest Darling,

It has been a few days since I have written also haven't rec'd any. As you can see by the heading, I am now in Germany. I suppose I needn't say any more. I finally found out what fighting is, and I am ready to go home. We are still in one piece. I mean the crew and right now nothing can separate us. We are a fighting team.

Honey, I don't want you to carry on after you read this letter, as I know you will. You can bet that I will be careful at all times, as I intend to be coming home soon. Of what I have seen of Germany, it is a battlefield they must have planned for a long time. I am wondering how you are getting along as the days go by and your time comes closer. So don't forget and quit that job pretty soon. As there is no need of taking any chances with your health.

I am hoping that you have rec'd the package I have sent. Also will send more the first chance I get. So until the next letter I close for now.

Your loving husband,
Ed

Grefarth fell to Task Force Walker by 1800 hours of the 2nd, with light opposition and few casualties. Darkness forced Task Force Walker to remain here during the night of 2 March.

Task Force Walker was ordered to proceed to Vinnbruck and secure this town. Task force Artman CCR jumped off at 0600 3 March and rolled eastward. Task Force Artman was ordered to capture the town of Schrephuysen, thus clearing the area for the lateral maneuver in the attack of Moers.

Task Force Walker captured the town of Saint Hubert, encountering light opposition, and moved to Vinnbruck. A blown bridge halted the column outside Vinnbruck. The engineers hastily constructed a tread way bridge and the leading tank of Company A, 80th Tank Battalion, had crossed over when the orders came to halt all forward movement, withdraw, and proceed to the Division bivouac area in the vicinity of Alderkerk-Wachtendonk-Zeigelheide. The Division had been completely "pinched out."

Meanwhile Task force Artman had been encountering stiffening resistance. A fierce fire fight, which developed in the vicinity of Saelhuysen, was quelled and Company A, 58th AIB, prepared to move out toward Schrephuysen. As the Task force entered this town the withdrawal order arrived and the unit began immediately to move to the bivouac area."[172]

The mental state of the German soldier in World War II was stated quite clearly in the book Frontsoldaten by Stephen Fritz, a history professor at East Tennessee State University. For soldiers faith in Nazism and loyalty to the Fuhrer were taken as "self-evident." In the ranks of the average German Soldier or Landser, there are certainly those who fight for the sake of the idea of National Socialism. Some landsers, in fact, saw in Nazism virtually mystical properties. When we set up our headquarters for the night, we set up our wireless set as usual…and we nearly fall flat on our faces when we realize that the furher is about to speak. No one knows what this beloved voice means to us…What a lift his words give us…Is there a finer reward after a day of battle than to hear the Fuhrer? Lieutenant P.G. wrote in 1943 that we live in a time whose value will be recognized only many years later. Here it is no longer a matter of the individual but the whole. Only so long as we are conscious of that can victory come. The Fuhrer made a firm promise to bail us out of here said a soldier in a perverse liturgy of faith. They read it to us and we believed in it firmly. Even now I still believe it, because I have to believe in something. If it is not true, what else could I believe in? All my life I believed in the Fuhrer. Indeed, claimed Pruller of a Hitler speech in December 1942. Every word was balm to our souls. With what enthusiasm we shall carry the attack forward to the enemy tomorrow. [173]

03 Mar. 45: 80th Tank Battalion arrived Wall, Germany 1815

Sunday, March 4, 1945

My Dearest Darling,

Have been moving so much that it has been impossible to write but today we finally stopped so here I am going to try and give an account of what has happen up to now. First, still in one piece, feeling fine. Getting use to this moving that now don't mind the change of climate as it does change. Also the scenery changes. By the looks of this country, these people have been preparing for us. As everywhere you look they have trenches, even in the back and front yards, roadblocks blocking every road. In fact all you can say is that it is just one big battlefield. Something else you may have heard of is how the German people don't have a thing. I mean all they raise goes to the Army. Well that is a lot of houy as I have seen for myself and they have all kinds of meat in their attics, enough to keep a family a long time. The same goes for other food stuff such as can goods, vegetables.

One of the reasons we know what they have is whenever we stop we kick the families out and take over. It is hard to do at first but after some of the sights, we see nothing is too hard on them. I just as soon kick them out as I would an animal out of the house.

Of course, you can imagine the fuss they put up. The way they put it, it ain't their fault. We have found out you can't trust a one of them, as they'll get you for sure the first chance they get.

I guess you can see by the way I write I am pretty bitter. I can say now I have reasons. Well so much for all that.

I got your package. The one which was mailed the 12th of January. We were on the road and during a short break, they managed to bring the mail around. It has been the same for some time. Just a matter of hit and run. Honey keep writing as your letters are the only thing I get here, even if delayed for days at a time. By now you'll know that letters from me are far and in between. Have been thinking of you all the time. So your on a diet. Well finally the Doc put his foot down. No wonder your getting as big as a barrel as you put it. One thing it won't be too long now and you can go back to the regular meals. So for now will close with love till next letter.

Love and kisses always,

Ed

05 Mar. 45: 80th Tank Battalion left Wall, Germany 0900 arrived Grefrath 0950

Monday, March 5, 1945

My Dearest Darling,

Rec'd two more of your packages last night. They both were mailed in December. Those cans are the ideal thing for sending candies and cookies as it keeps things fresh and also from melting and leaving a mess.

Today we moved and now occupying another house. Only this one is much better because it has running water.

Stove is also gas. You can just imagine how we are making out. I know I wouldn't want anyone taking my home but it serves these people right. I wonder if they thought about it when they went thru Poland and all those other countries. I have no pity for them what so ever.

. It doesn't seem possible here it is March the 5th. The days seem to go by pretty fast. The nights are pretty long especially when you have guard. Which reminds me I have to go on in a few minutes so will close now until tomorrow's letter.

Loving you always,

Ed

Tuesday, March 6, 1945

My Dearest Darling,

I guess your not the only one to get a lot of mail as I rec'd three from you. It is funny as by the time you hear that I am in a country, we move to another. But I guess from now on it will be Germany. All the way there. You asked if I have done any fighting, well the answer is yes and no. Suppose we just say I got close to a few Germans and perhaps killed a few but nothing to write about. When I get home and by the fire on some raining night I'll have some long tales. Something to put the children to sleep. Instead of the story "Little Red Riding Hood" I'll tell him of my experience in Germany or don't you approve of that?

Honey, I am feeling fine, in fact now we manage to clean all our clothes and also ourselves. So you can see how much we fight. Hey that size 18 has me worried. It sure is a big change from 9-12. Am waiting for that picture of you. I'll close for now.

Loving you always,

Ed

Wednesday, March 7, 1945

My Dearest Darling,

Here it is the close of another day. Spent a lazy day today. Trying to clean all my clothes and get ready in case we have to move again. As it is we now are resting up, having all the accommodations of home. Of course only one thing is missing (right) you. I keep saying to myself, it can't be too long and we'll all be going home. I know it sounds crazy, but I guess we all are hoping that.

I wish I could write like some fellows but you know what type of letters I write. I don't have to tell you that I miss you as you know it. Especially at this time_I keep wonder how you are getting along and if you are in need of anything. This being so far away is really hell. If anything should come up, have Leo help you, and I am sure he will.

As for myself, I am in the heat of battle. Oh yes, got one of those short haven'ts again. Reminds me of the good old camp days in the States. Hon will close.

Loving you always,

Ed

On the Western Front... The leading tanks of US 3rd Corps (part of US 1st Army) reach the Rhine River opposite Remagen and find the Ludendorff Bridge there damaged but still standing. Troops are immediately rushed across and a bridgehead is firmly established during the day. Other elements of the US 1st Army complete the capture of Cologne. Units US 12th Corps from US 3rd Army continue to advance rapidly.[174]

"On 11 March 1945 the Thundering Herd was detailed to perform a security mission. As outlined in Letter of Instructions Number 32, Headquarters, XVI Corps, dated 10

March 1945 1600 hours, the 8th Armored Division was to perform security missions in all the XVI Corps area between the Division rear boundary and Corps rear boundary with the exception of the town of Niekerk, Germany. All bridges, supply dumps, ammunition, and supply points were to be guarded. All houses in the area were to be searched for male civilians of military age and for civilians not carrying authorized identification cards. All such persons were to be taken into custody for screening.

During such screening the first evidences of an underground organization came to light. Skillful interrogation by Lieutenant Martin Bernstein of G-2 Section revealed complete plans of the underground. Cleverly camouflaged underground bunkers were discovered, each containing twelve to fifteen men, fully equipped and under orders to remain in place until the advancing troops had by passed them. These men would then receive secret orders to sabotage rear area army installations. These bunkers were cleared by the 7th AIB, and the German soldiers were sent under guard to the Division PW enclosure. Higher headquarters were apprised of the discovery, and the Thundering Herd claimed the distinction of being the first unit to uncover the existence of these secret "Werewolf" organizations.

The Germans also knew that the assault crossing of the Rhine in the Wesel area would not be long delayed. Their units which had escaped to the east bank were frantically regrouping and reorganizing. The 180th and the 190th Volks Grenadier Divisions had succeeded in withdrawing across the Rhine to the vicinity of Wesel. Supported by the 116th Panzer Division both Divisions remained in this position. The 130th Panzer Division, originally in the Wesel area, had moved to counterattack the 1st Army bridgehead which had been established on 7 March 1945

The German forces in this zone had been caught off balance when the 9th Armored Division, commanded by Major General John W. Leonard, seized the Remagen bridge, intact, on 7 March 1945 and rushed troops across it. The enemy in the Wesel sector thus became determined to repel the 9th Army assault so as to be able to counterattack the Remagen bridgehead."[175]

Sunday, March 11, 1945

My Dearest Darling,

Honey I am enclosing an money order for $60. I have been carrying the money around and can't seem to find any place to use it, so am sending it home. I hope it reaches you before Easter.

Our rations came in today, so now everyone has candy and gum. The only trouble is that it doesn't last only for one day. The boys are downstairs playing cards. It seems that the money is in too many hands. Before the night is over it will be in one mans hands. Someone said that Keaton was taken for a little. I know he was around trying to get enough for cigars. Honey, just had that can of soup and it really tasted good. It has been a long time since I had any. The years I am waiting for those cookies you sent. I hope they will get here soon.

You know by now that your packages have been coming slow but coming. Well honey I guess I better close for now. Until the next letter, I say goodnight.

Loving you always,

Ed

Tuesday, March 13, 1945

My Dearest Darling,

Was pretty busy last night as didn't get a chance to write. But doing my darnest to do so as tonight I am going on guard in a half-hour. So I will try and finish this before I do.

I am feeling fine and hoping that you are also. I am sure that by now the weather has changed and Spring is at your doorstep. As we here are enjoying the good old Spring weather.

Got my first look at a German plane today. Only it was going so fast that I couldn't describe it if I tried. Couldn't even get our guns on him.

I mailed a money order the day before yesterday. Keep an eye for it. Well honey, looks like I need to close. Keep your chin up and before you'll know it I'll be home. Then we can start where we left off.

Loving you always,

Ed

SOMEWHERE IN GERMANY

Thursday, March 15, 1945

My Dearest Darling,

I am out in an outpost and it really is a beautiful day. Johnnie and I just came back from a walk thru the woods. You should see the rabbits. Tried to get them but it is just a waste of ammunition. If I only had my shotgun!

We have been walking around in our shirts. In your last letters, you mentioned the cookies. Now you got me wanting them pretty bad. I just hope the mail isn't as slow as it was there for awhile, as at present it takes about nine days which is almost too good to be true. I suppose by the time you get this letter you'll be home taking life easy, as you did say you would do so about now. If not, you better do so. Hon, will close for now. I hope I have a letter when I get back tonight.

Always and Forever,

Ed

P.P.S. Am adding a few lines. Went back out and got one rabbit. Saw a bunch of deer but the gun was too small and couldn't kill them, but made a good attempt. Only shot 45 rounds at them. Can't wait to get home and see if I can shoot those deer upstate.

Love,

Ed

Saturday, March 17, 1945

My Dearest Darling Wife,

Spent rather a long day in the field today and feel down in the dumps. Here it is Saturday night at present it is only eight o'clock and no place to go unless you care to go to bed. But even that doesn't seem like a good idea. I pulled my guard last night so I don't have to tonight, which gives me a full night of sleep.

Right now Johnnie just came off his guard and now he is playing a mouth organ. He can really play one and of course he gives up the good old Polish music.

Tomorrow we have an easy day. We are having Mass at two o'clock in the afternoon and the rest of the day off.

We have had a few of the boys get passes to Paris. They really enjoy themselves and of course have some high tales when they come back but like every place that the soldiers go, they charge twice for everything they have.

Honey, I just took a cigarette as I thought that the boys would faint. Now don't get me wrong, just took one for fun. As I don't care for the damn things. Well, here it is.

Love and kisses
Ed

Sunday, March 18, 1945

Dearest,

Haven't had any mail from you in the last few days. I guess it's the same old story. The mail is held up someplace. When it does come, it will all come in a big pile. Nothing new has taken place here, the same old story. Today being Sunday, spent a quiet day doing just that (nothing).

We had a formation today, as one of the boys received a Purple Heart. We are now getting quite a few passes. Some to Paris and other places of interest. I don't believe that I'll take any, as I can see us going. The one that I am looking for is the one to the States.

Well honey, I will close for now. I hope that I hear from you tomorrow.

Loving you always,

Ed

"Pre-staging events came rapidly for the 8th as the time for assault crossing the Rhine grew nearer. On 20 March 1945 the tank battalions held blackout marches and practice river crossings over a pontoon bridge at Grefarth.

On 22 March 1945 Tornado's Division Artillery, commanded by Colonel Henry W. Holt, moved into firing positions to participate in the barrage to be made by elements of the 30th Infantry Division, commanded by Major General Leland S. Hobbs. Ammunition was stock piled during the 22nd and 23rd of March. "H" Hour, "D" Day was to be 0400 March 24; at H-1 hours the entire 9th Army front erupted with one tremendous roar. As far as the eye could see artillery, ranging from 75 mm to 240 mm, was hurling deadly steel at the Germans dug in on the east bank of the Rhine. Noise was so intense that the section chiefs could hardly hear commands coming in over their phones. Each minute during the hour-long barrage 1,087 shells were sent hurtling across the River, a total of 65,261 rounds being fired during that hour. From H-1 to H-4 hours the number of artillery rounds fired in support of the crossing was totaled at 131,450."[176]

Wednesday, March 21, 1945

My Dearest Darling,

Well, here it is, the 21st of March. Two years ago yesterday the Army decided that they could use me. Today I say that they made a big mistake. They could have done just as well if they had gotten someone else. Really honey, it seems like it has been years that I took my physical. A lot of things have happen in those few years. I just hope that before I say three years that I'll be home a free man. Remember the song I believe the title, In My Blue Heaven. That is what it is to be, just the three of us.

Personally, I believe that I am holding my own altho it has been said that I gained a few lbs. But can't be sure as there is no way of weighing. So we'll put it about the same. As for the "Tash" it has been off for some time. Feel better clean shaving.

By the letters, you haven't received any from me saying that I am in Germany and have been for a few weeks. While in Holland, we were in Volkanberg. That is about all I can say about Holland. (Oh yes some of the boys have been able to go on passes to Paris)

The weather has turned out beautiful. The days are warm. The nights still get a little cool but nothing like what we went thru in France. I hope that I don't have to spend another winter like it.

It seems I keep requesting that by the time you get this letter you'll have quit your job and staying home. So again, I hope that when you finish reading this, if you haven't finished working, you'll do so at once. Suppose we put it as an order. I wish I could see your face when you read this part. Well I close for now.

Loving you always,

Ed

Thursday, March 22, 1945

My Dearest Wife,

Received your most beautiful Easter card today. It also reminded me that up to now I haven't made any effort to send you any greeting of any kind. Did think of mother getting you flowers but I know how you feel about that. I know that this letter will get to you after Easter but remember the old saying, "Better Late Than Never." So now I'll say Happy Easter. I hope you'll have a nice day as it is a shame if it should be a stormy day.

It is surprising how many Polish people are here in Germany. I have checked quite a few and find most of them talk Polish but the question is, are they Polish. As it is the habit now, as soon as the Yanks enter, everyone becomes anything but German. Even soldiers when captured claim their Poles and not Germans.

Did I tell you of the hunting experience I had the other day. I believe I did mention something about it. Anyway, I was using a carbine, which is a small rifle. It was funny. Johnnie was using a machine gun, a clip holding thirty rounds.

Anyway, we went thru the woods seeing a few but unable to get a shot at any. On the way back, we see one. Johnnie tried to get a shot at it but his gun caught on his clothes. So then he carried the gun in front of him. It wasn't but a few feet further that this rabbit jumped up and started to run. Then Johnnie was shooting and hitting nothing. It was funny to see. Later during the day, we went out again. This time I finally got a chance at a few, finally getting one. Just before we had to leave for our (billets) (place where we stay), we seen a few deer. There I was shooting like mad, deer running every way, and I didn't get one. I only shot up 45 rounds.

Honey I finally am getting to believe that it will be a boy. As I have something that only a boy would take interest in. Today I was one of the six men to be awarded a decoration. It seems that in our last engagement with the enemy, we did a good deed. For it, I was awarded the Bronze Star, which I'll mail to you. I thought that I better tell you about it, as you may not understand just getting the star. Personally, what we did and it was the whole crew doing it, was what anyone would have done in our place. But it seems that it is the tank commander or whoever is in charge gets all the credit. That is why I don't believe I should have gotten it.

But I guess it is all in war. As alone we would have failed. Of course they had a formation, the men to be decorated in front of the companies. And of course all the Brass. When Our Name was called, we marched up to the General, gave him a salute, he then pinned on the medal, giving you a pep talk of how proud he was of you and what a splendid job you did. Then shook your hand. Standing there waiting for my name to be called, I had all kinds of things go thru my mind. Suppose I didn't go up right or maybe I would forget to salute but it turned out O.K.

Also, as the General pinned on the star, an Army cameraman took a picture. Now when you finish reading this don't get any ideas, as I am safe and sound. And I am not getting in any more danger than anyone else. In fact sometimes I am so far back that I keep wondering if we'll ever get even close to a Jerry.

Well honey, so much for that. Give my regards to all at home. Must close now.

Loving you always,

Ed

P.S. You are going to have trouble if the baby is a boy as he will be (Jr.) to me.

SOMEWHERE IN GERMANY

Friday, March 23, 1945 8 PM

My Dearest Darling Wife,

Just finished packing the medal. It will go out the same time this letter does. I hope that it gets home. The Company is having a fun party. I went over but stayed only a few minutes. It looks like the boys are really going to have a big one before it is over. The weather has been grand for the last few days. The people here are planting their gardens. Everywhere you look it is either in the garden or out in the field but everyone is working.

I finally am wearing summer undershirts as it is too warm during the day with winter ones. How is the weather at home? Warm enough for lighter clothes?

Well honey, I guess I better close for now. So until tomorrows letter.

Love and kisses,

Ed

Irving Odgers of the 58th Armored Infantry Bn., Company 'C' wrote that during the early morning of March 24 a tremendous artillery barrage to the east awakened us. We knew that the Ninth Army's assault of the Rhine River had started. The barrage was a continuous thunder that lasted for an hour and then subsided into intermittent blasts of called for fire support. On the 25th we received notice to be prepared to move out on thirty minutes notice.

24 March, 1945 SGT Walter John Linne Tank Commander of the 47th Tank Battalion B Company, B-11, 14th Armored Division was near Germersheim on the Rhine, Germany. The bridge leading into the town had been blown by the Germans. The attacking force of tankers and infantry were reassembled to the woods west of the town. About three in the morning the enemy began shelling the woods. The infantry had no where to hide and took a terrible beating. The attack advanced across an open field towards the town under heavy fire from antitank guns, machine guns, small arms, and the "kitchen sink". Walter had climbed out of the turret to load wounded infantrymen on to the back of his tank when he was killed."[177]

OPERATION PLUNDER

Sunday, March 25, 1945

Commencing on the night of 23 March 1945 during World War II Operation Plunder was the crossing of the Rhine river at Rees, Wesel, and south of the Lippe Canal by theBritish Second Army, under Lieutenant-General Sir Miles Dempsey(Operations *Turnscrew*, *Widgeon*, and *Torchlight*), and the U.S. Ninth Army(Operation *Flashlight*), under Lieutenant GeneralWilliam Simpson. XVIII U.S. Airborne Corps, consisting of British 6th Airborne Division and US 17th Aitborne Division, conducted Operation Varsity. All of these formations were part of the 21st Army Group under Field Marshal Sir Bernard Montgomery. This was part of a coordinated set of Rhine crossings.[178]

My Dearest,

Intended to write last night but was busy until very late, so will do so now. Just finished eating chicken, potatoes (with jackets), nuts, apples for dessert, and of course coffee, bread and butter. Now am waiting for two o'clock so that I can go to church. Will have to go alone, as I sent Johnnie and rest of the crew out on guard. Felt like putty myself so unable to go with them.

It is surprising the way these people dress on Sunday. I was under the impression they didn't have very good material, but it seems they are doing better than you are at home. Especially the stockings, they look like good silk.

We are supposed to have the Red Cross unit come around with coffee and doughnuts this afternoon. While here, we have been very lucky as they have had movies almost every night. So far I have only seen one.

I will have to stop for a short time but will con't later on. Well here I am back and to add more on. Went to church at two o'clock. Also rec'd three letters from you telling me you weigh 130 lbs. That is only 12 lbs. more than you weighed while I was home. Honey, let me know as soon as the packages get to you. Am still waiting for the rest of yours. Honey, will close for tonight.

Loving you always,

Ed

The following night we were off to cross the Rhine. On the night of the 26th of March at about 1800 we were told to mount up and prepare to move out. We climbed up into our track, arranged the gear inside and he placed his gun into the left side pintle and slipped in the hinge pin.

He dropped a box of ammunition into the gun mount bracket, popped the lid back and threaded the belt feed tab through the loading port on the left side of the receiver. He then pulled the bolt back once to secure the ammunition belt in the feed pawls of the gun but didn't pull it back a second time to put a round in the chamber. He preferred to run with the gun not fully cocked as a safety precaution since if he needed to fire it would only take a split second to chamber a round. He locked the mount with the gun facing forward and sat down and made himself comfortable for the long drive through the night that lay ahead. Within a few minutes Pastewka cranked up the motor and we slowly pulled out into a column and headed east. We later learned that the division was in a column of combat commands with CCA leading, CCR second and CCB bringing up the rear.

As we moved east the muttering of artillery got louder and louder. After grinding and clanking along for about three or four hours we got close enough to the Rhine to hear the reports of individual artillery pieces. We could see the glow of searchlights and the flashes of the big guns reflecting off of the overcast. We eventually crested a rise and there below us, at about three quarters of a mile away lay, the Rhine River. To our right we could make out a pontoon bridge in the reflected light of the antiaircraft searchlights. At each end there was a column of tracer streaks reaching vertically up into the night. The diameter of the columns must have been five or six hundred yards and it looked as if several hundred machine guns and 20 mm and 40 mm cannons were locked into a vertical position. They were firing continuously to provide an impenetrable screen at each end of the bridge thereby discouraging the German aircraft flying overhead from making a strafing or bomb run down the length of the bridge.

A German plane roared right over our track and it sounded as if we could reach up and touch him. When we caught a glimpse of him in the reflected light he was at least 200 feet above us. We could see the vehicles ahead of us slowly making their way up the shore ramp and onto the bridge. They were only moving about five miles an hour and the engineers were keeping them spaced out about 100 feet apart. Even so the individual pontoons bobbed up and down perceptibly as each tank or track passed over it. It took about fifteen minutes for us to work our way down the road that the engineers had cut into the river bluff. We were going south nearly parallel to the river until we reached the river plain that separated the river from the bluff by 70 yards. We swung to the left and slowly climbed up onto the ramp leading to the bridge. The bridge seemed to be nearly 800 yards long and as we crept onto it an engineer standing at the river end of the ramp caution us to not exceed 5 mph and to keep our spacing.

Why daddy did you not come home?

On Monday March 26 Brodowski's tank left Grefrath at 2005 and traveled 36 miles to the vicinity of Bruckhausen. It was now Tuesday March 27th at 0450. We waited there for our turn to go across the pontoon bridge and across the Rhine River.

We finally got our orders on the 28 of March. The Second Platoon and a Bull Dozer left Bruckhausen at 0730 leading the assault on Kirchhellen with Company "B" of the 58th Infantry. The Third Platoon was in support and the First Platoon was in reserve. We lined our tanks up along a dirt road leading into Kirchhellen. German artillery was raining down on us as we returned fire with our tank guns.

Sam Montean of C88 writes, "We jumped off on March 28th and must have gone only about a hundred yards when we seen some branches laying across the road. When we took a closer look we seen a couple of box mines on the road under the branches. We then heard bullets whizzing by followed by explosions in the tree tops over our heads. The road was lined with trees. I looked up and seen the flashes in the branches over our heads. McLinden and Dubois turned the jeeps around and the rest of us jumped in the jeeps and went back to the rest of the platoon. They then sent a lieutenant from the engineers up with a tank right behind him and he took away the branches and mines.

It was at this point that the order was given that we were to go in shooting and first squad was to lead with a tank right behind. My jeep may have been the only mortar jeep in the whole troop equipped with a 30 caliber machine gun on the hood right in front of the car commander. Blaker's gunner in his jeep was to fire on the right side of the road as we went into Kirchellen and I was to fire on the left side of the road. We were pretty close to the town when Blaker's jeep got hung up on some down power lines.

Rissmiller came up right behind me and yelled "Montean, take the point." He immediately said follow me and his armored car went around both of us. I followed him into Kirchellen. The tank followed me. There was a cemetery on the left side of the road and I was firing into the cemetery thinking that there might be Krauts behind some gravestones. I was also firing into a large brick building before I seen a large faded red cross painted on the side of the building. We were pretty much through the town when Rissmiller figured we went far enough. They sent the tank ahead and it was promptly knocked out.

Half tracks with infantry came up. The point was getting congested. Artillery started to come in. MeLinden came over to me and said people in the half tracks and armored cars were safe from the shelling but when the Krauts got zeroed in we in the jeeps were vulnerable. I said we couldn't dig in the cobblestone streets but if we had an ax. we could knock the door down on a building and get inside. McLinden said he had an ax on his jeep and asked if he should get it. I said "Let's do it". McLinden got the ax and promptly knocked the door in on a red brick building next to our position. We called other jeep crews to come inside. More and more people were coming inside. The shelling outside was becoming worse and a shell hit the machine gun mount on an infantry half track with the squad in the half-track. Many of the infantry were wounded. They brought one guy inside with a piece of gut sticking out of his lower belly. This guy was in pain. They knew they couldn't give a guy anything by mouth with a belly wound. They could sprinkle sulfa on the wound and bandage it and give him a shot of morphine. They didn't have morphine. I told them I had morphine in our first aid kit in our jeep and went out to the jeep and got it. I offered the tube of morphine to the guy who was taking care of his buddy. This guy said to me "you give it to him". I then jabbed the needle into this guy's arm and squeezed out the tube. It was then that McLinden said to me we need a medic up here and he was going back in the column to get one. McLinden went out the door that he had chopped down and that was the last time I seen him alive. There was a lot of shelling going on just outside the building. A little later on Joe Schneider came to me and said McLinden was sitting in his jeep outside and he was hit. He said he and Sgt. Downing was going out to get him and asked if I would go along. I said sure. Joe was leading this rescue attempt. Joe dashed out the door followed by Downing and I was following Downing when we heard a shell coming in. I hadn't gotten through the door yet so I just jumped to the side of the door opening and froze against the wall. Downing came diving back through the door and was about half way through the door when the shell exploded just outside. Downing came through the door with a flying cloud of dust and debris. Downing hit the floor and grimaced as he grabbed his leg. He got it in the leg. I looked through the door into a cloud of dust and yelled Joe a couple of times. Joe soon came walking out of the cloud through the door holding his arm. Joe had a grin on his f ace and said he was hit in the arm. Joe was holding one' arm with the other and said he had hit the gutter when the shell came in...

McLinden was still out there. I looked around and seen Pattengill and I told him Schneider and Downing were hit in an attempt to get to McLinden. I asked Pattengill if he would go out with me to see if we could bring in McLinden. Pattengill said he would. We waited for a lull in the shelling. The lull came and we dashed to McLinden's jeep. McLinden was laying back in the jeep and his eyeballs were rolled back in his eye sockets. I felt for a pulse and could get none. I tried to see if I could detect any breathing and couldn't. I said to Pattengill McLinden was dead and he agreed. We didn't feel there was a need to bring him in. I was going to go back in when Pattengill pointed to a couple of infantry guys sitting beside a building. Pattengill asked why they don't come inside the building. One of the guys said his buddy was hit and couldn't walk and he didn't want to leave him. Pattengill said we could help him get his buddy inside. Pattengill got on one side of the wounded infantry man and his buddy got on the other side and were able to get him inside. I followed carrying everybody's guns.

The shelling came to a stop. Maybe the Krauts were pulling back. There was no wind that day and we emerged from the building. There was a faint blue smoke cloud from the shelling around the area where we were and it had a sickening smell of burnt bacon."

Dick Kemp recalls that day in his story "A Pleasant Day in Deutschland." "We had just bypassed several Tellar mines hidden on the road when orders from our Task Force Commander, Major George Artman, came over the radio, "Bypass your recon." By 0725 in the town of Kirchellen we were in the basement of a house. I shall never forget that house! When the command came, "Avenelle" my tank moved out from behind a large building marked as a hospital because Lt. Martin wanted to draw enemy fire. The other 4 tanks and the infantry remained concealed. We were about 200 yards into the open when the German 88mm fired. The tank rocked and white hot steel was flying everywhere inside. Fire started almost immediately. Don Elshire and I flew out through our hatches. The sandbags on the front were being ripped with machine gun fire as we jumped over the side. "

Across the field a 58th armored infantry officer could see a large farm house with a fence surrounding the farm. Behind the farm house was smoke billowing up into the sky. The smoke was coming from a tank, Kemp's tank. No one knew at that time Kemp and his crew were in the basement of that farm house safely hidden from the Germans.

"I had Pfc. Hardenburgh by the hand and was trying to pull him off the back deck when another 88 skimmed the back deck killing him. Then Meyers hollered, "There's your officer in the middle of the road!" Martin had made it out, ran about 20 ft and collapsed, bleeding from a large piece of shrapnel in his chest. The white-hot steel had cauterized the wound. Part of the thumb and index finger on his left hand were gone. Meyers ran to him along with Elshire. Under enemy machine gun fire, they carried him back to safety beside the tank while I was crawling out from under Pfc. Hardenburgh.

God bless Meyers, he had a real presence of mind. I never was too bright! I hate to say this, but the fourth Infantryman; Buchett (I believe) was also swept off the back deck. The tank was really burning and starting to explode. We grabbed the Lt. and ran to the house. We left Buchett for dead but I found out later that he was just badly wounded and lived.

We were trapped in the upper basement with about 90 German civilians in the lower bomb shelter basement, while Panzer Grenadiers searched for us. They could smell the burning bodies of Cpl. Beckner and PFC Bean and could see the body of Pfc. Albert Hardenburgh, 58th AIB, and I believe that Buchett was still there at that time. There were five of us trapped in the basement until 1830 that evening when the town was retaken. The two 58th AIB soldiers with us along with Hardenburgh and Buchett had been riding 50 cal shotgun on the back deck. Damn fine soldiers.

Lt. Martin was close to death so we, with the aid of a very lovely young German girl, did all we could to keep him alive. The girl not only nursed him, but held the flashlight on his Wollboster while I put it in a Mason jar to go grum-grum. He was too weak to raise his hands. His mouth however kept saying, "Kemp – I'm going to kill you, not now, but someday." Other words he used were unprintable. It did as I hoped – made him too mad to die. He had made his fiendish plans for me!

It was after we were hit, that the Task Force withdrew and did not retake the town until dark. In the confusion we did not realize that our concealed tanks had laid down a rather heavy layer of smoke with 76 mm smoke shells and smoke mortars. The Germans were not the only ones fooled since all of our own men thought we were dead, until we crawled out of that basement at

1830. The men I owed cigarettes and money to all cheered. The rest looked discouraged!" T/5 Lloyd 'Dick' Kemp Co. 'A'., 80th Tank Battalion 6/9/00

The Second Platoon accomplished its mission of taking Kirchhellen. The Third Platoon with Ed Brodowski relieved the Second Platoon at 1700 and took up defensive positions in the town. Kemp could hear the gun fire and knew it was ours by the sound of the guns. Kemp left the basement of that farmhouse and down the column to Brodowski's tank. Brodowski looked down and yelled "Kemp, you're suppose to be dead. You better go tell Capt. Peterson." Kemp went to Peterson's tank and when Peterson saw him, he said" Kemp you're supposed to be dead." They then went back to the basement of the farm house to get the rest of the men.

At 1900 the First Platoon and "C" Company (58th Inf.) bypassed the Second and Third Platoons in Kirchhellen and traveled several miles southeast, took up positions outside of Overhagen.

March 29 began the first day of Passover for the Jews. A group of slave laborers were in a concentration camp on the Austrian Hungarian border. Before they went to sleep, they celebrated Passover with song, and a piece of Matzo. However, this Passover would begin a death march for them that would end at the Danube River. They marched during the day and slept in the open field at night.

When they had a chance, they picked up some of the grass from the fields and ate it. It was food. Fortunately, there was no rain. And they kept dry. It was three days of marching. Anyone who could not keep going was shot to death by the guards on the spot. Many perished and were left dead by the roadside. [179]

There was a historical Christ that walk on the face of the earth and left His footprints in the sand. That was 1945 years in the past. His existence was written about by historians such as Flavious Josephus, Phlegon, Thullus, Tertullian, et. al. Tertullian declares Christ to be the stone of Daniel 2 that will smite, at His second coming, the "secular kingdom" image. Phlegon and Thullus record that at the time of Christ's death, there was an elipse that darkened the sun. Flavious Josephus was a Jewish historian who wrote in his 'Antiquities' "Now there was about this time Jesus, a wise man, if it be lawful to call him a man, for he was the doer of wonderful works, a teacher of such men as receive the truth with pleasure.

Luke 22 7-8, 14-16 **7** Then came the *first* day of Unleavened
Bread on which the Passover *lamb* had to be sacrificed. **8** And
Jesus sent Peter and John, saying, "Go and prepare the Passover
for us, so that we may eat it. **14** When the hour had come, He
reclined *at the table,* and the apostles with Him. **15** And He said to
them, "I have earnestly desired to eat this Passover with you
before I suffer; **16** for I say to you, I shall never again eat it until it
is fulfilled in the kingdom of God."

On Thursday March 29th at 0630 the Third Platoon with Ed Brodowski moved out of Kirchhellen with Company "B" of the 58th, and moved to Zweckel a distance of 9 miles without meeting any stiff resistance.

Also, the First Platoon and Company "C" moved out of their positions at 0600 outside of Overhagen, proceeded through Zweckel and engaged the enemy on the outskirts at approximately 1430. At this time, tanks of the third Platoon went out on reconnaissance in an attempt to find an easier route of advance. They were forced to abandon the mission after being subjected to heavy direct fire for a considerable length of time because of heavy enemy concentrations in that area. The column retreated to a defilade position in the town for the night. The German 180th Volks Grenadier Division and the 116th Panzer Division withdrew to set up new defensive lines running through the fortress town of Rocklinghausen.

There was a Panzer Tiger somewhere out there and they knew it. It was blocking our forward progress. Kemp was supposed to drive lead tank for Lieutenant Kaz, even though his tank was destroyed on March 28th. Capt. Peterson gave the order to Lt. Kaz to send a lead tank with Kemp and the second platoon out against the enemy. Lt. Kaz. told Capt. Peterson that he did not want to go head on against 2 AT (anti tank) guns and a reinforced Panzer Grenedier Regt. He told Peterson that it was suicide. He ordered Kemp to take the lead tank in which Kemp yelled out "No I'm not! Are you crazy?" It was then that Brodowski and John H. grabbed Kemp under each shoulder, lifted him off the ground, and physically carried him out. "Kemp, Brodowski said, are you crazy or are you just trying to get court marshaled?" Brodowski then went back and volunteered to be the lead tank. It was then that Capt Peterson decided that Ed Brodowski would lead off. On that 29th of March, Peterson gave command of the Second Platoon to Sgt. Brodowski. S/Sgt. Edward Brodowski was moved over from the Third Platoon.

It was March 30. Good Friday. According to Catholic Tradition, today is the day that Christ was crucified and died at 3:00 P.M. That would be at 1500 hours Around 1600 Brodowski's platoon was moved up to support an Infantry company. It was thought that the enemy had a defense in that area and an attack was made to break through it. Kemp wrote, "Brodowski lead the attack on an area of houses and was met by a barrage of direct and indirect fire from enemy positions. It was a suicide mission. Lt. Kaz knew it and we knew it. As the attack neared the town a camouflaged German tank drove out from behind a building. Ed delivered a withering fire at the Grenadier ground troops surrounding the Tiger." The Tiger shot off a round that hit the right track of Ed's tank and disabled it." Johnny yelled out, we've been hit. We can't move the tank. Let's get the hell out. Then

Brodowski slipped down into the gunner's seat with McStay as his ammo loader. He knew there was no way that his 76mm could match up against the superior armor and firepower (88mm) of the "Tiger." He could have bailed out with the others to come back to fight another day but, in Dick Kemps words, " that hard headed Pollock Ed Brodowski was not going to back down against any damn Kraut." There was a chance that he might have been able to do some damage. Picking out the place from where the German tank had fired, he directed three rounds from his tank gun at the German tank before his tank was hit again. This time in the turret hitting McStay and Brodowski. S/Sgt. Brodowski, Tank Commander, was instantly killed doing what he was trained to do. To fight for freedom against the tyranny and evil that infiltrated into the world.

THE SON HE NEVER KNEW
Bruce Brodowski

Published in the Miami Herald February 4, 1985

Somewhere in Germany in 1945, close to the end of the war, a tank is hit, a soldier dies. His pregnant wife awaits his safe return in New York State only to receive the dreaded telegram – killed in action.

Several weeks later his son is born, the son he never knew.

It never seemed unusual to me that Dad wasn't there. Mom never remarried and I guess she told me early in life that Dad was buried in Holland.

When I was old enough to understand, Mom sat me down and showed me Dads' picture, his belongings that were returned, the Silver Star and Purple Heart. Somehow, now, these don't seem to be an adequate substitute for a Dad.

I often wonder what we would have done together. He liked deer hunting as attested by the mounted deer head hanging in his mother's dining room. Ah, those weekend hunting and fishing trips.

Just me and Dad.

Or maybe we would have thrown a baseball around in the summer; or a football; or played basketball or tennis. Yeah, tennis! I remember his old wooden tennis racket gathering dust in the attic. He would have taught me tennis and we would have played together.

Just me and Dad.

Someday a man will be standing in front of a grave in Holland with a flower in his hand, a lump in his throat, and a tear in his eye.

And it will be just me and Dad.

The dad I never knew. And the flower will be left behind by the son he never knew.

Colin Powell once said, 'Over the years, the United States has sent many of its fine young men and women into great peril to fight for freedom beyond our borders. The only land we have ever asked for in return is enough to bury those that did not return.'

CHAPTER SIX

Creation of an Orphan Heart

Although the precise numbers of deaths are impossible to determine, these are one set of figures for the number of deaths that occurred in World War II. These figures include military and civilian deaths where these were available. The countries were: USSR, China, Germany, Poland, Japan, Yugoslavia, Rumania, France, Hungary, Austria, Greece, United States, Italy, Czechoslovakia, Great Britain, Great Britain, Netherlands, Belgium, Finland, Canada, India, Australia, Albania, Spain, Bulgaria, New Zealand, Norway, South Africa, Luxembourg, and Denmark. The total was approximately 56,150,000 people. Thousands more were slaughtered in the trench warfare of World War I.

'By the end of the war about 13 million children in Europe were facing destitution, poverty, and hunger. These were children whose parents had been killed or who had been abandoned, kidnapped, or deported. Each country established their own policies on how to deal with the war child problem. "When perceived as a national issue, with dire consequences for the future, governments took action to resolve the 'war child problem.' When perceived as nothing but an ordinary social problem of poverty, illegitimacy, and related issues, governments took little interest in the welfare of these children. The children's immediate needs for food, love and protection did not receive attention. Children of enemy or occupation soldiers were especially vulnerable to this lack of interest in the child as 'being'. When public interest lacked or vanished, silence, shame and neglect fell upon the children

The war child welfare policies of each individual country are too extensive to present here but are well presented in "Children of World War II, the hidden enemy legacy." The countries of Norway, Denmark, Germany, Spain, France, occupied eastern territories and others all had their individual approach to solving the war child problem. It suffices to show that there was a significant paradigm shift that occurred due to the welfare of these children. The emotional and spiritual makeup of generations of children from these war orphans was significantly impacted by these events. Many may have developed into orphan hearts. Many are still looking for their father's or records of them to regain their true identity and family name.

Therefore, the possible number of forgotten fatherless orphans in the world that occurred from these wars is astounding. The consequence of World War I and II caused a paradigm shift in the spiritual culture that left a spiritual vacuum. This would forever change the spiritual makeup of the world. Children develop their image of God and understanding about love from their earthly fathers. For many of them, without the influence of their fathers in their lives, their image and understanding of God was altered. This was the consequence of the war. This created an orphan heart/spirit/spiritual orphan culture that had a major influence on their future generations. Some war orphans have experienced characteristics of an orphan heart/orphan spirit that encompasses a deep dark black empty hole of missing pieces in their lives. However, every fatherless orphan, whether male or female, may experience during his or her childhood the same orphan heart, orphan spirit mental attitude.

This opened the door for the deterioration of belief in God and religion through the generations to the point of what it is today. Moral degradation infiltrated into the social culture. As an example, it evolved over time into the 60's era. "The Sixties, denoting the complex of inter-related cultural and political trends which occurred roughly during the years 1956–1974 in the west, particularly United States, Britain, France, Canada, Australia, Spain, Italy, and West Germany. Social and political upheaval was not limited to these countries, but included such nations as Japan, Mexico, and others.

In the United States, the Sixties as they are known in popular culture today lasted from about 1963 to 1971. The term is used descriptively by historians, journalists, and other objective academics; nostalgically by those who participated in the counter-culture and social revolution; and pejoratively by those who perceive the era as one of irresponsible excess and flamboyance. The decade was also labeled the Swinging Sixties because of the libertine attitudes that emerged during this decade. Rampant drug use had become inextricably associated with the counter-culture of the era, as Jefferson Airplane co-founder Paul Kantner mentions: "If you can remember anything about the sixties, you weren't really there."[180] Weren't these the unaffirmed children from World War II now looking for the affirmation they needed?

Because my dad was killed in WWII before I was born, I didn't have a dad around to affirm to me that I was like him, that I was lovable, and that he loved me. This is what the results of World War II did for me. My mother never remarried, therefore, I didn't have strong male images in my life to teach me what it meant to be a male child. My grandfather was a strong willed Polish immigrant who ruled over his house of 10 kids with an iron hand. Even though I loved my grandfather dearly, I always had an intense fear of him and the day that I would do something to make him very mad. Unfortunately, that day came as my grandparents watch over me while mom went out of town. I hid in the barn where grandpa couldn't find me until my mom came looking for me. How was I to know that grandpa's kittens couldn't swim on top of the water in the rain barrel?

My aunts have repeatedly told me how much my mother loved me when I was a child even after she received the telegram in April of 1945 that dad was killed in action. I don't remember my mother being a hugging and loving person that affirmed to me I was lovable and that she loved me. In my mind, our relationship is what I will call the Karen Carpenter parents syndrome (from the movie) where the parents feel no need to tell the children how much they are loved because they just know. They don't need to be hugged and kissed as part of that love. The parents were always emotionally detached and distant. Maybe your parents were like that. Maybe you came from a country that has a cold culture.

"Rejection can even be felt by children of well-meaning parents who fail to hug, touch or express affection. This creates an environment of emotional neglect. When a sibling dies or parents separate, a vulnerable child may feel rejected by the departing family member and may even feel responsible for the loss, which then triggers self-rejection. Children who have never met their father or who were abandoned by him suffer from a very deep wound of rejection. All forms of abuse are types of rejections."[181]

I always knew I was different in some ways from other kids. I never wanted to socialize. I just wanted to be left alone in a corner all by myself. Probably because I didn't have my dad around that could play with me. I did well playing in a corner of a sand box by myself while the other kids played on the opposite side. From what I remember, I was always doing something for my mother that ended up proving myself to be worthy of something. I know that I was fascinated with pianos and music at an early age. I loved going to the neighbors and playing with their old player piano, which played from rolls of paper. I ended up later taking dance and ballet lessons for the purpose of which no one can tell me why to this day. It wasn't my decision. Mom would push me to achieve to be the best. One time when I refused to practice my dance steps, she locked me in our dark basement until I did. I knew in my head she loved me and that she did this out of that love. This left a permanent wound in my soul, which reinforced the orphan heart of being not loved and unlovable. I later became part of a dancing duet at the age of seven and a star of the dance school performing on stage at the Stanley Theater. Thus began the perfectionist, proving myself worthy of love and lovable, the over achiever part of my life. I was loved. Listen to the applause. Take a bow.

It was 1950 when we moved to New Hartford, New York. I think that it was that year that mom developed breast cancer and started her fight for life. During the next five years she wasn't around much. Most of the time she was in and out of hospitals for surgeries or treatments that made her ill. I was cared for by my grandmother and my aunts. My grandmother taught me how to crochet and hold balls of yarn for her knitting. Learning how to do guy things and how to play sports just wasn't part of my childhood. By the age of seven or eight, I was able to take a city bus to get to the YMCA for swimming classes and general swim. I didn't fit in well and the other kids didn't seem to like me much. By now, I was a little man in a kid's birthday suit. I was getting used to being a rejected unlovable person. I felt that I must have to become perfect. I must have to prove myself to everybody in the world that I am worthy to be loved and justified to be a person.

Then in 1955, the one person in this world who loved me sat me down in grandma's living room and told me that I must decide where I want to go live if she should die. I screamed and screamed that I didn't want to go anywhere but mom said I must choose. I chose Aunt Helen and Uncle Stan that wanted me and that I wanted to live with. However, my mother said I couldn't go live with them and then gave me several reasons why. I then said I would go to live with my cousins in Detroit in which my mom said that that was not an option. The one place I did not want to go and live was the only option my mother gave me.

Before October 7 of that year, I was taken to the hospital to visit my mom. The scene in the movie "Terms of Endearment" where the children are taken into the hospital room to see their dying mom for the last time still tears me up. That is what happened to me. That was the last time I saw her alive. She gave me a hug and then gave me the mothers curse. She said, go live with your aunt and uncle, be a big boy, be a good boy, study hard, and become a doctor. It took 53 years before I was able to grieve my mothers' death. At the funeral, I shed no tears and I made up my mind that from that time on I would feel nothing. The orphan spirit was now developing stronger in my life. I had been betrayed and abandoned. There was no one left I could trust and no one to love me. My safe and secure home was ripped out from under my feet. I had begun to develop an orphan heart/orphan spirit.

The Orphan Heart/Orphan Spirit

In researching the literature available on an orphan heart, I realized that every resource would have the reader believe that all orphans develop an orphan heart mental attitude during childhood development. Then I realized that it is not justified to lump all orphans into a category and then decide that all of them will have the same characteristics. If we interview several people born in June, such as me, and conclude that these people are introverted, shy, creative, late bloomers, etc., then we would be amiss if we assumed that all people born in June have these same characteristics. If that were so, when I met someone born in June, I could say to him or her, "oh you were born in June? Then you must be introverted, shy, creative, and a late bloomer." It may fit the majority of the group but not the total group. Therefore, assuming that all fatherless children would have characteristics of an orphan heart attitude would not be correct either. Only a portion of the sample group would experience these attitudes.

As I reviewed the characteristics of the orphan spirit, I found myself mentally checking off the ones that fit my personal situation, which was most of them. If this was the case, then I assumed that all orphans have an orphan spirit and need healing ministry. The logic was obvious to me. These are the characteristics of an orphan spirit. All orphans have an orphan spirit. We develop an orphan spirit because we are orphans. Therefore, all orphans have these characteristics.

However, the assumptions fell apart when I tried to obtain testimonials from orphans to support my supposition. One woman emailed to me and said, "You might want to look at your assumptions for your conclusions about this particular group of orphans as well as your own objectivity before proceeding much further. You cannot assume that every war orphan has your issues. I have found, knowing many among us very well, that among us all, each has his/her own issues, and I do too. Some of us have worked through them in one way or another and some have been more damaged than others have. We are a variable lot and cannot be painted with a broad brush. Most have none of the characteristics that you initially described.

You have read the stories of dads of some American World War II orphans in this book. In no way is it assumed that any of these orphans developed orphan heart mental attitudes during their childhood development. The orphans of WWII have specific issues related to the "Wall of Silence" under which most of us grew up.

However, many orphans during childhood development do establish an orphan heart/orphan spirit. This is not a spirit being or entity that can be cast out in the name of Jesus Christ just as the spirit of justice, the spirit of the game, in the spirit of friendship, in the spirit of the children, in the spirit of the season, in the spirit of Christmas, etc can not. It is the mood, attitude, the intent, the principle, and the soul of the condition. These are mental attitudes and not personal characteristics.

What are these characteristics based on and how were they determined to be correct. Not all orphans would have the same mental attitude. Shiloh Place Ministries has stated "we have based our teachings on our personal experience with those we have ministered to in our encounters where we share on orphan heart issues."

The orphan spirit is a heart attitude (how the heart feels) and a mental stronghold (what the mind thinks from the input of these feelings) that is a temptation for all of us.[182] This describes the orphan spirit-independent; hostel; contentious; with no sense of home, belonging, or of being a son.[183]

So what are the hallmarks of an orphan spirit? - Inability to have lasting relationships - Hatred of authority, general distrust for leaders - General lack of direction for your life - Inability to make key, strategic decisions - Drawing near, then backing away from intimacy - A sense that they're just going to reject you anyway - A gnawing sense of failure, never quite good enough - An inexplicable drive to succeed, win, prove yourself"[184] To affirm you are lovable and capable of being loved. Your daddy wasn't around to tell you that.

"The orphan heart sees things differently than those with the heart of a son. An orphan spirit does not have a safe and secure haven in God. He or she must strive for self, and hold tightly to what he has. The spirit of a son, in contrast, has a spirit of submission to the will of the father (John 5:19).

"Home" is where you are loved unconditionally. If you don't have a "home," a safe and secure place, you have to live life looking out for yourself, for number one, because no one else will.

When things go wrong, we try to handle things ourselves (orphan spirit) instead of throwing ourselves upon God (spirit of son)."[185]

"The orphan spirit will do everything to distract us away from being able to experiencing to hear the father's voice because then you are going to listen to his voice. God wants you to live in an everyday basis: to see his face, hear his voice, feel his love, living in his presence, experiencing his pleasure, living in security, love and I have come home. Then to bring that into a home, a marriage, into children, into churches, bring it into a community. That we are a family, we are all brothers and sisters, and we just want to enjoy our Daddy.

When you are afraid of intimacy (in-to-me-see) you can put on coverings to cover your nakedness. These are fear, insecurity, guilt, loneliness, escapism, anxiety, and failure. You are no longer able to see His face clearly and so you see many faces.. You are no longer able to hear His voice and therefore there are so many other voices. You don't feel His love so you are after passions. You no longer have His security, so you are going after possessions. You don't have His values so you are going after position and all these things as a by product because you are constantly looking for something that only Father God can give you."[186]

The Father's Blessing

John 14:18 "I will not leave you as orphans; I will come to you"

We receive our father's blessing when our earthly father affirms to us that we are lovable and capable of love. Without the presence of our father, some of us did not learn how to receive love, how to trust, how to be intimate in relationships and therefore we became emotionally dysfunctional. Our image of God evolves through our image of our father. Our image of a loving, caring, and nurturing father was fractured by the lack of our earthly father's presence in our lives. This image of our father in turn influenced our image of the characteristics of God. Unfortunately, as adults, we pass on to our children what we have learned as children about the father's love, which they then pass on from generation to generation.

The Search for Inner Healing

Every person in the world is influenced in some way by war. I couldn't help but think about the war orphans of the British, Germans, Italians, Polish, Russians, Yugoslavians, and all other countries that had soldiers fighting in the war. How many war orphans there are from all wars we may never know? I wanted to drop down to my knees and cry out with tears in my eyes, I am so very sorry that you had to grow up without your dad. As part of this human race, I stand in and ask for your forgiveness that this happened to you. Because I know the emptiness of it. I have experienced the orphan spirit. Moreover, all of us orphans would have been so much different if we had had our fathers in our lives. I would have learned so much from my father about love and about God.

We go through our childhood wanting to hear the same words that the Father said to Jesus, "Luke 3:22 – And a voice came from heaven which said, "You are my beloved Son (or daughter); with whom I am well pleased." However, for many orphans, for one reason or another, their fathers are not there. There is a void in their soul that cries out "Daddy."

It is a basic need for every human being to receive affirmation during childhood development. Every child needs to feel that they are loved. During World War II, the orphans in England's orphanages started to show signs of unusually physical development. They changed the babies, feed the babies, and bathed the babies but no one was holding the babies. The head of these babies continued to grow while the bodies did not. The babies began to die. These babies were starving for love. Then they brought in young women from the country side to hold the babies and nurture them with love. When they did, the babies began to grow. The basic need for love and affirmation was met. This condition was later named Marasmus.

Marasmus is a form of emaciation and wasting in an infant due to protein-energy malnutrition. It is characterized by growth retardation in weight more than height so that the head appears quite large relative to the body. The term "marasmus" is also used as roughly equivalent to "anaclitic depression," a term coined by René Spitz to refer to children who suffer from the early loss of a mother without a suitable substitute. In other cases such failure to thrive stems from emotional deprivation as a result of parental withdrawal, rejection, or hostility. It is hypothesized that the emotional experiences of the child lead to shifts in the production of growth hormone.[187]

Finally, a Dutch psychiatrist Dr. Anna A. Terruwe discovered *Emotional Deprivation Disorder* in the 1960's and was called the *Frustration Neurosis or Deprivation Neurosis* when translated into the English language by her colleague, Dr. Conrad W. Baars. EDD is described by the authors as follows: "A person is unaffirmed when he or she has been deprived of authentic affirmation. He or she may have been criticized, ignored, neglected, abused, or emotionally rejected by primary caregivers early in life, resulting in the individual's stunted emotional growth. Unaffirmed individuals are incapable of developing into emotionally mature adults without receiving authentic affirmation from another person. Maturity is reached when there is a harmonious relationship between a person's body, mind, emotions, and spiritual soul under the guidance of their reason and will."

EDD individuals are described as "incapable of establishing normal, mature contact with others. This abnormal emotional rapport with others causes the person to feel lonely and uncomfortable in social settings--he or she feels like a stranger, not part of the group."[188]

So how does a person receive inner healing for EDD and/or an Orphan Heart. Until we can experience the Father's love, for us as orphans, we will continue to live with the mindset of an orphan heart and orphan spirit. For more information on inner healing, see my book "My Father, My Son, Healing the Orphan Heart with the Love of the Father." Or refer to the other referenced material on the subjects in the reference section of this book.

But you have received the spirit of adoption" (Rom. 8:15 c.f Gal. 4:5)

If you are an American World War II orphan, contact www.AWON.com to meet others like you who lost their dads to the war.

Conclusion

War

Does the out come of war put a dent into the biggest crime against humanity, which is war? William C. McGuire II, a war orphan, says it best in his book, "After the Liberators: A Father's Last Mission, A son's Lifelong Journey": "And this war, war is abomination. Senseless killing, destruction, unspeakable horror in which none is the true winner and all are marked by the stain.

But look into the hearts of men to know their motivation and to weigh their action. Who would condemn those who raise their arms to fend the innocent, and smite the enemy who would destroy all if he himself is not destroyed?"[189]

Did we learn anything from this? Alternatively, is it that we have an unexplainable need to continue committing these crimes against humanity by an enemy we cannot define? Is it possible that there are principalities that we are not aware of that keeps us fighting amongst ourselves in the name of hatred, greed, and prejudice? Is war the instrument that turns us away from God, which is sin, and so makes us back sliders into the enemy's territory? Does spiritual warfare continue through the spiritual oppression of specific world leaders? Does the spirit of darkness pursue the creation of spiritual orphans through the inability to experience their earthly and heavenly father's love? Is ethnic cleansing now the new weapon of destruction for destroying God's children? Only God knows for sure.

How many years can some people exist
Before they're allowed to be free?
How many times can a man turn his head
And pretend that he just doesnt see?
How many times must a man look up
Before he can see the sky?
How many ears must one man have
Before he can hear people cry?
How many deaths will it take till he knows
That too many people have died?
The answer, my friend, is blowin in the wind
The answer is blowin in the wind.[190]

Some people want to call my dad a hero. He would not have wanted it that way. He was just one of many. In his words he wrote, "As for heroism, well I don't think much of that. As all I do is my job." As for me, my journey down inner healing highway continues daily directly to the Father's Heart. As for my dad, I now know him and can finally say from the son he never knew, "Thanks dad for what you did. I love you dad."

Bruce Brodowski

MEMORIAL

In memory of Lloyd "Dick" Kemp who passed away to be with his fallen comrades on February 25, 2008. Without Dick's invaluable information, much of the details of my dad's last days would not have been revealed to me. Rest now, in peace.

Story of: **A SOLDIER DIED TODAY**

Lloyd R. Kemp

We crossed the Rhine on the 26-day of March. My tank was hit by an 88mm German anti-tank gun on the 28th. Members of my crew and men of the 58th Armored Infantry were killed and throughout the day death lay all around.

Still the following poem depicts how the death of this young Infantry replacement affected me a few days later. Moving forward on a high farm road, the tanks and half tracks were all mixed in together. The fields were muddy on either side and we did not want to move into them until the last minute before attacking the town. 2 German 40mm anti personnel Guns opened up on us and we scrambled to reform. It was a mess. We took the town, but only with God's help.

This lad was killed alongside my tank on April 3 1945. We were moving down the roadway, the Infantry were on foot, they had just dismounted from their half Tracks and both tanks and infantry were getting ready to assault the town. Hell broke loose. Lt. Davis, the tank platoon leader was killed. 1 tank was disabled.

I saw this young man lifted up and thrown on his back. He never moved. We were jammed in by the disabled tank and the halftrack. Bill Hamersly and I picked the lad up. He looked like he was sleeping. We had to move him or we would have had to run over him with the tank tracks. I grabbed his legs, Bill got his arms. We actually counted to 3 while swinging him. I looked at Bill, he looked back and we gently laid him in the grass under the trees. His ultra clean uniform, new boots, his rifle still slung across his shoulder, have haunted me for 60 years. The bullet had caught him in the chest cavity. There was no blood to speak of. I believe it was because of the many layers of clothing. He was just sleeping! I believe he is also waiting and sometime, somewhere I will know his name!

In the meantime, "A SOLDIER DIED TODAY!"

...... A soldier died today.

I never heard him pray.

For he never knew that death,

Was about to take his breath.

A small hole round and neat,

Took away his heart's last beat.

He lay still and warm, though dead,

From a steel covered piece of lead!

A SOLDIER DIED TODAY!

The 58th was a fighting crew,

I doubt there were many lads he knew,

For he joined the group the day before,

A brand new replacement in an old, old war.

The 58th Armored Infantry, as tough as old shoe leather,

Were moving into battle - regardless of the weather.

They said, "Hang in there kid - it takes a week or two,

We'll do our very best to keep an eye on you."

A SOLDIER DIED TODAY!

He lay there in the German sun,

A lifetime ended that had just begun.

New combat boots were on his feet,

His uniform was clean and neat.

I could not bring myself to weep,

For it seemed to me, "He was just asleep."

His unfired rifle slung to his shoulder.

This boy of nineteen would grow no older.

A SOLDIER DIED TODAY

His first day of combat, also his last,

For death picks out the new men fast,

It leaves alone the unafraid,

For these are the lads who have learned the trade.

The trade of course is killing.

The results are rather chilling.

For killing is all that soldiers know,

Life for learning fast - death for being slow.

A SOLDIER DIED TODAY!

I never learned the soldier's name.
Death was his only claim to fame.
He lay so very quiet - under the roadside trees,
Blonde hairs from 'neath his helmet
shimmering in the breeze.

O'er half a century passed me by,
Since I saw this soldier die,
Yet every day near eventide,
I remember how this soldier died.
A SOLDIER DIED TODAY!

I know this lad rests peacefully.
I pray he thinks not ill of me,
For watching him die, day after day.
I cannot make it go away.

It's hell to watch a young man die,
He uttered not a simple sigh.
If only he had said one word, "Hell," "Damn," or "Mother."
Now he dwells within my heart as a Soldier Brother.
A SOLDIER DIED TODAY!

As long as I am still alive,
this much I can say,

Every day at eventide,

"A SOLDIER DIES TODAY!"

As I remember it

Your Dad has been in my thoughts all of my life. He was one Hell of a Man. I gather you are the son he never saw. I seem to remember you were born after we shipped out. John and I speak on the phone every so often. He of course was your Dad's driver. We have in common the fact that we both had tanks blown out from under us and lost our turret crew. It is weird, but I was supposed to be driving lead Tank for Kaz, even though my Tank was destroyed March 28th. Lt. Kaz. told Capt. Peterson that he did not want to go head on against 2 AT (anti tank) guns and a reinforced Panzer Grenedier Regt. He told Pete that it was suicide, why, I don't know but Pete backed down and told your dad that he would lead off. I admit to breathing a sigh of relief. Ed was the new platoon leader, as he had lost his platoon leader. He had been platoon Sgt. and platoon second section commander, so Pete moved him up. His promotion to 2nd Lt. came through about 4 days after he was killed. I know quite a bit as I wrote a 4-page story on Ed Brodowski for my journalism final in Jr. College. The yrs. have eroded some of my memories, but Ed's memory has never dimmed! If anyone ever wanted to know what a Hero in WWll was, it was spelled "Ed Brodowski".

Dick Kemp

September 11, 2008

Dear Bruce,

If your dad had not taken my Daddy's place in the lead tank on that fateful day then I would never have been born or had the privilege of meeting and knowing a man as good and great as my father. Yes I miss him immensely since his death just a few months ago, but then I think about your loss so I could have Daddy for 57 years and I thank you.

I know the story of your dad very well. I have heard the stories so often (and loved it every time) of our father's escapades, especially of my father's lapse in judgment the day before your dad died, I'm sure you know that he saved not only my father's life, but he kept daddy from getting court marshaled by volunteering for the lead tank. When they told Daddy he would be driving the lead tank again he spurted out, "No I'm not! Are you crazy?" I think were his exact words. That is when your father and another man picked him up, one on each shoulder and carried him away from the commanding officer. That's when he asked my dad if he was crazy or just trying to get court-marshaled. Brodowski then volunteered to drive the lead tank, saving my father's life and freedom. My father never forgot that, took it for granted or gave the credit to fate for not being in that tank on that day, Your father and only your father is the reason my daddy survived the war. He talked about Brodowski so much I've always felt like I knew your dad, just like I've always known Willie Glenn and Bean. Daddy just made them come alive in his stories.

Please don't think I am being disrespectful by calling your father by his last name only, but that's how Daddy always referred to him, and I know how highly my father thought of your Father. I don't know if it helps any to know that your Father lived on through the stories my Dad told to his friends and children. Brodowski was not forgotten. In our lives, my sister and I, your dad was the most important hero of the war. I know Daddy felt that way too, because he told me. He also felt a little bit guilty that he wasn't in that lead tank that day.

Thank you for letting me tell you all these things . I just wanted an opportunity to make sure you know you're not the only one who thinks he was great. My sister and I thank God for your father and we really appreciate his valor, HE IS A HERO.

Sincerely,

Cathy Kemp Periman

Endnotes

Prologue

[1] http://www.cuttingedge.org/NEWS/n1017.html

March 1943

[2] Boyles, Carolee Anita, "Savage Arms: the definition of accuracy: from riches to rags to honors," Shooting Industry, September 2003

[3] In Tornado's Wake, A History of the 8th Armored Division, by Capt. Charles R. Leach. Pg. 7

[4] http://www.8th-armored.org/division/8div-hist.htm

[5] Op. Cit. In Tornado's Wake, Pg. 9-10

April 1943

[6] http://www.onwar.com/chrono/1943/apr1943/f01apr43.htm

Article I. [7] Battle of El Guettar From Wikipedia, the free encyclopedia

[8] Op. Cit. In Tornado's Wake, Pg. 10

[9] http://www.onwar.com/chrono/1943/fmapr43.htm

[10] http://www.onwar.com/chrono/1943/apr1943/f07apr43.htm

[11] http://www.onwar.com/chrono/1943/apr1943/f14apr43.htm

[12] THE WOMEN'S ARMY CORPS: A COMMEMORATION OF WORLD WAR II SERVICE By Judith A. Bellafaire CMH Publication 72-15

[13] http://www.onwar.com/chrono/1943/apr1943/f17apr43.htm

[14] http://www.onwar.com/chrono/1943/apr1943/f22apr43.htm

[15] http://www.onwar.com/chrono/1943/apr1943/f26apr43.htm

[16] http://www.onwar.com/chrono/1943/apr1943/f30apr43.htm

May 1943

[17] http://www.onwar.com/chrono/1943/may1943/f01may43.htm

[18] Op. Cit. In Tornado's Wake, Pg. 11

[19] http://www.onwar.com/chrono/1943/may1943/f10may43.htm

[20] http://www.onwar.com/chrono/1943/may1943/f12may43.htm

[21] http://www.onwar.com/chrono/1943/may1943/f12may43.htm

[22] http://www.onwar.com/chrono/1943/may1943/f13may43.htm

[23] http://www.onwar.com/chrono/1943/may1943/f16may43.htm

[24] http://www.onwar.com/chrono/1943/may1943/f17may43.htm

[25] http://www.onwar.com/chrono/1943/may1943/f22may43.htm

[26] http://www.onwar.com/chrono/1943/may1943/f23may43.htm

[27] http://www.onwar.com/chrono/1943/may1943/f25may43.htm

[28] http://www.onwar.com/chrono/1943/may1943/f27may43.htm

June 1943

[29] http://www.onwar.com/chrono/1943/jun1943/f10jun43.htm

[30] http://www.onwar.com/chrono/1943/jun1943/f16jun43.htm

July 1943

[31] http://www.onwar.com/chrono/1943/jul1943/f09jul43.htm
[32] http://en.wikipedia.org/wiki/Allied_invasion_of_Sicily
[33] http://www.onwar.com/chrono/1943/jul1943/f10jul43.htm

[34] http://www.onwar.com/chrono/1943/jul1943/f11jul43.htm

[35] http://www.onwar.com/chrono/1943/jul1943/f12jul43.htm

[36] http://www.onwar.com/chrono/1943/jul1943/f13jul43.htm

[37] http://www.onwar.com/chrono/1943/jul1943/f16jul43.htm

August 1943

[38] http://www.onwar.com/chrono/1943/aug1943/f17aug43.htm

September 1943

[39] http://www.onwar.com/chrono/1943/sep1943/f03sep43.htm

[40] http://www.onwar.com/chrono/1943/sep1943/f09sep43.htm

[41] http://www.onwar.com/chrono/1943/sep1943/f10sep43.htm

[42] http://www.onwar.com/chrono/1943/sep1943/f13sep43.htm

[43] http://www.onwar.com/chrono/1943/sep1943/f16sep43.htm

[44] Op. Cit. In Tornado's Wake, Pgs. 12-13

October 1943

[45] http://www.onwar.com/chrono/1943/oct1943/f01oct43.htm

[46] http://www.onwar.com/chrono/1943/oct1943/f03oct43.htm

[47] http://www.onwar.com/chrono/1943/fmoct43.htm

[48] http://www.onwar.com/chrono/1943/oct1943/f19oct43.htm

[49] http://www.onwar.com/chrono/1943/oct1943/f22oct43.htm

[50] http://www.onwar.com/chrono/1943/oct1943/f27oct43.htm

[51] http://www.onwar.com/chrono/1943/oct1943/f28oct43.htm

November 1943

[52] http://www.onwar.com/chrono/1943/nov1943/f04nov43.htm

[53] http://www.onwar.com/chrono/1943/nov1943/f05nov43.htm

[54] http://www.onwar.com/chrono/1943/nov1943/f06nov43.htm

[55] http://www.onwar.com/chrono/1943/nov1943/f12nov43.htm

[56] http://www.onwar.com/chrono/1943/nov1943/f15nov43.htm

[57] http://www.onwar.com/chrono/1943/nov1943/f19nov43.htm

[58] http://www.onwar.com/chrono/1943/nov1943/f22nov43.htm

[59] Op. Cit. In Tornado's Wake, Pg. 13

[60] http://www.onwar.com/chrono/1943/nov1943/f28nov43.htm

December 1943

[61] http://www.onwar.com/chrono/1943/dec1943/f01dec43.htm

[62] http://www.onwar.com/chrono/1943/dec1943/f02dec43.htm

[63] http://www.onwar.com/chrono/1943/dec1943/f08dec43.htm

[64] **Op. Cit. In Tornado's Wake, Pg.'s 13-14**

[65] http://www.fortunecity.com/tinpan/parton/2/tooyoung.html, Lyrics as reprinted ibid. © 1943 M. Witmark & Sons

(Lyrics: Frank Loesser, Music: Arthur Schwartz) (1943) © 1943 M. Witmark & Sons

[66] http://www.onwar.com/chrono/1943/dec1943/f18dec43.htm

[67] http://www.onwar.com/chrono/1943/dec1943/f20dec43.htm

[68] http://www.onwar.com/chrono/1943/dec1943/f21dec43.htm

[69] http://www.onwar.com/chrono/1943/dec1943/f26dec43.htm

[70] http://www.onwar.com/chrono/1943/dec1943/f31dec43.htm

January 1944

[71] Op. Cit. In Tornado's Wake, Pg. 14-16

[72] http://www.onwar.com/chrono/1944/jan44/f11jan44.htm

[73] http://www.onwar.com/chrono/1944/jan44/f14jan44.htm

[74] http://www.onwar.com/chrono/1944/jan44/f15jan44.htm

[75] http://www.onwar.com/chrono/1944/jan44/f20jan44.htm

[76] http://www.onwar.com/chrono/1944/jan44/f22jan44.htm

[77] http://www.onwar.com/chrono/1944/jan44/f23jan44.htm

[78] http://www.onwar.com/chrono/1944/jan44/f30jan44.htm

February 1944

[79] http://www.onwar.com/chrono/1944/feb44/f02feb44.htm

[80] http://www.onwar.com/chrono/1944/feb44

[81] http://www.onwar.com/chrono/1944/feb44/f25feb44.htm

March 1944

[82] http://www.onwar.com/chrono/1944/mar44/f03mar44.htm

[83] http://www.onwar.com/chrono/1944/mar44/f06mar44.htm

[84] http://www.onwar.com/chrono/1944/mar44/f08mar44.htm

[85] http://www.onwar.com/chrono/1944/mar44/f15mar44.htm

[86] http://www.onwar.com/chrono/1944/mar44/f20mar44.htm

[87] http://www.onwar.com/chrono/1944/mar44/f22mar44.htm

[88] http://www.onwar.com/chrono/1944/mar44/f24mar44.htm

[89] http://www.onwar.com/chrono/1944/mar44/f30mar44.htm

April 1944

[90] http://www.onwar.com/chrono/1944/apr44/f17apr44.htm

[91] http://www.onwar.com/chrono/1944/apr44/f18apr44.htm

May 1944

[92] http://user.pa.net/~cjheiser/ct9/339f1.htm

[93] AWON Fathers Tribute

[94] http://www.337thinfantry.net/337history.php

[95] http://user.pa.net/~cjheiser/ct9/339f1.htm

[96] http://www.337thinfantry.net/337history.php

[97] http://user.pa.net/~cjheiser/ct9/339f1.htm

June 1944

[98] http://www.ww2-airborne.us/units/506/506.html

[99] Op Cit, AWON

[100] Op. Cit. In Tornado's Wake,. Pg. 36-44

August 1944

[101] http://www.onwar.com/chrono/1944/aug44/f01aug44.htm

[102] http://www.onwar.com/chrono/1944/aug44/f15aug44.htm

[103] http://www.onwar.com/chrono/1944/aug44/f25aug44.htm

[104] http://www.onwar.com/chrono/1944/sep44/f01sep44.htm

September 1944

[105] http://www.onwar.com/chrono/1944/sep44/f10sep44.htm

[106] http://www.onwar.com/chrono/1944/sep44/f12sep44.htm

[107] http://www.onwar.com/chrono/1944/sep44/f17sep44.htm

[108] http://www.onwar.com/chrono/1944/sep44/f25sep44.htm

October 1944

[109] Op. Cit, AWON

[110] Op. Cit, AWON

[111] Reardon, Mark, Battle of Hürtgen Forest: The 9th Infantry Division Suffered in the Heavily Armed Woods, December 2006 issue of World War II magazine, quoted material is reprinted with permission of Weider History Group (http://www.historynet.com/battle-of-hurtgen-forest-the-9th-infantry-division-suffered-in-the-heavily-armed-woods.htm#high_2)

[112] Op. Cit, AWON

November 1944

[113] Op. Cit. In Tornado's Wake,. Pg. 45

[114] Op. Cit. In Tornado's Wake, Pg. 45

[115] http://www.onwar.com/chrono/1944/nov44/f07nov44.htm

[116] http://www.history.army.mil/books/wwii/lorraine/lorraine-ch09.html

[117] Op. Cit, AWON

[118] Ratliff, Tom. "Now I Know"

[119] http://www.onwar.com/chrono/1944/nov44/f16nov44.htm

[120] Op. Cit. In Tornado's Wake, A History of the 8th Armored Division, by Capt. Charles R. Leach. Pg. 47

[121] OP. Cit, AWON

[122] http://www.491st.org/491hist4.html

[123] Op. Cit, 491st.org

[124] OP. Cit, AWON

December 1944

[125] http://www.onwar.com/chrono/1944/dec44/f02dec44.htm

[126] http://www.thetroubleshooters.com/80th/farebersviller0013.html

[127] Op Cit, AWON

[128] http://www.8th-armored.org/books/leach/tw03.htm

[129] http://www.onwar.com/chrono/1944/dec44/f16dec44.htm

[130] http://www.onwar.com/chrono/1944/dec44/f17dec44.htm

[131] http://www.onwar.com/chrono/1944/dec44/f20dec44.htm

[132] http://www.onwar.com/chrono/1944/dec44/f22dec44.htm

[133] http://www.onwar.com/chrono/1944/dec44/f24dec44.htm

[134] Op. Cit, AWON

[135] http://www.onwar.com/chrono/1944/dec44/f25dec44.htm

[136] Op. Cit. In Tornado's Wake,. Pg. 57

[137] http://www.onwar.com/chrono/1944/dec44/f26dec44.htm

January 1945

[138] http://www.onwar.com/chrono/1945/jan45/f01jan45.htm

[139] McCarthy, Peter and Mike Syron. Panzerkrieg, The Rise and all of Hitler's Tank Divisions, pp231-232.

[140] Op. Cit. In Tornado's Wake,. Pg. 57 and 58

[141] http://www.onwar.com/chrono/1945/jan45/f02jan45.htm

[142] http://www.onwar.com/chrono/1945/jan45/f03jan45.htm

[143] http://www.onwar.com/chrono/1945/jan45/f04jan45.htm

[144] http://www.onwar.com/chrono/1945/jan45/f05jan45.htm

[145] Op. Cit. In Tornado's Wake, Pg. 58

[146] http://www.onwar.com/chrono/1945/jan45/f10jan45.htm

[147] Op. Cit. In Tornado's Wake,. Pg. 59

[148] Op. Cit, AWON

[149] http://www.onwar.com/chrono/1945/jan45/f16jan45.htm

[150] Op. Cit. In Tornado's Wake, A History of the 8th Armored Division, by Capt. Charles R. Leach. Pg. 59-61

[151] http://www.onwar.com/chrono/1945/jan45/f21jan45.htm

[152] Op. Cit, AWON

[153] Op. Cit, AWON

[154] http://www.onwar.com/chrono/1945/jan45/f27jan45.htm

February 1945

[155] Op. Cit. In Tornado's Wake,. Pg. 83

[156] Op. Cit. In Tornado's Wake,. Pg. 83

[157] Op. Cit. In Tornado's Wake,. Pg. 83 and 84

[158] Op. Cit. In Tornado's Wake, Pg. 88 and 90.

[159] Op. Cit, AWON

[160] Op. Cit. In Tornado's Wake,. Pg. 89

[161] Op. Cit. In Tornado's Wake, Pg. 90

(a) [162] http://www.lonesentry.com/usdivisions/history/infantry/division/84th_infantry_division.html

[163] Op. Cit. In Tornado's Wake,. Pg. 90

[164] Op. Cit. In Tornado's Wake,. Pg. 91

[165] Op. Cit. In Tornado's Wake, Pg. 92

[166] Op. Cit. In Tornado's Wake, Pg. 93

[167] Op. Cit. In Tornado's Wake, Pg. 93

[168] Op. Cit, AWON

[169] Op. Cit. In Tornado's Wake,. Pg. 109-110

[170] Op. Cit. In Tornado's Wake, Pg. 110

[171] Op. Cit, AWON

March 1945

[172] Op. Cit. In Tornado's Wake, Pg. 111

[173] Fritz, Stephan. Frontsoldaten, The German Soldier in World war II. pp 200-201

[174] http://www.onwar.com/chrono/1945/mar45/f07mar45.htm

[175] Op. Cit. In Tornado's Wake,. Pg. 135-137

[176] Op. Cit. In Tornado's Wake,. Pg. 137

[177] Op. Cit, AWON

[178] http://en.wikipedia.org/wiki/Operation_Plunder

1) [179]http://www.ask.com/bar?q=+passover+1945&page=1&qsrc=2417&zoom=%3CKW%3EPassover%3C%2FKW%3E+Recipes%7CLearn+about+the+Holiday+%3CKW%3EPassover%3C%2FKW%3E%7C%3CKW%3EPassover%3C%2FKW%3E+Food&ab=0&u=http%3A%2F%2Fwww.hellers.ws%2Fborrowed-time%2Fpassover-*1945.shtml*
The above is part of the book of On Borrowed Time, in preparation

[180] http://en.wikipedia.org/wiki/1960s

[181] Why do I feel so down when my faith should lift me up? Dr. Grant Mullen, M.D. p 259

[182] Spiritual Slavery to Spiritual Sonship. Jack Frost, p69

[183] Ibid.

[184] Robert I Holmes, Dealing With An Orphan Spirit

[185] http://lifewaychurchnotes.blogspot.com/2007/02/exposing-roots-of-spiritual-orphans.html Rev. David Kirschke

[186]Excerpts from Leif Hetland on the Orphan Spirit 2007.
[187] http://social.jrank.org/pages/378/Marasmus.html fair use.
[188] http://www.healthieryou.com/mhexpert/exp1082503b.html

[189] After The liberators: A Father's Last Mission, A Son's Lifelong Journey, William C. McGuire II, p173

[190] Lyrics from Blowing in the Wind by Peter, Paul, and Mary http://www.lyricsfreak.com/p/peter,+paul+&+mary/blowin+in+the+wind_20107667.html

Bibliography

1 *AWON Fathers Tribute, Awon.com, permission granted by each individual author.

2 *Bellafaire, Judith A., THE WOMEN'S ARMY CORPS: A COMMEMORATION OF WORLD WAR II SERVICE by Center of Military History Publication 72-15

3 *Boyles, Carolee Anita, "Savage Arms: the definition of accuracy: from riches to rags to honors," Shooting Industry, September 2003

4 *Cutting Edge Ministries, STUDY ANTICHRIST THROUGH STUDY OF HITLER.

5 *Fritz, Stephan. Frontsoldaten, The German Soldier in World War II.

5A *Frost, Jack, Spiritual Slavery to Spiritual Sonship

6 *Hetland, Leif Excerpts from DVD on the Orphan Spirit 2007.

7 *Holmes, Robert I, Dealing with an Orphan Spirit

8 *Leach, Charles R. Capt. In Tornado's Wake, A History of the 8th Armored Division, by Pg. 7

---

9 Lyrics from Blowing in the Wind by Peter, Paul, and Mary, (Lyrics: Frank Loesser, Music: Arthur Schwartz) (1943) © 1943 M. Witmark & Sons

9a McGuire II, William C., After The liberators: A Father's Last Mission, A Son's Lifelong Journey

10 McCarthy, Peter and Mike Syron. Panzerkrieg, The Rise and Fall of Hitler's Tank Divisions

11 *Mullen, Grant, M.D. Why do I feel so down when my faith should lift me up

12 *Ratliff, Tom. "Now I Know"

LaVergne, TN USA
25 June 2010
187393LV00001B/1/P